KU-465-225

The Fiction of Chinua Achebe

JAGO MORRISON

Consultant editor: Nicolas Tredell

palgrave
macmillan

© Jago Marrison 2007

All rights reserved. No reproduction, copy or transmission of this publication may be made without written permission.

No paragraph of this publication may be reproduced, copied or transmitted save with written permission or in accordance with the provisions of the Copyright, Designs and Patents Act 1988, or under the terms of any licence permitting limited copying issued by the Copyright Licensing Agency, 90 Tottenham Court Road, London W1T 4LP.

Any person who does any unauthorised act in relation to this publication may be liable to criminal prosecution and civil claims for damages.

The author has asserted his right to be identified as the authors of this work in accordance with the Copyright, Designs and Patents Act 1988.

First published 2007 by
PALGRAVE MACMILLAN
Houndmills, Basingstoke, Hampshire RG21 6XS and
175 Fifth Avenue, New York, N.Y. 10010
Companies and representatives throughout the world

PALGRAVE MACMILLAN is the global academic imprint of the Palgrave Macmillan division of St. Martin's Press, LLC and of Palgrave Macmillan Ltd. Macmillan® is a registered trademark in the United States, United Kingdom and other countries. Palgrave is a registered trademark in the European Union and other countries.

ISBN-13: 978–1–4039–8671–9   hardback
ISBN-10: 1–4039–8671–1   hardback
ISBN-13: 978–1–4039–8672–6   paperback
ISBN-10: 1–4039–8672–X   paperback

This book is printed on paper suitable for recycling and made from fully managed and sustained forest sources. Logging, pulping and manufacturing processes are expected to conform to the environmental regulations of the country of origin.

A catalogue record for this book is available from the British Library.

Library of Congress Cataloging-in-Publication Data.

Morrison, Jago, 1969–
    The fiction of Chinua Achebe/Jago Morrison.
        p. cm.
    Includes bibliographical references and index.
    ISBN 1–4039–8671–1 (alk. paper) – ISBN 1–4039–8672–X (alk. paper)
        1. Achebe, Chinua–Criticism and interpretation.   I. Title.

PR9387.9.A3Z827 2007
823'.914—dc22   2007018263

10   9   8   7   6   5   4   3   2   1
16   15   14   13   12   11   10   09   08   07

Printed and bound in China

4/22

£4·95

READERS' GUIDES TO ESSENTIAL CRITICISM

CONSULTANT EDITOR: NICOLAS TREDELL

Published

Lucie Armitt	George Eliot: *Adam Bede – The Mill on the Floss – Middlemarch*
Richard Beynon	D. H. Lawrence: *The Rainbow – Women in Love*
Peter Boxall	Samuel Beckett: *Waiting for Godot – Endgame*
Claire Brennan	The Poetry of Sylvia Plath
Susan Bruce	Shakespeare: *King Lear*
Sandie Byrne	Jane Austen: *Mansfield Park*
Alison Chapman	Elizabeth Gaskell: *Mary Barton – North and South*
Peter Childs	The Fiction of Ian McEwan
Christine Clegg	Vladimir Nabokov: *Lolita*
John Coyle	James Joyce: *Ulysses – A Portrait of the Artist as a Young Man*
Martin Coyle	Shakespeare: *Richard II*
Michael Faherty	The Poetry of W. B. Yeats
Sarah Gamble	The Fiction of Angela Carter
Jodi-Anne George	Chaucer: The General Prologue to *The Canterbury Tales*
Jane Goldman	Virginia Woolf: *To the Lighthouse – The Waves*
Huw Griffiths	Shakespeare: *Hamlet*
Vanessa Guignery	The Fiction of Julian Barnes
Geoffrey Harvey	Thomas Hardy: *Tess of the d'Urbervilles*
Paul Hendon	The Poetry of W. H. Auden
Terry Hodgson	The Plays of Tom Stoppard for Stage, Radio, TV and Film
Stuart Hutchinson	Mark Twain: *Tom Sawyer – Huckleberry Finn*
Stuart Hutchinson	Edith Wharton: *The House of Mirth – The Custom of the Country*
Betty Jay	E. M. Forster: *A Passage to India*
Elmer Kennedy-Andrews	The Poetry of Seamus Heaney
Elmer Kennedy-Andrews	Nathaniel Hawthorne: *The Scarlet Letter*
Daniel Lea	George Orwell: *Animal Farm – Nineteen Eighty-Four*
Philippa Lyon	Twentieth-Century War Poetry
Merja Makinen	The Novels of Jeanette Winterson
Jago Morrison	The Fiction of Chinua Achebe
Carl Plasa	Tony Morrison: *Beloved*
Carl Plasa	Jean Rhys: *Wide Sargasso Sea*
Nicholas Potter	Shakespeare: *Antony and Cleopatra*
Nicholas Potter	Shakespeare: *Othello*
Berthold S	
Nick Selb	

SOUTHWARK LIBRARIES

SK 2180595 4

Nick Selby	Herman Melville: *Moby Dick*
Nick Selby	The Poetry of Walt Whitman
David Smale	Salman Rushdie: *Midnight's Children – The Satanic Verses*
Patsy Stoneman	Emily Brontë: *Wuthering Heights*
Susie Thomas	Hanif Kureishi
Nicolas Tredell	F. Scott Fitzgerald: *The Great Gatsby*
Nicolas Tredell	Joseph Conrad: *Heart of Darkness*
Nicolas Tredell	Charles Dickens: *Great Expectations*
Nicolas Tredell	William Faulkner: *The Sound and the Fury – As I Lay Dying*
Nicolas Tredell	Shakespeare: *Macbeth*
Nicolas Tredell	The Fiction of Martin Amis
Angela Wright	Gothic Fiction

Forthcoming

Pascale Aebischer	Jacobean Drama
Simon Avery	Thomas Hardy: *The Mayor of Casterbridge – Jude the Obscure*
Paul Baines	Daniel Defoe: *Robinson Crusoe – Moll Flanders*
Annita Bautz	Jane Austen: *Sense and Sensibility – Pride and Prejudice – Emma*
Mathew Beedham	The Novels of Kazuo Ishiguro
Justine Edwards	Postcolonial Literature
Jodi Anne-George	Beowulf
Louisa Hadley	The fiction of A. S. Byatt
William Hughes	Bram Stoker: *Dracula*
Mathew Jordan	Milton: *Paradise Lost*
Sara Lodge	Charlotte Brontë: *Jane Eyre*
Aaron Kelley	Twentieth-Century Irish Literature
Mathew McGuire	Contemporary Scottish Literature
Timothy Milnes	Wordsworth: *The Prelude*
Stephen Regan	The Poetry of Philip Larkin
Mardi Stewart	Victorian Women's Poetry
Michael Whitworth	Virginia Woolf: *Mrs Dalloway*
Gina Wisker	The Fiction of Margaret Atwood
Mathew Woodcock	Shakespeare: *Henry V*

Palgrave Readers' Guides to Essential Criticism
Series Standing Order
ISBN 1–4039–0108–2
(*outside North America only*)

You can receive future titles in this series as they are published by placing a standing order. Please contact your bookseller or, in the case of difficulty, write to us at the address below with your name and address, the title of the series and the ISBN quoted above.

Customer Services Department, Macmillan Distribution Ltd
Houndmills, Basingstoke, Hampshire RG21 6XS, England

for Bevan

For Kirsten

Contents

Things Fall Apart (1958): Challenging the Canon

Chapter 1 begins by looking at some early responses to *Things Fall Apart*, by critics including Honor Tracy, G. D. Killam, Eustace Palmer and A. G. Stock. Much of this work is challenged by later scholars: Oladele Taiwo, Nahem Yousaf and C. L. Innes are important examples. The third part of the chapter discusses the 'language debate' which has occupied many critics, not least Gareth Griffiths, Ngũgĩ wa Thiong'o and James Snead. Finally, the chapter examines three of the most influential feminist readings of *Things Fall Apart*, by the critics Rhonda Cobham, Kirsten Holst Petersen and Florence Stratton.

Things Fall Apart (1958): The Novel and Nigeria

Continuing the discussion, this chapter addresses two key historical contexts for Achebe's first novel. The first part examines the novel's turn-of-the century setting, with five distinctive readings by Robert Wren, Raisa Simola, Herbert Ekwe-Ekwe, Neil ten Kortenaar and Richard Begam. The second part views *Things Fall Apart* as a text reflecting the debates of Nigerian independence: the three critics discussed are Chinua Achebe himself, Ode Ogede and Romanus Okey Muoneke.

No Longer at Ease (1960)

This chapter begins by comparing early and later criticism of *No Longer at Ease*. A key point of discussion in the first part is the complex structure of intertextual allusion in Achebe's novel. The work of Arthur Ravenscroft, David Carroll, Philip Rogers and Arnd Witte are the examples selected.

The second part goes on to explore some of the historical contexts of the novel, through the critics Umelo Ojinmah, Michael Valdez Moses and Simon Gikandi.

The discussion of Achebe's third novel begins with the author's own account of *Arrow of God* as an attempt to 'revaluate my culture'. Through the critics Robert Wren, Charles Nnolim and C. L. Innes, it goes on to explore the novel's key intertexts and influences. The chapter concludes with three quite different critical readings, by K. Indrasena Reddy, David Carroll and Tejumola Olaniyan.

This chapter begins by exploring the background to *A Man of the People* through Achebe's biographer, Ezenwa-Ohaeto. Two early, political readings are offered, by Bernth Lindfors and Ngũgĩ wa Thiong'o. The chapter then explores three more recent treatments of the novel, by Joe Obi, Onyemaechi Udumukwu and Jago Morrison. The final part of the chapter deals with Achebe's 1972 short story collection *Girls at War and Other Stories*, exploring the responses of critics C. L. Innes, Umelo Ojinmah and Ode Ogede.

The discussion begins, using Achebe's own commentary, by considering the changed sense of the author's role that informs the writing of *Anthills of the Savannah*. It then compares three different, political readings of the novel, by Simon Gikandi, Supriya Nair and Neil ten Kortenaar. The final part of the chapter examines the feminist response to Achebe's fifth novel, through the critics Ifi Amadiume, Rose Acholonu and Elleke Boehmer.

ACKNOWLEDGEMENTS

T he author would firstly like to thank the many critics of Achebe's work whose varied and provoking contributions made this book possible, and in particular Rose Acholonu, Ifi Amadiume (especially in helping to locate her article 'Class and Gender in *Anthills of the Savannah*: A Critique'), Richard Begam, Elleke Boehmer, David Carroll, Rhonda Cobham, Herbert Ekwe-Ekwe, Ezenwa-Ohaeto, Simon Gikandi, Gareth Griffiths, C. L. Innes, G. D. Killam, Neil ten Kortenaar, Charles R. Larson, Bernth Lindfors, Michael Valdez Moses, Romanus Okey Muoneke, Supriya Nair, Ngũgĩ wa Thiong'o, Charles Nnolim, Joe Obi, Emmanuel Obiechina, Ode Ogede, Umelo Ojinmah, Tejumola Olaniyan, Femi Osofisan, Eustace Palmer, Kirsten Holst Petersen, Arthur Ravenscroft, K. Indrasena Reddy, Philip Rogers, Raisa Simola, James Snead, A. G. Stock, Florence Stratton, Oladele Taiwo, Honor Tracy, Onyemaechi Udumukwu, Arnd Witte, Robert Wren and Nahem Yousaf. The staff and resources of the British Library and the School of Oriental and African Studies, as well as the university libraries of Chichester, Sussex, Southampton and Leeds, were invaluable. For his excellent editing of the first draft and many useful suggestions, I am indebted to Nicolas Tredell. For their practical help, in various ways, during the writing of this book, thanks to Sonya Barker, Isla Duncan, Sue Morgan and Susan Watkins. Thanks finally to Alison Morrison for her love, encouragement and support.

Introduction

S ince the emergence of *Things Fall Apart* in 1958, Chinua Achebe has acquired a reputation as the 'Godfather' of modern African writing. With combined book sales for his novels running to tens of millions of copies, his work has become a staple of the college and university curriculum throughout the English-speaking world. It is difficult to imagine a course on postcolonial writing, or on the post-war novel, which did not include one of Achebe's novels, and the spread of criticism on his work is correspondingly vast and bewildering.

This book is intended to enable readers of Achebe's work to navigate the field of Achebe criticism, setting out the key areas of critical debate, the most influential alternative approaches to his work and the controversies that have so often surrounded it. As Achebe's most influential and widely studied text, *Things Fall Apart* provides an important focus of discussion. Chapter 1, '*Things Fall Apart*: Challenging the Canon', explores the novel's extraordinary international critical impact as a milestone in post-war fiction, whilst chapter 2, '*Things Fall Apart*: The Novel and Nigeria', sets the novel against its West African historical background. Chapters 3 to 6 focus on the novels *No Longer at Ease*, *Arrow of God*, *A Man of the People* and *Anthills of the Savannah*, respectively. In order to provide some discussion of the less often studied short fiction, a short section on the collection *Girls at War* is included in chapter 5, providing an interesting postscript to the troubled career of *A Man of the People*.

Albert Chinualumogu Achebe was the fifth of six children born to a church catechist and his wife, Isaiah and Janet Achebe, in the Ibo village of Nneobi in 1930. His childhood was spent in his father's ancestral village of Ogidi, where Ibo tradition and colonial culture rubbed shoulders. Achebe attended a school whose regime was based – to judge by the account of biographer Ezenwa-Ohaeto (1958–2005)[1] – on a brutal enforcement of Christian values. As is

1

suggested by his name, the school's headmaster, Mr Okongwu, may have provided one of the models for the figure of Okonkwo in *Things Fall Apart*:

■ The strict nature of Okongwu and his adherence to discipline was immediately established when he addressed the teachers and pupils, enumerating a list of prohibitions which he stressed with the refrain, 'A raa eme ya eme!' – 'It is never done!' That phrase became the nickname of the new headmaster and one day, soon after the public address, as he was going to the Iyienu hospital to give the Europeans there some lessons in Igbo, some pupils began shouting, 'It is never done! It is never done!'

The next day Mr. Okongwu gathered the pupils after the morning service at the school. After locking the doors he produced some canes with which he proceeded to flog every child to punish the offenders that no one was willing to identify.[2] □

After an early education partly overshadowed by World War Two, Achebe attended a government college for his secondary education, and University College, Ibadan, a daughter college of the University of London, for his undergraduate studies. On graduation, his application for funding for postgraduate work at Trinity College, Cambridge, was unfortunately rejected, forcing Achebe to quit university and to start work as an English teacher at a school in Oba. Only a few months passed in this employment, however, before he was contacted by the controller of the Nigerian Broadcasting Service (NBS), with the offer of an interview in Lagos:

■ At the interview Achebe found out how his name had been forwarded to the Broadcasting Service. The Director of the NBS in Lagos, Tom Chalmers, who had been seconded from the British Broadcasting Corporation (BBC), had made inquiries of James Welch at the University College, Ibadan. Chalmers wanted Welch to recommend somebody who would become their senior broadcasting officer in the Eastern Region. It was necessary to make such plans, in the opinion of the authorities at the NBS, since impending political independence held the implication that expatriates would make their exits soon after that event. It did not take James Welch long to come up with the name of the young Ogidi graduate he had earlier recommended to the University of Cambridge.[3] □

After Welch's recommendation, the job at the NBS gave Achebe direct access to the professional networks which would later enable him to secure the publication of his first novel. As chapter 1 of this book describes, it was thanks to a work–experience trip to the BBC in London that Achebe made the specific editorial contacts which ultimately brought *Things Fall Apart* to Heinemann.

If his early career was blessed with both luck and the privilege of professional recommendation, the critical success of *Things Fall Apart* and its successors can by no means simply be ascribed to such advantages. As *West Africa* magazine reported in a 40-year retrospective,[4] critic Donald MacRae, editorial adviser to Heinemann in 1957, was only the first to recognize that Achebe was an outstanding literary talent. On the basis of MacRae's assessment that Achebe's novel was 'The best first novel since the war',[5] the publisher decided to take an unusual chance, printing a full run of 2,000 copies in hardback. *West Africa*'s reporter Idowu Omoyele records that 'since then, over three million copies have been sold through the years. Translations of the novel can also be read in languages as diverse as French, Hungarian, Czech, Hebrew, Russian, Slovene, Spanish, Italian and German. Forty years on, *Things Fall Apart* is as historically significant as ever'.[6]

As Stephanie Newell observes in her recent study *West African Literatures* (2006),[7] many critics have seen the publication of *Things Fall Apart* as a major watershed in African fiction, setting the tone for much later writing, especially in its handling of colonialism. Half a century after the novel's emergence, it remains the most canonical of African texts. In terms of the reception and understanding of West African literature, however, the enormous impact of Achebe's novel has had some negative as well as positive effects, Newell argues. Certainly, its status as the 'founding text' of modern African literature has tended to obscure the importance of his precursors. As she says, critics have tended to condense the decades *before* Achebe's emergence into an 'expectant, Achebe-shaped pause'.[8] Similarly, the empire–writes–back model of *Things Fall Apart,* as well as its thematic emphases, has often been taken as a blueprint against which all other African writers should be judged. In fact, the African literary scene in the mid-twentieth century was far more varied and developed than many critics have assumed:

■ If elite authors in the empire were 'writing back' to the colonial centre at this time, as Ashcroft, Griffiths and Tiffin claim [in *The Empire Writes*

Back (1989)] for 'first generation' authors such as Achebe, many other West African writers were also writing novels, poems and plays for their own local communities, not primarily for metropolitan markets. . . . [T]hese other 'first-generation' authors produced a great deal of literature for their own consumption, not designed for – nor acceptable to – European publishing houses. The Yoruba novelist, D. O. Fagunwa [1903–63], who gained fame among Yoruba Nigerians for his work in the 1930s and 1940s, exemplifies the *localism* of this literature. Fagunwa's style of writing in the 1930s and 1940s inspired later international novelists, including Amos Tutuola [1920–97], whose *The Palm-Wine Drinkard* [1952] drew many themes from Yoruba-language texts and tales. . . .

Many other West African authors in the late colonial period also defied the 'empire writes back' model. One immensely influential branch of West African literature that tends to be neglected by literary scholars is the booming local market in self-help pamphlets, popular fiction, and religious literature by African authors writing in French and English. . . . Unfortunately, however, the 'starter' status conferred on *Things Fall Apart* tends to obscure the literary contexts in which Achebe was situated when he started to write.[9] □

As Newell suggests, the virtually incomparable literary status of *Things Fall Apart* has profoundly shaped the reception of Achebe's later works and those of other writers. Partly because of its relationship with the English literary canon and its more general intelligibility to an international audience, the novel has helped to define the ways in which outsiders approach African literature.

Newell's argument certainly raises questions about the wider implications of Achebe's positive critical reception, especially in the West. On the positive side, however, it must also be balanced by a recognition of his unique importance in promoting the work of many other African writers. As the publisher Alan Hill suggests in an interview with Kirsten Holst Petersen,[10] Achebe's indirect, and later direct, role in getting the international book trade to pay attention to African literary production is undeniable. Stressing his own pivotal role as well as Achebe's, Hill recalls the circumstances under which Heinemann's legendary African Writers Series was established in the wake of *Things Fall Apart*:

■ Achebe could not be unique. I felt there must be other potential authors among the new university-educated generation in Nigeria. So the following year, 1959, I went to West Africa and I took the book around with me. . . . I then went on to travel round the whole of sub-Saharan Africa, and when I got back it was clear I needed specialized help if we were to find and publish new African authors – a feat which none of the famous British publishers who were long-established in Africa had ever attempted.

Fortune favoured me. In 1960 Nelson's talented West African specialist Van Milne had a flaming row with his boss and resigned. I at once invited him to join me. Though he was only to stay two years, his contribution was crucial. We decided to make a really cheap paperback of *Things Fall Apart* – 25p in fact – and look for some other books to go with it so that we could put out a package. Achebe by now had written a second book, and Van picked up Kenneth Kaunda [born 1924; President of Zambia 1964–91] who was just out of prison and was writing a book about the independence struggle in Zambia. Van finally approached Cyprian Ekwensi [born 1921] who had made something of a name for himself by writing for Hutchinson, and he dug out a manuscript from his bottom drawer called *Burning Grass* [1962]. This made a group of four books, and by 1962 we were able to launch them as the first of 'The African Writers Series'.[11] □

Achebe himself became the editor of the series, a job he continued without pay for the following ten years. If, as Newell suggests, the success of *Things Fall Apart* was in some ways a distorting influence on African fiction, the author's role in bringing the continent's writers to international attention was nonetheless of immense importance. As Hill says, 'his name was the magnet that brought everything in, and his judgment was the decisive factor in what we published. And in addition to that, the fantastic sales of his own books . . . provided the economic basis for the rest of the series'.[12]

This book explores the critical reception of Achebe's fiction from *Things Fall Apart* in 1958 to *Anthills of the Savannah* in 1987. As the following chapters will illustrate, the critical treatment of Achebe's work has been extraordinarily varied. Well over a hundred book–length studies devoted to Achebe have been published worldwide over the last 40 years, together with hundreds of shorter pieces. Responses to Achebe's work range from interventions by some of the most influential figures in contemporary literary studies, to lightweight and hagiographic commentary. Because of the broad and disparate array of critical material on Achebe, library holdings are unfortunately often patchy and idiosyncratic. Much of the most thought-provoking critical material, especially that by Nigerian academics, is out of print and hard to access, whilst the existing 'casebooks' are inevitably limited in scope. A few excellent studies, such as those by C. L. Innes and Simon Gikandi, circulate widely, but it is important to set such work against the wide range of other treatments and interpretations of Achebe's work that exist. In writing this book, I have attempted to provide readers with a sense of this range. Whilst, inevitably, the book proceeds by selection rather than blanket coverage, the bibliography which concludes it is intended to help readers to further explore the work of this important and complex writer.

CHAPTER ONE

Things Fall Apart (1958): Challenging the Canon

A s we saw in the introduction, Achebe's first novel was written in the mid–1950s whilst he was working as a broadcaster for the Nigerian Broadcasting Corporation (NBC). As Ezenwa-Ohaeto relates in his excellent biography,[1] in 1956 Achebe was sent to attend a radio production course run by the BBC in London, followed by a period working in one of the company's departments. Achebe was encouraged by a Nigerian colleague to show his manuscript – which at that stage was a lengthy novel consisting of both *Things Fall Apart* and *No Longer at Ease* – to the established English novelist Gilbert Phelps (1915–93), a tutor on the course. Back in Nigeria, he decided to prune back the text severely and eventually sent a much shorter manuscript to Phelps under the title *Things Fall Apart*.

According to Ezenwa-Ohaeto, the manuscript was rejected by a string of London publishers. Even at Heinemann, with their well-developed West African markets, there was hesitancy about the sales potential of such an unusual offering. Eventually the book came to the attention of Alan Hill, one of the company's most innovative editors, who sent the text out to specialist readers. As we saw in the introduction, the terse verdict of one of Heinemann's educational advisers, Professor Donald MacRae, finally tipped the balance:

> ■ Heinemann's normal fiction reader read it and did a long report but the firm was still hesitating whether to accept it. Would anyone possibly buy a novel by an African? There are no precedents. So the rather

doubting bunch at the top of Heinemann's thought of the educational department, who after all sold books to Africa and were supposed to know about Africans. So they showed it to one of our educational advisers, Professor Donald MacRae, who was just back from West Africa. He read it in the office and ended the debate with an eleven word report: 'This is the best novel I have read since the war'.[2] □

As Ezenwa-Ohaeto describes:

■ Thus *Things Fall Apart* was published in hardback on 17 June 1958 with a print run of 2,000 copies. The publishers did not 'touch a word of it' in order to correct it and 'it achieved instant acclaim in the British national press, with enthusiastic reviews by such critics as Walter Allen [1911–95] and Angus Wilson [1913–91]' . . . It changed the direction of Alan Hill's publishing life and added a new dimension to the list of books published by Heinemann.[3] □

EARLY CRITICAL RESPONSES

In fact, initial responses to the novel in the London press combined praise for Achebe's vivid writing style with reservations about his handling of both traditional Ibo culture and the colonial encounter. According to the *Times Literary Supplement* on 20 June 1958, for example, the novel's conclusion was flawed by its 'confusion of attitude'. After his powerful depiction of African village life, the *TLS* reviewer maintains, Achebe loses his way when portraying the European missionaries: 'For Mr Achebe owes much to missionary education, and his sympathies are naturally more with the new than the old. His picture of the collapse of tribal custom is perhaps less than compassionate'.[4]

For Honor Tracy, reviewing for the BBC's own literary organ *The Listener* the following week, this initial sense of ambivalence towards *Things Fall Apart* is amplified, with admiration for the author's stylistic accomplishment tempered by an open, colonial disdain for his subject matter. Achebe's Iboland is, for Tracy, 'mindless, dominated by vague and preposterous terrors . . . incapable of advancement by itself'.[5] Would 'Mr Chinua' and his professional friends prefer to abandon their careers in order to wear raffia skirts and tend yams, she asks? Or is this essentially a work of hypocrisy? Whilst the novel might be a refreshing change from the usual diet of fiction, Tracy concludes, its portrait of the destructive effects of British colonialism is ultimately 'facile . . . mere sentimentality'.[6]

Amongst academic critics, Achebe met with a much more positive welcome. According to G. D. Killam, who first writes about the novel in the 1960s, *Things Fall Apart* is to be hailed as 'the first novel by a Nigerian writer to have serious claim to consideration as literature'.[7] Killam's main aim with Achebe's work, in liberal humanist fashion, is to establish its literary credentials with reference to the standards of the Anglo-Irish English literary canon. Ultimately, he argues, the value of all Achebe's novels as works of art must be disassociated from their particular '"anthropological" or "sociological" biases',[8] and judged instead on their 'universality' and fidelity in reflecting the 'human condition'.[9] These are works which 'bring news of a strange part of the world and of the values and attitudes of a group of people who have only recently achieved prominence in world affairs'.[10] Whilst the novels' meditations on themes of colonialism and cultural imperialism are likely to be of 'local' interest to Africans, what is far more important is to assess Achebe against the 'general' standards of the literary traditions of England. In Killam's analysis of *Things Fall Apart*, therefore, the overriding concern is to establish Achebe's technical proficiency and the soundness of his aesthetic judgement:

■ Achebe's prose has been described as 'leisurely' and 'stately' and a casual reading of the book, especially the first part, supports such judgment. Because Achebe refuses to take sides in the issues he describes and dramatizes, his presentation is disinterested and this quality is reflected in the writing. Yet, restrained as the pace may be, it moves the story forward with a sense of inevitability, the momentum gradually increasing, until the first climax is reached, Okonkwo's third sin against the Earth Goddess and his subsequent banishment. The casual approach and style quite belie the intensity of the life the novel evokes and from the outset Achebe's absolute certainty of approach is established.[11] □

Killam's commentary on characterization in the novel, similarly, is primarily motivated by a concern to identify the protagonist Okonkwo's 'universally' human qualities and to discuss him in terms of his 'representativeness' as a figure of his time:

■ Okonkwo was 'one of the greatest men of his time', the embodiment of Ibo values, the man who better than most symbolized his race. His stature is presented as heroic. His story, as was mentioned above, is presented in terms which resemble those of Aristotelian tragedy – the working out in the life of a hero of industry, courage and eminence, of an insistent fatality (in this book symbolized by the *chi,* or personal god) which transcends his ability to fully understand or resist a foreordained sequence of events. Achebe suggests as well the flaw, or flaws in his nature – his inordinate ambition and his refusal to tolerate anything less than excellence, taken in conjunction with an impulsive rage to which he easily gives way and which produces irrational responses to situations.[12] □

Dealing with the nineteenth-century West African context of *Things Fall Apart,* once again, the movement of Killam's analysis is always from the particular to the general, and from the general to the 'universal'. Discussing the cultivation of yams, for instance, he is keen to stress the ways in which Achebe's representations of farming and cooking invoke a more abstract opposition of male and female principles in Umuofian life, and through them a sense of the larger ethical and spiritual structures within which the clan understands its existence. In the following extract, for example, Killam analyses a passage from the novel in which Okonkwo asks for seed yams from the senior clansman, Nwakibie:

■ The images again are chosen from nature and suggest the continuum of the natural world of which man is part and at the centre. There are several references in this passage which require further comment because they lead into a deeper consideration of the way in which Achebe uses environment not only to symbolize character and theme but also to define the moral and ethical principles on which Ibo society is based and which is his ultimate concern in the book.

The yam is king: a man's wealth, status and reputation depend upon his possession of yams. Yams are food, true, and 'he who could feed his family on yams from one harvest to another was a very great man indeed'. But as well, 'yams stood for manliness'. With yams, which are wealth, a man could take titles in the clan; that is, he could achieve power and influence the conduct of the affairs of the clan. Conversely a man without yams was not able to take titles: he is described as *agbala* a word which as we have seen denotes 'a woman' and a man without titles. The two concepts are linked: to possess a female disposition is undesirable if not wholly unacceptable. Yet in the opposition between the man who possesses yams and the one who does not a paradox is apparent. While a continuing emphasis on male activities – acquisition of wealth and wives, the production of children, courage and resourcefulness in sport and war – informs the surface interest of the novel, all activity in *Things Fall Apart* is judged by what is or is not acceptable to *'Ani,* the Earth Goddess and source of all fertility . . . ultimate judge of morality and conduct' in the clan. In other words a powerful 'female principle' pervades the whole society of Umuofia and sits in judgement of events in the community.[13] □

For Killam, the ultimate tragedy of the novel is seen in terms of the interplay of these male and female principles. He is not unaware that the novel might in some way be concerned with the colonial encounter. The arrival of the white man in Umuofia, as he observes, signals the introduction of an alien religion and also a new system of trade. The importance of the latter, however, is that it brings out 'the male principle of acquisitiveness',[14] upsetting its traditional equilibrium with the female principle of nurture and respect for the earth. In this context, the death of Okonkwo is less caused than fated. As a representative of Ibo society, his demise represents nothing less than Achebe's recognition of 'the inevitable, irrepressible forces which determine historical change'.[15]

G. D. Killam's analysis of *Things Fall Apart*, then, attempts to establish the novel's status as a work of art, through the trademark 'universalism' of liberal humanism. The project of other early critics such as Eustace Palmer and A. G. Stock, meanwhile, is to further confirm the text's literary credentials by tracing relationships of influence between Achebe and canonical figures from the Anglo-Irish canon.

In Palmer's *An Introduction to the African Novel* (1972)[16] Achebe's relationship with Thomas Hardy (1840–1928), and especially with *Tess of the D'Urbervilles* (1891), is the focus of attention. Like *Tess*, Palmer argues, *Things Fall Apart* is structured around the interaction between its individual protagonist on the one hand and the imposition of inexorable, external social forces on the other. Like Killam, Palmer is resistant to an 'anthropological' approach to the narrative, but for different reasons. One of the strengths of the novel, he argues, is its unsentimental representation of traditional Ibo culture, which resists co-option to anticolonial orthodoxy:

■ There is a school of social anthropologists who rhapsodize over traditional African society seeing it as a welcome antidote to the materialism and commercial technology of Western society, with its morbid preoccupation with worldly possessions, status symbols, rapid promotion, and all the trappings of the rat-race. Such anthropologists are likely to have second thoughts on reading *Things Fall Apart,* for this society is just as competitive, just as materialistic, and just as concerned with status as any to be found in the Western world. This is a society in which a man's prestige is in direct proportion to the number of yams he has in his barn, the number of huts he has in his compound, the number of his wives and children, the 'titles' he has taken, and the number of human heads he has to his credit. Indeed, the struggle for the acquisition of titles is the equivalent of modern technological society's rat-race, and like the latter it can be an expensive, soul-destroying process in which the weak and the introverted are easily left behind. Modern technological societies (e.g. the U.S.A.), tend to evaluate a man according to his own achievement rather than his ancestry. This is exactly the situation we find in Umuofia, where '. . . a man was judged according to his worth and not according to the worth of his father'. As in any modern, competitive, and acquisitive society, age is respected, but achievement is revered.[17] □

Comparing *Things Fall Apart* to *Tess*, Palmer detects a strong strand of social determinism in Achebe's writing that reflects – and indeed outstrips – that of Hardy. If the fate of Tess is determined by colossal forces against which she struggles but over which she has no ultimate control, Achebe's Okonkwo is, for Palmer, even more radically defined by his environment.

■ Okonkwo is what his society has made him, for his most conspicuous qualities are a response to the demands of his society. If he is plagued by fear of failure and of weakness it is because his society puts such a premium on success; if he is obsessed with status it is because his society is preoccupied with rank and prestige; if he is always itching to demonstrate his prowess in war it is because his society reveres bravery and courage, and measures success by the number of human heads a man has won; if he is contemptuous of weaker men it is because his society has conditioned him into despising cowards. Okonkwo is the personification of his society's values, and he is determined to succeed in this rat-race.[18] □

In the novel, Okonkwo's fear of failure and weakness, his brutality and tendency towards self-destruction are balanced by the qualities of gentleness, generosity and serenity embodied by other characters, such as Unoka. As Palmer argues, therefore, one of the masterstrokes of the novel in terms of structure is Achebe's decision to have the white man's arrival in Umuofia coincide with Okonkwo's period of banishment, after he commits the crime of killing a kinsman. By the time Okonkwo returns from his seven-year exile, the unfolding of a new *status quo* is well under way. In contrast to his previous position of social dominance, Okonkwo's attitude of violent opposition is, on his return, inflected with a sense of belatedness and impotency. According to Palmer, the inherent 'inhumanity'[19] of traditional society has already rendered it so vulnerable to exploitation by the missionaries and the colonial administration that resistance is doomed to failure.

For Palmer, the presence of what he terms 'sociological' information and even 'sociological' scenes does raise a question mark over the literary quality of Achebe's novel: 'Critics object not only because such information makes the novel tedious, but also because the novel form ought to exist in its own right, not as a sociological document, but as a medium for the treatment of personal relationships'.[20] It is a mark of Achebe's novelistic skill, he argues however, that the author is able to incorporate such material in a way which does not detract from the dramatic impact or the aesthetic balance of his text.

The assumption here that *Things Fall Apart* requires validation against the yardstick of English Literature might seem, to more recent readers, decidedly problematic: Palmer's comparison of Achebe's style with that of his compatriot Flora Nwapa (1931–93) raises a parallel set of questions. For Palmer, Nwapa's work is to be dismissed out of hand. African fiction may be very acceptable to the English reader, Palmer implies, provided it does not dwell on African culture for its own sake. This fastidious and sometimes patronizing attitude is communicated quite clearly, for example, when he describes a scene in which Okonkwo and Ogbuefi Ezenwa share some snuff:

■ Achebe does more than convey the friendly custom of snuff taking among Ibos. This, and the ensuing scene are presented in terms of dialogue, deliberate gestures, and movements, and are therefore fully 'realized'. Indeed, scenes like these do not bore or annoy the reader because of the superb skill with which Achebe handles them. The incidents are related in such a way that we feel their relevance, and they are dramatically evoked in such powerful prose that their reality is enacted, and we do not stop to question either their relevance or their authenticity. We only have to contrast Achebe's technique with that of an inferior novelist, Flora Nwapa, the author of *Efuru* [1966], to see how skilful he is. Miss Nwapa's sociological descriptions, which are almost always irrelevant, are often prefaced by some comment like this: 'They organized themselves in groups and sang from door to door. Their song went like this' . . . And then follows an Ibo song or an elaborate recipe for some kind of soup. The introductory comment, 'their song went like this' detaches the song or whatever follows from its context, and it becomes purely sociological information.[21] □

In A. G. Stock's idiosyncratic but influential early essay 'Yeats and Achebe' (1968),[22] *Things Fall Apart* is again read through the lens of the Anglo-Irish canon, and specifically through the particular conception of history described in the 1925–37 text *A Vision* by W. B. Yeats (1865–1939). Stock begins by describing Yeats' notion of time and change, before attempting to establish its structuring influence on Achebe's novel:

■ For Yeats the whole of potential being is a vast chaos, a 'fabulous formless darkness'. Every civilization is an ordered structure which mind builds up, the cumulative mind that is in tradition, by defining a hierarchy of values and imposing it on experience. The chaos is always beating on its walls, but is kept out so long as the hierarchy holds its own integrity – which shapes its artefacts, its speculative thought, its codes of conduct, and moulds its children by giving a language to their experience. But to define is to limit, and mind cannot be contained for ever within any one enclosed order; mind belongs also to the outer darkness. In every hierarchy there are some impulses made shameful because others are exalted, some types of personality frustrated which would have been fulfilled in a different mould, beliefs made nonsensical which could have made sense in another context of thought. In the end these negligible-seeming cracks make up the 'opposing gyre' which becomes its nemesis: they widen, coalesce, form a breach in the walls letting in the 'mere anarchy' of the kingdom of darkness. Thus, no civilization can either remain static or evolve for ever towards a more inclusive perfection. It must both collapse from within and be overwhelmed from without, and what replaces it will appear most opposite to itself, being built from all that it overlooked or undervalued.[23] □

With reference to Yeats' poem 'The Second Coming' (1921), invoked by Achebe's title, Stock reads the first part of *Things Fall Apart* as an exposition of traditional Ibo culture as a 'ceremony of innocence',[24] an account of a cultural equilibrium in which the 'seeds of disintegration'[25] are initially hidden but gradually rise to visibility. Again Okonkwo is read as a representative figure, who encapsulates not only the pride and strength of the clan, but also its intolerance of weakness:

> ■ The code of Umuofia might tolerate gentleness but it expected strength, and because of his father's inadequacy Okonkwo was afraid to live by his merely natural strength; he must be strong to the repression of all patience with weakness [*sic*]. So it came about that his own son was driven from mere mediocrity to conscious alienation, and found in the white man's religion a different code which turned his weakness into a kind of strength.[26] □

Once again, rather than viewing the collapse of traditional Ibo civilization as an effect of colonization and cultural imperialism, Stock uses the Yeatsian model of the spiralling gyre to read Achebe's novel in a different way. Instead, it is seen as a study of a culture ruining itself, descending towards anarchy against the background of great historical change.

WRITING BACK: LATER CRITICISM

Amongst later scholarship on *Things Fall Apart*, the approach to Achebe's writing taken by A. G. Stock, Eustace Palmer and others comes in for a significant amount of criticism. In Oladele Taiwo's book *Culture and the Nigerian Novel* (1976),[27] indeed, the very practice of appointing European 'literary godfathers'[28] for African writers is seen as unhelpful to the development of either African literature itself or its critical appreciation. Taiwo stresses the importance of addressing such literature in relation to the differing cultural environments of the nations and regions from which it emerges. His own approach to Achebe is to read his fiction as 'a serious artist's interpretation of the history of his people'[29] across a historical range from the nineteenth century to the present, with a vision encompassing both rural and urban life. In the case of *Things Fall Apart*, Taiwo views Okonkwo as a historically representative (if not typical) figure, who 'embodies in a magnified form the strengths and weaknesses of his society'.[30] Whilst he wants to insist on the wider validity of the novel, he is also keen to relate the breakdown of Umuofian society to the specific historical circumstances of South Eastern Nigeria, and

even more closely than that, to a specific confrontation between Ibo
culture and Christianity at Aro-Ndizuogu in 1916:

■ This brought about widespread dislocation of tribal life in the same
way that the events in *Things Fall Apart* mark the beginning of the
eventual liquidation of an old way of life. To limit our interpretation of
tragedy only to the fate of Okonkwo is, therefore, to ignore the profound
human issues raised in the novel, unduly narrow its scope, misread its
title *(Things* not *Something)* and undermine the achievement of the
novelist in this impressive work.[31] □

As we will see in chapter 2, Taiwo's call for more wide-ranging
readings of Achebe as a historical novelist is answered by several more
recent critics. In his rejection of scholars who unthinkingly subordinate Achebe's work to the question of his European literary models,
moreover, Taiwo's argument is also echoed in much subsequent
criticism. In his 2003 study *Chinua Achebe*,[32] for example, Nahem
Yousaf shows that the relationship of influence between Achebe and
the Anglo-Irish literary canon is in fact far more complex and
two-way than earlier critics had allowed. In an important way, he
suggests, Achebe's works can be seen as not merely reflecting but
(in the now familiar phrase) 'writing back' to authors such as Joseph
Conrad (1857–1924) and Joyce Cary (1888–1957), repudiating the
colonialist image of Africa that novels like *Heart of Darkness* (1902)
and *Mister Johnson* (1939) worked to produce and perpetuate.

In his 1977 essay 'An Image of Africa: Racism in Conrad's *Heart
of Darkness*',[33] Achebe himself attacks Conrad's novel for the way it
silences and dehumanizes Africans, presenting Africa in terms of a
cultural and metaphysical darkness which the European enters at his
peril. Yousaf picks up on this critique, reading Achebe's own writing as a serious engagement with African culture at the end of the
nineteenth century, and at the same time as a gesture of resistance to
the colonialist discourse that had so violently overwritten it during
the period of colonial rule. In this way Achebe's works are seen as
contesting the entire regime of representation foisted on Africans as
part and parcel of the colonial encounter:

■ The ideologies of imperialism that Achebe rejects have a long
literary tradition. Characters who make their fortunes in 'the colonies'

include Victorian capitalists in Jane Austen's [1775–1817] *Mansfield Park* (1814) and Charles Dickens's [1812–70] *Dombey and Son* (1847) and, later, intrepid heroes who could almost be based on Henry Morton Stanley and his travels as recounted in *In Darkest Africa* (1890). Empire adventurers are best represented in those texts which utilize the literary form of the romance or the 'boy's own' adventure story as the structuring framework for male penetrations into Africa's interior, like the novels of H. Rider Haggard [1856–1925] and John Buchan [1875–1940]. Africa is fetishized, if not invested with desire and eroticism; in *She* (1887), and in Joseph Conrad's *Heart of Darkness* (1902) a demonic, sensual African woman can overwhelm a sophisticated European like Kurtz. Holly and Leo in Haggard's *She,* Marlow and Kurtz in *Heart of Darkness,* and David Crawfurd in Buchan's *Prester John* (1910) all journey with a similar set of imperialist preconceptions to an 'Other' world that is the African continent. The journey is always a physical journey – the novels pseudo-travelogues – but also a psychological, exploratory journey towards the heart, or *Kor* in Haggard's case, of the imperial venture and the human condition (Sigmund Freud [1856–1939] even refers to Haggard's *She* in *The Interpretation of Dreams,* 1900, as the heart of the unconscious).[34] □

The characteristic manoeuvre of empire writing when dealing with Africa, Yousaf argues, is to commodify Africans, rendering them interchangeable. For many critics, this charge can certainly be levelled at *Heart of Darkness*, and Conrad is often seen as the prime target of Achebe's critique in *Things Fall Apart*. As Yousaf says, however, the equal importance of Joyce Cary as a 'negative influence' on him, and in particular the 'Nigerian' novel *Mister Johnson*, should also be recognized. Cary was a colonial civil servant who worked as an Assistant District Officer between 1913 and 1920. *Mister Johnson* is the story of a young Nigerian who variously steals, borrows and murders his way through the lower echelons of the British colonial administration, before meeting an ignominious end at the hands of (yes) the local Assistant District Officer. Comparing Cary's representation of the figure of Johnson to Conrad's depiction of Africans in *Heart of Darkness*, Yousaf describes the cultural complex against which Achebe is attempting to 'write back':

■ Cary seems to visualize Johnson out of the tradition of minstrelsy in the United States and 1930s cinematic depictions as much as European stereotypes. Johnson's self-dramatizing is the stuff of *Gone with the Wind* (1936) and his demeanour that of an obsequious Stepin

Fetchit. On discovering he may be taken to court to honour his debts, he responds:

> 'Oh, Gawd! Oh, Jesus! I done finish – I finish now – Mister Johnson done finish – Oh, Gawd, you no fit do nutting – Mister Johnson too big dam' fool – he fool chile – oh, my Gawd'. He hits himself on the forehead with his fist. 'Why you so bloody big dam' fool, you Johnson? You happy for Fada – you catch government job – you catch good pay – you catch dem pretty girl – you catch nice gentlemen frien's – you catch new shoes – you big man – now you play de bloody fool. . . '

> . . . Johnson is a caricature with incongruous dress sense and affected English mannerisms and whereas Conrad's Congolese are inarticulate cannibals ('catch im . . . eat im'), Cary's Nigerians are pidgin-speaking incompetents. Johnson is a commodification in the way of Conrad's risible 'fireman', who is an 'improved specimen' because 'to look at him was as edifying as seeing a dog in a parody of breeches and a feather hat walking on his hind legs' . . . In order to simplify the Africans, Cary imposes a double bind from which they are powerless to escape: they are either 'savages' whose society is petrified or the 'assimilated' (like Johnson), marginalized Nigerians who suffer the ridicule of the Europeans they seek to emulate. It was left to Achebe and the generation of African writers that followed Cary to open up such closed and caricatured representations.[35] □

In C. L. Innes' book *Chinua Achebe* (1990),[36] the relationship between Cary and Achebe is explored in more detail. For Innes, Achebe's language, as much as his narrative technique, can be seen as a form of creative appropriation. In his hands, she argues, the English novel is 'Africanized'. As she informs us, *Things Fall Apart* was, in fact, initially planned by Achebe as an alternative version of Cary's *Mister Johnson*. In lots of ways, it is *No Longer at Ease* which seems to provide the clearer narrative parallel, dealing as it does with a young Nigerian clerk who experiences the same temptations and dilemmas as Cary's hero. For Innes, however, *Things Fall Apart* must also be seen as a novel 'written back' to Cary. If *Mister Johnson* centers on an opposition between 'intuitive feeling and rigid social codes,[37] this is reflected in *Things Fall Apart* as an opposition between the 'femininity' of Unoka and Nwoye and the 'masculinity' of Okonkwo. Cary's novel sets up a schematic contrast between the rule-bound 'correctness' of British officials and the emotional energy of Africans. In *Things Fall Apart*, Innes claims moreover, it is a deliberate strategy of Achebe's to abandon this (essentially racist) equation and to locate the conflict instead within the Umuofian community itself:

■ The fact that the conflicts are located *in* the African community and then shadowed by the British characters makes an important difference, for at once the Africans become something more than symbols of qualities which, however important, are nevertheless subordinate elements in the total complex of the European psyche. Achebe's characters are complex individuals, types rather than archetypes, the resolution of whose conflicts is central to the plot. Okonkwo's role is not to Save the British administrator and it is clear that Achebe's Europeans, even the more liberal ones like Mr. Brown, will never dream that they have anything to learn from Africans – who may be studied but never imitated. That is part of the tragedy for the Africans, who find it almost impossible to comprehend the depth and consequences of the white man's arrogance.[38] □

In the course of her analysis, Innes compares several key elements in the two novels, beginning with their portrayal of marriage arrangements. By contrast to the brutally business like marriage of Johnson to Bamu in Cary's novel, in which the girl is bartered by her family like a 'choice piece of horseflesh',[39] Innes stresses the elaborate etiquette described in Achebe's novel:

■ One may contrast Achebe's depiction of the agreement and discussion over the marriage contract for Obierika's daughter, Akueke. First there is a long period of drinking and chatting before the business of settling the bridal dowry is brought up. As if to make the contrast quite explicit, one of the men compares their traditional method of using a bundle of sticks to settle the dowry with the customs of other clans such as Abame and Aninta: 'All their customs are upside down. They do not decide bride price as we do, with sticks. They haggle and bargain as if they were buying a goat or a cow in the market'. Achebe does not let the point rest, for we are shown yet another part of a marriage ceremony in part 2, the consummation of the marriage of Uchendu's youngest son; in part 3 the question of the marriage of Okonkwo's daughters is discussed, and we learn of their willing agreement to await their return to Umuofia. We are also reminded several times of the special relationship between Okonkwo and Ekwefi.[40] □

Similarly, Innes contrasts Cary's portrait of corruption and despotism amongst African rulers with Achebe's intricate portrait of Ibo

self-government, where decision making centres around the democratic consultation of elders, and power is exercised with detailed
regard for the peace and equilibrium of the community as a whole.
As importantly, she also focuses on Achebe's Africanization of character and the detailed attention the novel lavishes on its representation of a family and social context for Okonkwo:

> ■ Perhaps one of the most significant things about *Things Fall Apart*
> is the way in which it demonstrates the intricate relationship between
> a man's individual psychology and the social context in which he has
> grown up. And that is where the novel makes its firmest response to
> Cary. Mister Johnson is representative of the free and unfettered spirit;
> he is an earlier version of Gulley Jimson, the carefree artist in Cary's
> later and more successful novel, *The Horse's Mouth* [1944]. So in
> terms of the theme of the novel it is appropriate that he have no family,
> no background, no social context other than the vague suggestion
> of a mission education. He is a man without roots, belonging to
> romance rather than to historical narrative. The European reader, long
> accustomed to such figures in literature if not in life – wandering poets,
> Synge's tramps and playboys [e.g. in *The Playboy of the Western
> World* (1907) by J. M. Synge (1871–1909)], bohemian artists – does
> not readily question Mister Johnson's rootlessness. But Mister Johnson
> is essentially a European creation. To the Nigerian reader, according
> to Achebe, such a figure is hard to imagine; no Southern Nigerian (as
> Johnson is supposed to be) in the early part of the twentieth century
> could be without a family or relatives to care for him and come to his
> assistance when he is in trouble.[41] □

For Innes, the central strategy of Achebe's novel is thus to reinterpret Cary's opposition of reason versus feeling in *Mister Johnson*, as
a tension between masculine and feminine principles in traditional
Ibo culture. Okonkwo's tragedy, for her, is precipitated by his fear
of, and inability to embrace, the feminine within himself. Nowhere
in the novel is this more starkly represented than in the killing of his
foster-son, Ikemefuna. For Innes, indeed, this is the pivotal moment
of the entire novel. As a figure who represents the perfect balance
of masculine and feminine principles – who is both a hunter and a
skilled musician – Ikemefuna is read as 'the embodiment of the clan's
potential'.[42] His sacrifice thus symbolizes the end of the cultural equilibrium which makes Umuofia resilient in the face of internal strife
and external threat.

In contrast to Cary's work, which represents a kind of 'domestica-tion' of African characters for the consumption of Europeans, one of the achievements of Achebe's novel is its insistence on the *otherness* of Ibo culture, Innes argues. In part this is achieved by the inclusion of Ibo vocabulary, sayings and proverbs, which without mystify-ing it, serve as a reminder of the cultural distinctness and integrity of the community being described. At the same time, on the level of style, Achebe's constant changes of time and tense effectively prevent the reader from being passively 'swept along by events', she suggests. Achebe's technique encourages a more active and reflective readerly attitude in which aesthetic and political engagement go hand in hand:

■ For Achebe, the problem of artistic expression and the problem of social change are inextricable, for language is central to both. The reader's task is to be aware of the limits of language, to be alert to the ways in which words, formulas and rhetoric can obscure understanding. He is not allowed to separate feeling and judgement, to swim unreflecting before emerging on the shore to look back and criticize, but must continually combine criticism and sympathy.[43] □

LANGUAGE

If, as we have seen, there is a schism between the comparatively conser-vative, early criticism of *Things Fall Apart* and later 'revisionist' accounts which stress the text's resistance to colonialism and colonial liter-ary culture, these arguments are crystallized in the so-called 'language debate' that came to prominence in the early 1960s. In his own criti-cism, such as the essay 'English and the African Writer'(1965),[44] indeed, Achebe takes up the question 'what is African literature?' and sets out his own distinctive position. Reference is made to a 1962 conference in Makerere, in which the future of English as a literary language in Africa had been a central point of contention. Importantly, he draws a funda-mental distinction between the notion of 'ethnic' and 'national' litera-tures, respectively. His own literary production is clearly situated in terms of the latter, as a body of writing based in the Ibo cultural tradition, but written in English and reflecting the rise of the modern nation state:

■ A national literature is one that takes the whole nation for its province, and has a realized or potential audience throughout its territory. In other words a literature that is written in the *national* language. An ethnic literature is one which is available only to one ethnic group within the nation. If you take Nigeria as an example, the national literature, as I see it, is the literature written in English; and the ethnic literatures are in Hausa, Ibo, Yoruba, Effik, Edo, Ijaw, etc., etc.

Any attempt to define African literature in terms which overlook the complexities of the African scene and the material of time is doomed to failure. After the elimination of white rule shall have been completed, the single most important fact in Africa in the second half of the twentieth century will appear to be the rise of individual nation states. I believe that African literature will follow the same pattern.[45] □

In this sense, at the same time as acknowledging its capacity for resistance to colonial ideology, Achebe casts his own writing as a product of colonialism. The English language has been thrust on Nigerians for good or ill, he argues, and it is a legitimate choice for writers to extract what is valuable from that legacy, without losing sight of the evils that came alongside it:

■ What are the factors which have conspired to place English in the position of national language in many parts of Africa? Quite simply the reason is that these nations were created in the first place by the intervention of the British which, I hasten to add, is not saying, that the peoples comprising these nations were invented by the British. . . . I believe that in political and economic terms . . . this arbitrary creation called Nigeria holds out wonderful prospects. Yet the fact remains that Nigeria was created by the British – for their own ends. Let us give the devil his due: colonialism in African disrupted many things, but it did create big political units where there were small, scattered ones before. Nigeria had hundreds of autonomous communities ranging in size from the vast Fulani Empire founded by Usman dan Fodio in the North to tiny village entities in the East. Today it is one country.

Of course there are areas of Africa where colonialism divided a single ethnic group among two or even three powers. But on the whole it did bring together many peoples that had hitherto gone their several ways. And it gave them a language with which to talk to one another. If it failed to give them a song, it at least gave them a tongue, for sighing. There are not many countries in Africa today where you could abolish the language of the erstwhile colonial powers and still retain the facility for mutual communication. Therefore those African writers who have chosen to write in English or French are not unpatriotic smart alecs with an eye on the main chance – outside their own countries. They are by-products of the same processes that made the new nation states of Africa.[46] □

One of the most important ongoing effects of colonialism is that it has given the English language a communicative power that outstrips that of all the indigenous languages of Africa, Achebe argues. It is for this reason that writers should not be castigated by their fellows for adopting 'the world language which history has forced down our throats'.[47] Against the claims of critics such as Obi Wali that African literature written in English 'can only lead to sterility, uncreativity and frustration',[48] Achebe suggests that there is much to be gained from a creative practice which adopts the language but also reshapes it for new purposes. Citing the poets Christopher Okigbo (1932–67) and J. P. Clark (born 1935), he demonstrates ways in which English can be successfully and beautifully 'Africanized' by skilled writers. Citing specific instances such as the latter's poem 'Night Rain' (1961), Achebe pushes his case by saying:

■ I do not see any signs of sterility anywhere here. What I do see is a new voice coming out of Africa, speaking of African experience in a world-wide language. So my answer to the question, Can an African ever learn English well enough to be able to use it effectively in creative writing? is certainly yes. If on the other hand you ask: Can he ever learn to use it like a native speaker? I should say, I hope not. It is neither necessary nor desirable for him to be able to do so. The price a world language must be prepared to pay is submission to many different kinds of use. The African writer should aim to use English in a way that brings out his message best without altering the language to the extent that its value as a medium of international exchange will be lost. He should aim at fashioning out an English which is at once universal and able to carry his peculiar experience. I have in mind here the writer who has something new, something different to say. The nondescript writer has little to tell us, anyway, so he might as well tell it in conventional language and get it over with. If I may use an extravagant simile, he is like a man offering a small, nondescript routine sacrifice for which a chick or less will do. A serious writer must look for an animal whose blood can match the power of his offering.[49] □

Amongst the other delegates to the 1962 Makerere conference was a young student called James Ngũgĩ (born 1938) who was to become Achebe's most celebrated antagonist in the language debate. Renamed Ngũgĩ wa Thiong'o in the Kenyan tradition of patrilineage, his later publications on English and its uses could not differ more sharply from Achebe's. In recognition of the diverse cultural and linguistic geography of Africa and its history of violent homogenization under European imperialism, it is Ngũgĩ's contention that a renewed focus on self-determination in language must be central to any programme of social renewal. For Ngũgĩ, differently from Achebe, struggles over language are seen as indivisible from the broader struggle over colonialism and independence themselves:

■ The contention started a hundred years ago when in 1884 the capitalist powers of Europe sat in Berlin and carved an entire continent with a multiplicity of peoples, cultures, and languages into different colonies. . . . The Berlin-drawn division under which Africa is still living was obviously economic and political, despite the claims of bible-wielding diplomats, but it was also cultural. Berlin in 1884 saw the division of Africa into the different languages of the European powers. African countries, as colonies and even today as neo-colonies, came to be defined and to define themselves in terms of the languages of Europe: English-speaking, French-speaking or Portuguese-speaking African countries.

Unfortunately writers who should have been mapping paths out of that linguistic encirclement of their continent also came to be defined and to define themselves in terms of the languages of imperialist imposition. Even at their most radical and pro-African position in their sentiments and articulation of problems they still took it as axiomatic that the renaissance of African cultures lay in the languages of Europe.[50] □

Looking back with a critical eye at the 1962 Makerere conference, Ngũgĩ notes the anomalous nature of its organization: as a meeting of 'African Writers of English Expression', it embraced students like himself, with only a couple of short stories in English to his credit, whilst excluding some of the most important figures in African literature, such as Shabaan Robert (1909) and D. O. Fagunwa (1903–63), because they wrote in Kiswahili and Yoruba, respectively. The conference's central debate about language and the future of African literature was thus, he argues, radically skewed from the outset towards a recoronation of English and other major European languages as the indispensable tools for African writers:

■ English, like French and Portuguese, was assumed to be the natural language of literary and even political mediation between African people in the same nation and between nations in Africa and other continents. In some instances these European languages were seen as having a capacity to unite African peoples against divisive tendencies inherent in the multiplicity of African languages within the same geographic state. Thus Ezekiel Mphahlele later could write, in a letter to *Transition* number 11, that English and French have become the common language with which to present a nationalist front against white oppressors, and even 'where the whiteman has already retreated, as in the independent states, these two languages are still a unifying force'. In the literary sphere they were often seen as coming to save African languages against themselves. Writing a foreword to Birago Diop's [1906–89] book *Contes d'Amadou Koumba* [1947] Sédar Senghor [born 1906] commends him for using French to rescue the spirit and style of old African fables and tales. . . . The fact is that all of us who opted for European languages – the conference participants and the generation that followed them – accepted that fatalistic logic to a greater or lesser degree. We were guided by it and the only question which preoccupied us was how best to make the borrowed tongues carry the weight of our African experience by, for instance, making them 'prey' on African proverbs and other peculiarities of African speech and folklore. For this task, Achebe (*Things Fall Apart; Arrow of God*), Amos Tutuola (*The Palmwine Drinkard*; *My Life in the Bush of Ghosts* [1954]), and Gabriel Okara [born 1921] (*The Voice* [1964]) were often held as providing the three alternative models.[51] □

Against this hardening consensus, Ngũgĩ is concerned to ask why African writers should be so keen to embellish the literary traditions of erstwhile colonial powers, whilst neglecting to develop the cultural resources implicit in indigenous languages such as Ijaw, with its distinctive philosophical traditions, ideas and legacy of experience. Importantly, Ngũgĩ distinguishes the physical force of colonialism from the differently invasive effects of cultural imperialism in the nineteenth and twentieth centuries. He argues that, with regard to the latter, language itself must be recognized as the most potent tool of Africa's subjugation. The task for writers and intellectuals, then, is to understand the processes by which this cultural hegemony was established and the means by which it might begin to be undone:

■ How did we arrive at this acceptance of 'the fatalistic logic of the unassailable position of English in our literature', in our culture and in our politics? What was the route from the Berlin of 1884 via the Makerere of 1962 to what is still the prevailing and dominant logic a hundred years later? How did we, as African writers, come to be so feeble towards the claims of our languages on us and so aggressive in our claims on other languages, particularly the languages of our colonization?

Berlin of 1884 was effected through the sword and the bullet. But the night of the sword and the bullet was followed by the morning of the chalk and the blackboard. The physical violence of the battlefield was followed by the psychological violence of the classroom.[52] □

He recalls the regime of corporal punishment dealt out to him and fellow pupils in their colonial school in Kenya during the 1950s, whenever they were caught speaking Gikuyu in the environs of the school. By contrast, he records the ways in which proficiency in English was recognized with praise, school prizes and other rewards. Whilst the literary curriculum was dominated by texts of the Anglo-Irish canon, study of the orature of Kenya was completely suppressed. For Ngũgĩ, there is a direct relationship between the practice of cultural imperialism exercised by the colonial school system and what he sees as the quasi-colonial *status quo* represented by writers like Achebe in contemporary Africa. Such literature cannot, he argues, be separated from the ongoing cultural domination of the continent, continued after independence by a new bourgeoisie who remain umbilically tied to the culture of imperialism:

■ The twenty years that followed the Makerere conference gave the world a unique literature – novels, stories, poems, plays written by Africans in European languages – which soon consolidated itself into a tradition with companion studies and a scholarly industry.

Right from its conception it was the literature of the petty-bourgeoisie born of the colonial schools and universities. It could not be otherwise, given the linguistic medium of its message. Its rise and development reflected the gradual accession of this class to political and even economic dominance. But the petty-bourgeoisie in Africa was a large class with different strands in it. It ranged from that section which looked forward to a permanent alliance with imperialism in which it played the role of an intermediary between the bourgeoisie of the western metropolis and the people of the colonies . . . to that section which saw the future in terms of a vigorous independent national economy in African capitalism or in some kind of socialism, what I shall here call the nationalistic or patriotic bourgeoisie. This literature by Africans in European languages was specifically that of the nationalistic bourgeoisie in its creators, its thematic concerns and its consumption.[53] □

In Gareth Griffiths' essay 'Language and Action in the Novels of Chinua Achebe' (1971),[54] a third way is found which (in retrospect) indicates the possibility of common ground between these two important writers. Griffiths argues that, although *Things Fall Apart* is written in English, one of its most important effects as a narrative is to draw attention to the very questions of language, accessibility and power with which Ngũgĩ is concerned. Griffiths begins by focusing on the final scene of Achebe's novel, in which the hanging body of Okonkwo is seen from two contrasting viewpoints, that of Obierika and that of the commissioner:

■ To the commissioner the inability of Okonkwo's fellow tribesmen to handle the body of a suicide is fascinating. He is, we are told, 'a student of primitive customs'. Transferred momentarily by the phrase from an 'inside' to an 'outside' view of the action we become aware more decisively than before that the words we have been reading in English are reproducing Ibo thoughts and speech-patterns.

Obierika, who had been gazing steadily at his friend's dangling body, turned suddenly to the District Commissioner; and said ferociously: 'That man was one of the greatest men in Umuofia. You drove him to kill himself; and now he will be buried like a dog'. . . He could not say more. His voice trembled and choked his words. 'Shut up!' shouted one of the messengers, quite unnecessarily.

The command is unnecessary for two reasons. First, because Obierika, overcome by his feelings, can say no more; and, secondly, because anything he does say, including the speech he has just made, will be quite incomprehensible to the commissioner who has had to speak 'through an interpreter'. To the commissioner anything that he says sounds like a series of primitive grunts. They are speaking, we recall ironically, in a savage tongue. Through a simple pointing device Achebe can demonstrate the commissioner's exclusion from the society he 'rules'. It is a linguistic exile, and the staple of the novel is language. Achebe can recreate the bitter history of his people through the history of words.[55] □

If the novel's conclusion dramatizes the vexed relationship between English and Ibo, it partly does so through the implicit contrast

Achebe sets up between his own work of cultural archaeology, *Things Fall Apart*, and that of the commissioner, *The Pacification of the Primitive Tribes of the Lower Niger*. Again, Griffiths suggests, the effect of Achebe's narrative is to destabilize us as readers, forcing us to question the status of the text we have just read:

■ By the very act of writing Achebe's stance is contiguous to that of the commissioner. Both seek to reduce the living, oral world of Umuofia to a series of words on the page; and they are English words, for Achebe as well as for the commissioner. In his attempt to present a picture of the destruction of tribal Iboland Achebe is aware that in gaining the voice to speak he reveals his involvement with the destruction which he records. That is why there is no simple condemnation possible, not for Okonkwo, nor Nwoye, nor even for the commissioner. Neither is there any temptation to sentimentalise. The search is not for a lost idyll, nor an historical excuse, but for a meaningful appraisal of what has been lost and what gained, and a clear analysis of where the writer and his contemporaries stand in the list of residual legatees.[56] □

Clearly, this reading would contrast significantly with Ngũgĩ's dismissal of all anglophone writing in Africa as weak, bourgeois and neoimperialist. For Griffiths, the novel is a vehicle of historical enquiry which is ultimately directed towards contemporary political action. In order to discover what they can be or can do, he argues, literary intellectuals in Africa need to assess the legacies of the past, both good and bad, so as to understand the cultural complex that has arisen from it. At the centre of this enquiry, for each writer, is the problem of language:

■ The very choice of language involves him in a deliberate public stance; his use of dialect, or of phrases in his native language, are cultural gests [*sic*] as well as rhetorical devices; while his movement from one register to another in the recording of speech is a direct sociological comment. Inevitably in such a situation the writing of a novel, even more than usual, becomes an act of self-definition. It is Achebe's distinction that he recognizes this more clearly than any other African writer, and uses his situation to define the history of his own rhetoric.[57] □

Reading Achebe unambiguously as a 'committed' writer, Griffiths sees *Things Fall Apart* as part of a larger effort at cultural rehabilitation. For him, that project necessarily involves a recognition of the

Janus-faced role of English as a tool not only of colonialism, but also of independence. Once again, the figure of Nwoye is seen as of pivotal importance in the novel, especially as a bridge between traditional culture and the new colonial order:

■ In *Things Fall Apart* the central character is Okonkwo. But, as the novel develops, we realize that it is Nwoye not Okonkwo who takes the first step that will lead the Ibo writer to be able to record in 'a world language' the disintegration of his tribal past. Okonkwo's 'success' leads to his destruction, Nwoye's 'failure' ensures his survival in the changing world of Umuofia. The modern African intellectual is the descendant of the tribal underdog, an ironic variation on the theory of social Darwinism which has played such a prominent and derisory role in the colonial view of the Afro-Asian world.

This is a concomitant of the central irony of the book, that Okonkwo is destroyed because he performs more than is expected of him, and sacrifices his personal life to an exaggerated, even pathological, sense of communal duty. . . . Nwoye, on the other hand, puts personal feelings above social responsibility. He and Okonkwo's father, to whom he is considered a 'throwback', are more comprehensible to the post-tribal world. In this respect Nwoye's greater capacity for personal relationships and his deeper feelings for personal value is clearly a gain; but one which is accompanied by a loss of pride, of social unity and clarity of purpose. It involves the destruction of the tribe as the unit of value. Nwoye's movement away from the tribal values that Okonkwo defends is the first stage of the journey for the Western-educated Nigerians of Achebe's own generation. Achebe is the inheritor of Nwoye's revolt as well as of Okonkwo's sacrifice. He can celebrate the 'depth and value and beauty' of tribal Ibo culture, but he must do so with the tools gained in the act of destroying it.[58] □

Reinforcing Griffiths' position, James Snead[59] is one of several critics to notice how *Things Fall Apart* works to destabilize the viewing position of European readers. Writing in Homi Bhabha's influential essay collection *Nation and Narration* (1990), Snead points not only to the novel's range of unfamiliar cultural reference and its skilful manipulation of point of view, but also to its use of language, in which Ibo words and phrases are constantly incorporated but frequently left untranslated. Like Innes, Snead sees Achebe as 'Africanizing' the novel in ways which render it disconcertingly strange/familiar:

■ The European reader, feeling at the outset at home in a literary form that Europe has developed, is made to assume, without warning, the vulnerable position of the African in a European culture which he or she is expected to understand and absorb. Whites, perhaps for the first time, see themselves as Africans see them: 'It is like the story of white men who, they say, are white like this piece of chalk. . . . And these white men, they say, have no toes'. The words 'white body' are no longer synonymous with 'innocence' (as Jahn might suggest), but (in the Ibo conception reported in *Arrow of God*) with 'leprosy'.

Perhaps most importantly, Achebe's ability to shift points of view and narrative centring between white and black characters (there is no longer any question of simply peering into the machinations of a putative 'African mind') increases the ironic distance from both perspectives, and intensifies Achebe's ongoing elegy to segregationist discourse and narrative.[60] □

For Snead, *Things Fall Apart* is a work of linguistic appropriation, reversing the colonial gesture with which British culture overwrote the orature of the Ibo. Like Griffiths, he locates the climax of this strategy at the novel's end, where Achebe seeks to usurp the position of authority assumed by the District Commissioner, replacing his blinkered and partial representation with a historically authentic account of the 'tribes of the lower Niger'.

Amongst other scholars, it is certainly possible to find support for the less compromising line taken by Ngũgĩ. A prime example of such work is Ode Ogede's book *Achebe and the Politics of Representation* (2001),[61] which questions the entire project of *Things Fall Apart* as an (ostensibly) counter-colonial work which, in fact, proves to be steeped in the aesthetic traditions of colonialism. A discussion of Ogede's argument is included in chapter 2, together with several other interesting, alternative readings of Achebe's novel.

CHALLENGING ACHEBE: FEMINIST READINGS

As we have seen, *Things Fall Apart* has been read by many critics as a challenge to the Anglo-Irish literary canon, especially to the writings of Joseph Conrad and Joyce Cary. Arguably, this relationship of antagonistic connection to canonical works has aided *Things Fall Apart*'s own incorporation into the literary curriculum at school, college and university level, thereby securing canonical status for Achebe himself. In more recent years, however, increasing interest in questions of gender has led to a reappraisal of texts like *Things Fall*

Apart, bringing a more detailed examination of their representations of masculinity and femininity.

Amongst these, Rhonda Cobham's essay 'Making Men and History: Achebe and the Politics of Revisionism' (1991)[62] is an interesting example. Looking at the figure of Okonkwo, Cobham asks us to consider Okonkwo's obsession with courage, and in particular the simplistic equation he seems to draw between his own manliness and 'the ability to do difficult, even distasteful, jobs without flinching'.[63] In the novel, the pivotal dramatization of the latter is provided by Okonkwo's killing of Ikemefuna, in which affection for his foster-son is overwhelmed by the fear of displaying 'feminine' weakness.

As Cobham points out, the novel's portrayal of Okonkwo's continual struggle to affirm his masculinity takes place against a background in which a much wider and more complex range of cultural values than his own are represented. The contrast between Okonkwo's tendency to anger and aggression, on the one hand, and Obierika's openness, sensitivity and compassion, on the other, forms one of the axes along which gender identity is explored in the text. For Cobham, moreover, the novel's handling of the colonial encounter is directly entwined with its gendered concerns. Okonkwo is placed in an antagonistic relation to the democratic, tolerant and culturally accommodating characteristics of the Ibo tradition, she argues, and in this sense the novel partly aligns him with the position of the District Commissioner, with whom he shares a number of assumptions and values:

■ Okonkwo's most complex conflation of brute force with the 'masculine' virtue of courage occurs in the final pages of the story, when he beheads the court messenger and then hangs himself. Here courage is dissociated from those other 'manly' attributes: caution, diplomacy, and the ability to weigh both sides of an argument. Ironically, none of these 'higher' values in his society has any effect on the superior military might of the colonizers. Thus, in a twisted sense, Okonkwo and the District Commissioner share the same worldview: that, ultimately, physical strength and the ability to inflict one's will on another human being – a wife, a son, or a native – are the only significant forms of social differentiation in establishing a masculine identity.[64] □

Whilst Cobham by no means simply conflates Okonkwo's perspective – in its violence and misogyny – with that of Achebe, she does draw a significant parallel between the portrayal of Okonkwo as a socially rootless figure and Achebe's own unstable position as a hybrid of colonial and traditional culture. Interestingly, this leads her to read *Things Fall Apart* itself as a profoundly 'wilful' work, in which the author attempts to mould his cultural inheritance to match a particular self-image:

■ Okonkwo's final solution brings us back to the dilemma of his creator. Like Okonkwo, who attempts to carve out a relation to his clan in the absence of an inherited sense of identity, Achebe must renegotiate a relation to traditional Igbo society, a connection his education, religious training, and internalized moral standards have made tenuous. Like Okonkwo, he often proceeds by isolating specific aspects of a society to which he has access and allowing them to stand for many other possible readings of a given social situation. Achebe has said that his mission in writing *Things Fall Apart* is to teach other Africans that their past was neither so savage nor so benighted as the colonizers have represented it to be. In other words, Achebe wants to prove to himself that the best values of his Christian upbringing are compatible with the values of traditional Igbo society.[65] □

Returning to the death of Ikemefuna, Cobham points to the way in which Achebe's narrative draws upon Christian tradition to understand – and indeed, to ameliorate – his ethical qualms about Ibo culture. Whilst the death resonates partly with the sacrifice of Jesus by the Father in the New Testament, the most telling parallel she draws is with the Old Testament story of Abraham and Isaac, in which the notion of a father's willingness to sacrifice his son is played out in a rather different way. By drawing from his own faith position, she argues, Achebe's text effectively works to 'sanitize' aspects of Ibo culture which the author finds difficult to face:

■ In describing Ikemefuna's death, Achebe, like Okonkwo, must find a way of synchronizing the qualities he wishes to represent with the values he has internalized. While Achebe shares the mission-school horror at the idea of human sacrifice, an attitude he also attributes to the converts in *Things Fall Apart,* he must find ways of addressing this issue without jeopardizing the reader's sympathy for the community as a whole. Thus he structures the story of Ikemefuna's death so that it parallels the biblical story of Abraham's near sacrifice of his son Isaac. The journey out of the village, the boy's carrying of the vessels

associated with the sacrifice, and his last disarming words, 'My father, they have killed me!' all echo the biblical story. . . .
   For Achebe's readers to share the tragedy of Ikemefuna's death as a moment of pathos rather than one of revulsion, the parallel with Abraham must function as a shared archetype. The object of sacrifice must be a sentient individual, bound to the person who makes the sacrifice by bonds of affection. In this way the act of sacrifice becomes a symbol of devotion to a principle higher than earthly love rather than the brute machination of a culture incapable of elevated sentiments. Though Okonkwo's personal intervention in Ikemefuna's death remains tragically wrongheaded, the context in which he acts retains its dignity.[66] □

The parallelism forged here between Judeo-Christian and Ibo cultures is explicitly reinforced, Cobham argues, in the faith conversations between Akuna and the missionary Mr Brown towards the end of the novel, in which an equivalence is established between Chukwu and the Christian God. In the novel's representation of relationships, she argues moreover, this process of conflation is once again reflected. Thus, whilst the novel does formally acknowledge the practice of polygamy, with Okonkwo's three wives, only one relationship is given detailed colouring, the one between Okonkwo and Ekwefi. Once again, the ideological trajectory of the novel is towards establishing a convergence between Western, especially Christian, values and those of the Ibo. In this, she suggests, Achebe's text contrasts sharply with the more challenging representations of gender relations offered by women writers such as Flora Nwapa:

■ Although the novel tells us of Okonkwo's many wives and children, the male–female relationships in Okonkwo's family that Achebe isolates for our scrutiny are almost indistinguishable from those of monogamous couples in Western tradition. Okonkwo has three wives, but we come to know only one: Ekwefi, the mother of Ezinma. She marries Okonkwo for love, having run away from her first husband. Her relationship with her husband, for better or worse, has all the passion, violence, and shared trauma we associate with the Western romantic tradition. Achebe clearly intends to show that all these emotions existed in traditional Igbo society, but, as with the situation he chooses to illuminate the issue of human sacrifice, the relationship he describes between Okonkwo and Ekwefi is by no means normative. We never really see Okonkwo's wives interacting with one another the way we see the men interacting among themselves or even Okonkwo interacting with his children. From a Western perspective the omission is hardly experienced as a loss, as the reader can identify effortlessly with the structure if not the content of the relationship described between Okonkwo and Ekwefi. Indeed, its similarity to Western versions of marriage may help explain why students spontaneously empathize with Ekwefi when Okonkwo mistreats her and why they often read the text as misogynistic.[67] □

More generally, according to Cobham's analysis, Achebe's tendency in *Things Fall Apart* is to minimize, rather than to expand upon, the position of women in Ibo society. Whilst the novel does mention the *umuada* or 'daughters of the clan' and their role in managing livestock and in betrothal and marriage rituals, for example, it neglects to describe the *umuada*'s other historic function as regulators of town markets or their pivotal judicial role in settling civic and marital disputes. Instead, Achebe's attention to women focuses much more intensively on questions of decoration, from the drawing of henna patterns on young women's skin to the plaiting and embellishment of their hair:

■ We do not see them planting their farms, bartering their goods in the marketplace, sitting in judgment on members of their community, or taking action alongside or against their men. The only woman we see acting with any authority is the priestess of Chielo, and she is represented, in terms consistent with Western practice, as a witch – a force for good or evil who is separate from the regular women rather than part of a chain of ritual and social female authority.[68] □

For Cobham, the ways in which Achebe's text shapes and skews itself to Western and Christian models of gender relations is a weakness that limits its imaginative reach. Considered as the novel of an Ibo Christian seeking to define a cultural heritage that can contain him, this need not be a problem for *Things Fall Apart*, she argues. What it does call into question, however, is the novel's widespread reception as an 'authentic' or 'objective' representation of Ibo (or even African) culture in the nineteenth century.

Amongst other critical discussions which examine the relationship between the anti-colonial dynamics of *Things Fall Apart* and its negotiation of gender, it is useful to mention Kirsten Holst Petersen's discussion of feminism and African literature, published in 1984.[69] Like Cobham, Petersen points out that Achebe's 'unsentimental' portrayal of traditional Ibo society, so much praised by early critics, begins to seem rather more problematic when viewed from a feminist perspective. Whilst Achebe's cultural nationalism is admirable in some respects, Petersen argues, it is seriously flawed by his ideologized and inauthentic representations of women and their roles:

■ An important impetus behind the wave of African writing which started in the '60s was the desire to show both the outside world and African youth that the African past was orderly, dignified and complex and altogether a worthy heritage. This was obviously opting for fighting cultural imperialism, and in the course of that the women's issue was not only ignored – a fate which would have allowed it to surface when the time was ripe – it was conscripted in the service of dignifying the past and restoring African self-confidence. The African past was not made the object of a critical scrutiny the way the past tends to be in societies with a more harmonious development, it was made the object of a quest, and the picture of women's place and role in these societies had to support this quest and was consequently lent more dignity and described in more positive terms than reality warranted. Achebe's much praised objectivity with regard to the merits and flaws of traditional Ibo society becomes less than praiseworthy seen in this light: his traditional women are happy, harmonious members of the community, even when they are repeatedly beaten and barred from any say in the communal decision-making process and constantly reviled in sayings and proverbs. It would appear that in traditional wisdom behaving like a woman is to behave like an inferior being. My sense of humour has always stopped short at the pleasant little joke about Okonkwo being punished, not for beating his wife, but for beating her during the week of peace. The obvious inequality of the sexes seems to be the subject of mild amusement for Achebe.[70] □

The feminist analysis pioneered by Cobham, Petersen and others is developed in more detail by the critic Florence Stratton, in her 1994 study *Contemporary African Literature and the Politics of Gender*.[71] Like them, Stratton is interested in asking whether such readings of *Things Fall Apart* through the prism of gender should lead us to question the judgement of influential critics such as Eustace Palmer. She begins by examining an early passage in which Okonkwo begs Nwakibie for some seed yams to start his farm. Nwakibie's wives file into his Obi, kneel and drink in their turn, then respectfully and silently withdraw:

■ Eustace Palmer chooses this excerpt as one of the passages he particularly admires, stating that from it 'the reader gains a sense of an alien, but nevertheless strong, self-assured, and civilized society'. But where in this passage is the gendered African reader to locate herself? For while she will immediately recognize the strength and self-assurance of the male culture of Umuofia, she will have no such experience of its female culture. Might she not wonder if the abject servitude of women is the hallmark of a 'civilized society'? . . . For with the notable exception of Chielo, the powerful priestess of Agbala, Achebe's women are, indeed, 'down on one knee', if not both, before their menfolk and they are regularly making an exit, no doubt 'in their proper order', from all the spaces in which power, economic or otherwise is exercised.

The status of women in Umuofia is very low: 'He had a large barn full of yams and he had three wives.' They are mere objects circulated among their menfolk, willed, for example, by a father to a son as part of an estate, or traded for a bag full of cowries. The only escape, it would seem, from this demeaning classification is for a woman to outlive the men who could own her. . . .

Women are also systematically excluded from the political, the economic, the judicial, and even the discoursal life of the community. This is indicated not only through the composition of the governing council of elders, the *ndichie,* or the membership of the powerful *egwugwu* cult, which is, in both cases, all male. For a repetition of the meaning underlying the closing sentence of the passage Palmer admires so much – 'The other wives . . . went away' – provides the novel with a kind of semantic refrain.[72] □

For Stratton, as for Cobham, one of the weaknesses of Achebe's text is its consistent subordination of women characters. On the death of a townswoman in the novel, it is the men of Umuofia who are summoned to a meeting. When the ancestral spirits meet, Achebe's women accept their exclusion unquestioningly. As Stratton argues, citing the respected cultural historian Ifi Amadiume, Achebe's representations of the religious culture of the Ibo in the nineteenth century by no means transparently reflect the historical evidence:

■ In Amadiume's analysis, Idemili was 'the central religious deity' of the Igbo living in the Nnobi area of Eastern Nigeria where both she and Achebe were born. Associated with female industriousness, assertiveness, and prosperity, as well as other qualities, Idemili embodied the matriarchal principle, a principle which, in its ideological opposition to the patriarchal principle embodied in 'the cult of ancestral spirits' (Achebe's *egwugwu*), ensured that Igbo gender construction was flexible. Furthermore, the qualities associated with

Idemili ensured that women were not marginalized either politically or economically. Hence the 'male daughters' and 'female husbands' of Amadiume's title – women who, through inheritance or self-generated wealth, acquired the status and power of men. There was also a title reserved for women, the *Ekwe* title, which was associated with Idemili and which prosperous women could take, after which they 'would wear a string anklet . . . like all titled men' and become members of the Women's Council. This Council, Amadiume writes, 'appears to have been answerable to no one', not even to '*ozo* titled men' (Achebe's elders or *ndichie),* its special strength residing in its authority to order mass strikes by all women.[73] □

Even where the novel turns to a betrothal ceremony – traditionally the province of women – Achebe swiftly turns away from the main preparations and towards the specific part of the proceedings that concerns men and their negotiation of the bride price. Throughout the novel, Stratton argues, his tendency to reinforce and naturalize patriarchal assumptions is constantly repeated.

Certainly, there are moments when the hierarchical gender relations of Umuofian society are thrown into crisis. When Okonkwo beats his wife during the Week of Peace, when Ozoemena's wife dies as if 'in sympathy' with her husband's death and when Okonkwo is forced to return to his motherland, Achebe's narrative brings questions of gender to the fore in different ways. In each case, however, the novel retreats from any serious consideration of male/female power relations. Indeed, as Stratton goes on to suggest, it frequently reveals a strong masculinist bias in its handling of the narrative voice. Achebe goes out of his way to distance the narrator's perspective from that of Okonkwo, for example in the portrayal of his relationship with Nwoye. But when it comes to the portrayal of women, the narrative frequently appears to endorse Okonkwo's patriarchal assumptions, leaving little or no room for a balancing point of view, for example from Ojiugo. If femininity is indeed an important theme in the novel, Stratton argues therefore, its role seems to be largely as a balancing facet of the male personality, manifested for example as Obierika's conscience or Nwoye's sensitivity:

■ But this male heart is not moved by the oppression of women, by their degradation in their definition as chattel, or by their marginalization in society. Nor is Achebe's. For although he avoids idealization by including in the novel an implicit criticism of certain aspects of life in Umuofia, that criticism, which is in part expressed through the reflections of male characters such as Nwoye and Obierika, does not cover the condition of women in Umuofia. Moreover, not only does the male inner voice fail to question the harsh injustice done to women, the female inner voice is utterly mute. . . .

The women of Umuofia, then, are content with their lot. In their silence they assent to their status as the property of a man and to their reduction to a level lower than a barn full of yams in their role as signifiers of their husbands' wealth. So, too, does Achebe. For although he exposes, through the defection of *osu*, the injustice of Umuofia's social class system, he remains silent (mute like his women) on its gender hierarchy. And while critics continue to eulogize Achebe for the balance he has achieved in his portrayal of Umuofia's strengths and weaknesses, they have generally avoided pointing to the subjugation of women as one of those weaknesses or to the novel's failure to make the same point. This critical silence on the work's sexism can be attributed to the same cause as that to which Achebe assigns responsibility for the silence on Conrad's racism: sexism 'is such a normal way of thinking that its manifestations go completely undetected'.[74] □

It may be right to celebrate Achebe's text for the boldness with which it overturns the colonialist perspective of texts like Conrad's *Heart of Darkness*, Stratton argues. If Conrad is, in the author's words, 'a bloody racist',[75] however, for Stratton the endorsement of gender inequality in *Things Fall Apart* renders Achebe vulnerable to the balancing charge that he is 'a bloody sexist'. In this sense, for Stratton, it is crucial for readers to approach the novel with a critical eye to its shortcomings, as well as an appreciation of its achievements. Achebe should not be read in isolation, or fetishized as the only and definitive literary voice of Nigeria. Instead, he needs to be considered alongside women writers, such as Buchi Emecheta (born 1944), who have extended the gendered engagements of Nigerian fiction in ways that *Things Fall Apart* does not even begin to envisage.

Against the backdrop of Achebe's reputation as the 'Godfather' of African literature, it is easy to assume that *Things Fall Apart* would have been treated to uncritical celebration from the outset. In fact, as we have seen in this chapter, a growing appreciation of the richness and complexity of the novel has been accompanied by frequent challenges to the political and aesthetic choices it embodies. As we will see, some of the most interesting and important of these critical debates revolve around two key questions about the novel's project. Firstly, how should we consider Achebe's account of his people's past — what kind of history is this, which offers itself as fiction? Secondly, how might we think about this novel politically, as it emerges out of the independence struggle in Nigeria — what sort of a manifesto for change is *Things Fall Apart*? It is to these questions that we turn in chapter 2.

CHAPTER TWO

Things Fall Apart (1958): The Novel and Nigeria

As we saw in chapter 1, much of the early criticism of *Things Fall Apart* focussed tightly on the relationship between Achebe's text and the existing Anglo-Irish literary canon. Around questions of language and also of gender, the initial, rather self-satisfied reception of the novel as an interesting African 'take' on familiar literary models began to break down in the 1970s. From the 1980s, alongside feminist readings of the novel, a range of excellent historical criticism of *Things Fall Apart* began to emerge, placing the novel within a much more complex sense of cultural context. This chapter explores some of this later criticism, considering Achebe's novel in relation to two key historical contexts. Firstly, it explores the novel as a work of (perhaps problematic) historiography, an attempt to reclaim Ibo culture at the end of the nineteenth century. In this section, five alternative readings of the novel are explored – each with a distinct focus – by the critics Robert Wren, Raisa Simola, Herbert Ekwe-Ekwe, Neil Ten Kortenaar and Richard Begam, respectively. Secondly, this chapter explores *Things Fall Apart* as a text of its own time, one intimately tied to the aspirations and ambitions of Nigerian Independence. Here, we set Achebe's description of his own project against the biting critique offered by Ode Ogede, as well as Romanus Muoneke's analysis of the novel in relation to the radical black movement, Negritude.

THINGS FALL APART AND HISTORICAL RECLAMATION

Amongst the wide variety of scholarship which explores the nature of *Things Fall Apart*'s historical engagements, Robert Wren's early study *Achebe's World* (1980)[1] remains one of the most useful. The specific context within which Wren's book places *Things Fall Apart* is that of the British colonial doctrine of 'pacification' to which the end of the novel ironically alludes. Conventionally, *Things Fall Apart* is read as an account of the encounter between the Ibo and the colonizing British in the late nineteenth century, before the phase of formal colonization which led to the establishment of the state of Nigeria. Wren's focus, however, is on a slightly later period, between 1900 and 1920, during which the British made aggressive incursions into Iboland, hanging Ibo priests and burning down religious buildings.

In the novel itself, Wren draws a comparison between the massacre at Abame, of which Okonkwo hears when he is in exile, and specific historical events in 1905 at Obezi and Eziudo. The account he draws from colonial office records throws interesting light on the novel, illuminating the background of ignorance and prejudice against which the colonial project was pursued in this period:

■ The one case is that of Dr. J. F. Stewart, who at 1:00 p.m. November 16, 1905, set off on his bicycle from Owerri (today the capital of Imo State) intending to ride to Calabar via Bende. At a branch in the 'road' (really a track), he turned toward Obizi – a serious error, according to a letter to the Colonial Office from H. M. Douglas. 'Natives', he said, who reported the matter to Owerri, reported that Stewart was stripped, bound, and beaten, and afterwards 'his body was cut up and shared. His bicycle also was broken up and shared'. A. E. Afigbo investigated local tradition about the death of Stewart and found that the Ahiara people 'took him to their neighbours. To show them what they had caught'; 'they did not know he was a human being', though he might have been a ghost.

On December 13 – nearly a month later – a Captain Fox, commanding two groups of black soldiers (if each had a white officer this would meet Obierika's 'three white men'), came, intending a surprise attack. He found few people and concluded his surprise had failed. (Perhaps the scarcity of people merely indicated that there was no market that day). Fox removed 'cooked' leg bones which he took to be Stewart's.

On December 16, a force 'managed to kill 19 Obezi's and Eziudo's' – that is, people of villages where Stewart was thought to have been captured. Probably – the records do not say – the towns were destroyed.[2] □

As Wren points out, official British records pertaining to Stewart are patchy and inconsistent. In the file, alternative accounts report variously that he was hung or else killed whilst asleep and eaten by cannibals. The importance of Stewart's death, notwithstanding the dubious status of the evidence surrounding it, is that it was one of the key justifications used by the colonial military after 1905 for the destruction of the Oracle at Akwa and the 'pacification' of the Ahiara people, making way for a road-building project that helped to consolidate colonial control over the region.

In his discussion of British tactics in Iboland in this period, one of the important themes that Wren brings out is the contrast between the principles of jurisprudence practiced at home and those of 'pacification' practiced in the West African colonies. Typically, records reveal, little or no concern was given to identifying particular resistance fighters among the Ibo, or to mounting trials of individuals accused of particular crimes. Instead, a policy of 'collective punishment'[3] was used, in which soldiers would target and destroy whole villages and their inhabitants. The connection between such actions and the pursuit of larger infrastructural projects such as road building becomes clear in such cases as Obezi and Eziudo. In the novel, Achebe paints a complex picture in which violent 'pacification' and legal procedures form two complementary arms of the colonial apparatus. When Okonkwo and the other village elders are arrested and imprisoned by the District Commissioner, a facade of legal process is skillfully balanced by a sense of the commissioner's duplicity and arbitrary power.

Partly because of the democratic structure of Ibo culture, Wren argues, the British found it difficult to adopt local leaders (as they did in the north) as puppet authorities through which colonial power could be exercised by proxy. Instead, the practice of 'pacification' was institutionalized in British law, in the 'Collective Punishment Ordinance' of February 2, 1912. Because of the lack of a fixed hierarchical structure of authority in Ibo culture, the practice developed of incorporating Christian converts into the lowest levels of the colonial administration, for example as 'court messengers' who acted as

intermediaries between the British and the indigenous people. In
the novel, the importance of the messengers is brought out to great
effect – the final act of Okonkwo's tragedy is set in motion when he
kills one of them. As Wren suggests, therefore, one of the insights
into colonial rule offered by Achebe's text concerns the dependence
of District Commissioners on such functionaries, and the power that
thus accrued to the latter:

■ The D.C., in a way, was helpless. The political system in Umuofia
provided no means by which he could by indirect rule impose his will.
The *ndichie,* the elders, would not obey one of their own number; the
ndichie ruled collectively, and collectively they would not blindly obey
the white men.

The D.C. was helpless too when he attempted to function as chief
magistrate. Though he could interrogate witnesses, he could do
so only through an interpreter. Achebe illustrates the problem in a
story Obierika tells Okonkwo. A land dispute leads Aneto to fight with
Oduche, and by accident to kill him. In accord with custom, following
the accidental murder, Aneto is to flee to Aninta – presumably his
mother's town – 'to escape the wrath of the earth'. But the D.C. learns
of the murder, sends the Kotma to arrest Aneto, and – evidently –
puts the case to trial. Aneto was sent to Umuru to be hanged, and
the land was awarded to those who had bribed the messengers and
interpreters.

Such errors were inevitable, and a District Commissioner might be
forgiven his ignorance, if it be assumed that colonial officers were men
of good will. Achebe challenges this assumption in the treachery of his
D.C., who invites the leading men of the town to a 'palaver', and when
they are unarmed and seated, arrests them. Has the author loaded the
dice against the British? Alas, no. The practice was so commonplace
that as early as 1900 a Major Gallway wrote to Sir Ralph Moor,
Commissioner and Consul General, in protest. . . Nothing indicates
that Gallway's protest was heeded. Corruption of the morals of the
colonial officers themselves was one of the fruits of 'pacification'.[4] □

At the same time, Achebe's novel also brings out the economic
development and expansion of trade that accompanied colonialism.
The products of palm culturation – oil and kernel – become 'things
of great price' in Umuofia and can be traded for cloth, porcelain,
iron pots and other manufactured products. Likewise, Wren argues,
the novel very clearly acknowledges the relationship between
missionary culture in Iboland and the expansion and formalization
of education in the period. Missionary schools were founded on a

powerful Protestant ethic and often reflected a wide range of orientalist and racist assumptions, but also had the effect of spreading
literacy amongst converts. As a direct product of the colonial school
system, Achebe's writing explores the implications of missionary
education in a fascinatingly nuanced and ambivalent way.

As Wren points out, then, under British colonialism the culture of
Iboland was transformed through the interconnected influences of
trade, religion and (English-language) education. At the same time
however, this process of change must be understood in relation to
the simultaneous, violent practices of 'pacification'. For Wren, the
novel very successfully brings out the nature of this colonial equation between 'pacification' and 'civilization' under British rule. As he
argues, whilst the specific contents of Achebe's text are fictive, *Things
Fall Apart* can still be regarded as an authentic representation of the
colonial encounter in Iboland at the turn of the twentieth century.

Wren's analysis of the historical background to Achebe's first
novel is usefully complemented by that of Raisa Simola in her study
World Views in Chinua Achebe's Works (1995).[5] The aim of Simola's
book is to piece together as detailed an account as possible of Ibo
culture at the turn of the century. On an ideological level, she is particularly concerned to give us a better understanding of the encounter between Ibo spirituality and Christianity that runs to the heart of
Achebe's novel.

In this work of historical reclamation, it should be said, Simola
is not unaware of the problems implicit in 'translating' between
radically different religious traditions. As she observes, even for
words like 'God' and 'spirit' in English, 'precise corresponding
Igbo words hardly exist'.[6] Despite this problem, the somewhat
paradoxical task Simola sets herself is to document the Ibo worldview from an insider's point of view. Drawing on the work of
well-established cultural historians such as T. Uzodinma Nwala,
she makes an attempt to construct an outline of the Ibo outlook
at the turn of the century, stressing the nature of the relationship
between humans and the supernatural:

■ According to Nwala, the Igbo world view implies two basic ideas:
(1) unity of all beings and (2) organized interaction between all
beings in the universe. Cosmic structure, understood in the light of

unity and interaction, can be divided into three big categories which, in their part, have their subcategories: (1) spirits and forces (*Nmuo na ogwu*); (2) human beings *(Madu);* (3) things; plants and animals (*Ihe*). . . . The impulse to maintain order, harmony and peace belongs to human nature, according to Nwala. Thus the disorder, chaos and misery people encounter are explained in a way that does not disturb belief in the element of order. The Igbos believe that only spirits, gods and medicine-men have the power to transform natural laws.[7] □

Although she acknowledges his importance as a scholar of Ibo culture, Simola is not uncritical of Nwala. For Nwala, humans are organized into eight subcategories, in a hierarchical order of importance. These are, respectively, priests, diviners, medicine men, elders, titled men/'big artists'/the initiated, ordinary men, women and the yet unborn. The explicit designation of women as the least significant of all living humans is, at the very least, a questionable reading of Ibo culture, Simola contends, even once its masculinist tendencies are acknowledged. At the same time, she identifies a disturbing tendency in much established scholarship on the Ibo to represent their culture as 'timeless' and historically unchanging. Nevertheless, the work of scholars such as Nwala and others is immensely useful in terms of their ability to illuminate the nature of 'being' in Ibo tradition, including the relationships between the human and the divine, the physical and the spiritual:

■ The Igbos recognize three kinds of reality . . . the physical, the spiritual, and the abstract. They do not accept the claim that every thing is made of matter. And further, 'the standard posture of contemporary African metaphysics' which claims that reality can be divided into the physical and the spiritual, does not, either, explain satisfactorily the experience of the Igbo. The physical is what we can touch, weigh, eat, what we can reach through our general senses; the spiritual is what may be seen or touched only by specially 'washed' eyes, and the abstract is what exists and may affect reality by becoming realized in either physical or spiritual form. These different sides of being come out at different times due to differing circumstances. Deity represents the abstract form of being. *Ala* is the concept of earth as deity. The land we are treading on is the physical form of the earth. All in all, *Ala* can be seen as an abstraction (deity), or as various items (which symbolize *Ala*), or as a place (for example, the shrine in the square). *Ala* thus manifests itself in a combination of physical and abstract forms.[8] □

As Simola says, this notion of the complementarity of the physical and the spiritual contrasts sharply with the European opposition between body and mind, associated with the philosopher René Descartes (1596–1650). Similarly, Ibo understandings of the nature of deities differ sharply from those associated with the Christian tradition. As she explains, 'Deities . . . can be the supernatural counterparts of natural phenomena such as earth, river, hill, tree, sky, lightning. They can be created by human thought as supernatural counterparts to man made objects . . . The ancestors *are* present'.[9]

In Achebe's novel, as Simola shows, much of this worldview is represented with reasonable faithfulness. The importance of *Ani* the earth goddess, for example, is explored by Achebe both as a transcendent godhead, the 'ultimate judge of morality and conduct', and in terms of her embodiment in earth and flesh. Thus, when Unoka dies of a strange swelling disease, he cannot be buried in the earth, since to do so would be a corruption to *Ani*. Yet the evil forest, where lepers and twins are taken to die, appears in some way to be outside *Ani*'s domain.

Whilst Simola is keen to bring out the complexity of Achebe's presentation, she also notes some of the ways in which the novel seems to look for accommodation between the traditional Ibo belief system and the terms and structures of Christianity. One example of this is the author's handling of the notion of *chi*. Within Ibo spirituality, as she says, the *chi* can be thought of not only as an individual's 'personal god' or 'spirit double', but also in terms of duality or transition between different states of being. In *Things Fall Apart,* however, the notion of *chi* almost always invokes the former sense:

■ In *Things Fall Apart, chi* clearly is seen in the role of a 'guardian angel' in several cases. When Ekwefi tells Chielo that Okonkwo had almost killed her during the Week of Peace, Chielo remarks: 'Your *chi* is very much awake, my friend'. And while telling about the massacre of the Abame people, Obierika claims *chi* saved those who survived: 'Everyone was killed, except the old and the sick who were at home and a handful of men and women whose *chi* were wide awake and brought them out of that market.'[10] □

Similarly, she stresses the way in which Achebe's characterization of Chukwu, particularly in the conversation between Akunna and the missionary Mr Brown, seems to render him as 'the highest God' in a way that is as amenable as possible to the Christian worldview. Fascinatingly, she discusses claims by some Ibo historians that, in fact, Chukwu may even have been a god imported by the white man in the period before formal colonization:

> ■ Nwoga's view in *The Supreme God as Stranger in Igbo Religious Thought* (1984) is that the Igbos have not always believed in one supreme god. A certain group of people (the Aro people) recognized Chukwu as their god; but it was the missionaries who made him the supreme god of the whole ethnic group. Thus, Chukwu served as the Igbo counterpart for their Christian god.[11] □

As she points out, it is possible to read Achebe's novel as an examination of the ways in which Christians sought to reinterpret Ibo belief 'in accordance with their own interests'.[12] Overall, Simola's account of Ibo culture in this period describes a people with not only a powerful ethic of personal achievement, but also a strong receptiveness to cultural change. In the novel, she concludes, Achebe's exploration of these qualities and their shaping role in determining the Ibo reaction to invasion faithfully reflects the changing cultural dynamics brought by colonialism at the end of the nineteenth century.

Like Robert Wren and Raisa Simola, the critic Herbert Ekwe-Ekwe[13] approaches *Things Fall Apart* as a complex work of historical reclamation. For Ekwe-Ekwe, however, one of the great achievements of Achebe's novel which tends to go unnoticed in this context is the sense of beauty and simplicity it manages to conjure, in far-from-simple circumstances. 'Despite the centuries of hostility directed by the guardians of eurocentricism on the African humanity', he argues, Achebe's genius is to recognize that 'the African story does not require some pretentiously nor ornamentally turgid sociological or narrational *oeuvre*'.[14] The narrative simplicity of *Things Fall Apart* can only be fully appreciated, Ekwe-Ekwe argues, when we have gained a full awareness of the scale of the genocide committed against West Africans, especially the Ibo and Yoruba, in the period of the novel's setting. Citing the Yoruba critic Kole Omotoso, he is scathing towards scholars whose work seems to minimize the importance of this history in their assessment of Nigerian writers such as Wole Soyinka (born

1934) or Achebe. According to Omatoso, he says, the difference
between the Yoruba and Ibo responses to colonialism and to slav-
ery is that the former broadly 'accepted' the negative aspects of
dealing with Europe, whilst the latter typically acted with greater
hostility. For Ekwe-Ekwe, such a reading of the period is completely unacceptable:

> ■ Omotoso does not however specify what he means by the Yoruba
> acceptance of the 'negative' component or spheres of the conquest.
> The conquest broadly had three distinct junctures – namely, the
> genocide, the dispersal or the exportation of peoples, and the
> occupation of the lands of those who remained. Which of these have
> the Yoruba 'accepted'? Just one of the three, or two of the three, or all
> of them? What exactly does it mean for an African people to 'accept'
> *any* or *all* of these 'negative' attributes of a devastating holocaust?
> Apart from perhaps the Akan, the African holocaust had the gravest
> impact on the Yoruba. Arguably, more Yoruba than any other Africans,
> *including* the Igbo, were exported to the Americas and elsewhere by
> European slavers during the period. . . . The consequences on the
> Yoruba nation were horrendous. It is therefore an outrage for any
> scholar, particularly a Yoruba for that matter, to describe this history
> as 'mere episode, a catalytic episode only'.[15] □

For Ekwe-Ekwe, what must be recognized by any reader of
Achebe's work is that Africans today are still wrestling with the
legacies of colonialism and genocide, in the form of continued mass
impoverishment, in the political fragility of their nation states and
in the continued refusal of European powers to acknowledge their
responsibility. Africa's rehabilitation and future development, he
argues, need to be based on control of Africa's resources by Africans
themselves, together with a sustained commitment to retrieving
and reaffirming African history, 'especially in the wake of centuries
of eurocentric distortions, fabrications, and evasions'.[16] In this context, intellectuals must be 'uncompromising and untiring in setting
the record straight'.[17] For Ekwe-Ekwe, *Things Fall Apart* stands as a
milestone in this crucial reconstructive effort.

In the novel, accordingly, he stresses the ways in which Achebe
avoids romanticizing Ibo history, laying its tensions and contradictions open to plain view. For example, the threat of poverty and
deprivation is constantly a presence in the novel: Achebe takes
time to depict the complexity of Umuofian attitudes to economic

development and to inequality. One such instance of this is provided by the text's presentation of Unoka, Okonkwo's father:

■ He is heavily indebted, poor, and an unsuccessful farmer. Why? He is 'lazy and improvident and was quite incapable of thinking about tomorrow'. But Unoka surely has other talents to offer society! He is after all a cultural worker – flutist and dancer especially during those three months' 'season of rest' after the end of the yam harvest and the beginning of the new planting season. He would travel around Umuofia and elsewhere performing with various dance troupes and exchanging and learning new compositions. But his entertaining skills do not help to improve his standing in society because 'his wife and children had barely enough to eat'. Indubitably, the accomplishment of this crucial family task is a benchmark for measuring the relevance and the success of the choice of one's occupation or indeed vocation in Umuofia.[18] □

As Ekwe-Ekwe argues, Achebe's novel powerfully evokes the meritocratic ethos in Ibo culture and is careful in its depiction of family structure and marriage, both as axes of emotional commitment and as structures of social cohesion. At the same time, a great deal of time in the novel is devoted to the industrious and competitive spirit embodied by Okonkwo himself. For Ekwe-Ekwe, Achebe's characterization of his protagonist in these terms can partly be seen as a riposte to European stereotypes of Africans, 'the Unoka-type profile of indolence and "entertainer" . . . cultivated in children's literature, in schools, in the media (particularly television) and through other agencies of cultural life'.[19] If we consider the killing of Ikemefuna, the complexity of Achebe's presentation of Okonkwo's situation, caught as he is between the edict of the Oracle, the dictates of his *chi* and the emotional dynamics of his involvement with both the boy and his fellow clansmen, comprehensively disallows such a stereotypical reading. In his discussion of this episode, Ekwe-Ekwe focuses particularly on the intervention of Okonkwo's friends Obierika and Ezeudu, who each counsel against his rash action. As Ekwe-Ekwe argues, this interaction in the novel enables Achebe to portray the ethical and spiritual framework of Umuofian society as distinct from those of Europe and Christianity, at the same time as dramatizing Okonkwo's unique personal situation:

■ What these two respected members of Umuofia's leadership are highlighting in their respective interventions on this issue is a cardinal feature in Igbo religion/spirituality which expects a person to worship all the gods in the Igbo pantheon equally all the time, in contrast to the liberty of selectiveness which exists among other nations and peoples. Hence, the Igbo adage: 'You may worship Udo to perfection and still be killed by Ogwugwu'. Okonkwo could thus feel that he has dutifully carried out the decree of the Oracle of the Hills and Caves as we have seen, but risks unmitigated sanctions from say, *Ani,* the earth goddess, if his action(s), whilst implementing the directive of the oracle, are in breach of *Ani's* moral code![20] □

In the narrative as a whole, Achebe patchworks a wide range of Ibo beliefs, proverbs, stories and images, but does so with a lightness of touch which seldom feels didactic. Importantly, Ekwe-Ekwe argues, the novel also witnesses the flexibility and relative resilience of Ibo culture. Contrary to the assumption of many critics, Ibo resistance did not simply collapse in the face of the European invasion, but continued for decades into the twentieth century. One particular passage he highlights is the conversation between clansmen and a church official at Mbanta, in which the latter is ridiculed for his silliness and ignorance. Although it ends with Okonkwo's suicide and with the District Commissioner's musings as he imagines his task complete, the novel by no means shows Umuofian society in ruins. Its members are divided, but not completely stripped of dignity or a sense of self-determination. The text leaves us with no more than an intimation of the looming threat experienced in this period by all African states.

Discussing Okonkwo's belligerent and uncompromising response to the British invasions when he returns from exile, Ekwe-Ekwe stresses the heroic character of his stance. For other critics, including Ernest Emenyonu, Kalu Ogbaa and Gareth Griffiths, the moral to be drawn from Okonkwo's resistance concerns his blindness to the inevitable and/or misapprehension of his own weakness. According to Ekwe-Ekwe, however, another reading is possible:

■ The underlining spur for these critics' condemnation of Okonkwo's resolute position to defend Umuofia from a possible British military and political take-over, emanate from their collective awareness of the preponderant military superiority of the invader; nothing else. Yet, bound by the sole preoccupation on the balance of military forces of both sides, these scholars lose sight of the salient features in history that characterise the defence by peoples, any peoples, of their homeland from external invasion whatever the odds – even when this defence might appear 'too obviously suicidal', to quote from C. L. R. James [1901–89], a leading philosopher of the African resistance and liberation wars. As history has shown, each and every invader of some other person's lands is potentially militarily superior to their would-be victims. But the latter's response to the event is the defence of the homeland under attack despite the odds and even when these are known by the defenders as overwhelming. As the European invasion got underway in Africa during the period, African armed resistance, expectedly, was the most featured element of Africa's initial or first phase of the defence of its homeland. It is this fact of African history that Chinua Achebe captures so dramatically in Okonkwo's steadfast response to the British invasion of Umuofia which the array of critics referred to surprisingly overlook.[21] □

If Okonkwo's violent resistance results in his death, Ekwe-Ekwe argues, this in itself need not be read as an indication of defeatism on Achebe's part. Indeed, Obierika's more pragmatic and careful response to the invasion can be seen as anticipating the varied pattern of underground resistance to colonialism that continued right up until Independence in the mid-twentieth century. The importance of the District Commissioner's book *The Pacification of the Primitive Tribes of the Lower Niger*, in this reading, is that it reminds us of the extent to which such struggles will be occluded by the flood of Africanist discourse, authored by Europeans, that will dominate understandings of the continent for a generation. 'As a student of literature and history at Ibadan's London University College of the late 1940s/early 1950s', Ekwe-Ekwe argues, 'Chinua Achebe would have been confronted with endless shelf-rows of [this] africophobist literature of lies, triumphalism and denial'.[22] Ekwe-Ekwe's project is thus to resituate *Things Fall Apart* as a text of resistance to imperialist discourse. In his reading, Achebe's novel is offered as one amongst many efforts by Nigerians and other Africans to reclaim their history, in its often-unpalatable complexity, and to assert a right to self-determination in the shaping of their future.

If it is Herbert Ekwe-Ekwe's concern to position *Things Fall Apart* as an act of historical affirmation, his analysis contrasts interestingly with that of Neil Ten Kortenaar,[23] who approaches the novel from the more sceptical theoretical viewpoint of New Historicism. As Kortenaar says, the discourse of history has two principal components. Firstly, it attempts to gather traces of the past by collecting pieces of verifiable 'evidence'. Secondly, it arranges those fragments into narrative forms that communicate historical meaning. The focus of Kortenaar's essay is to examine Achebe's historiographic method in the second sense, tracing the ways in which he attempts to build an impression of historical authenticity or authority into his representation of the disappearing Ibo past. For reasons that he makes clear, Kortenaar begins with the novel's conclusion:

■ *Things Fall Apart* ends with the decision taken by a historian to recount the process whereby a whole world was overturned. The narrative this historian will write is not, however, the one the reader has just finished reading, but a less objective and necessarily less accurate narrative. In the final pages the new District Commissioner walks away from the site of Okonkwo's suicide and wonders whether to make Okonkwo's death a chapter or a paragraph in his projected book, *The Pacification of the Primitive Tribes of the Lower Niger*. This appeal to an obviously false authority deploys irony to establish Achebe's own credentials as a historian of Igboland. We do not ask why we should trust the narrative we have just read: the District Commissioner's projected history and by implication other texts on Africa stand condemned as manifestly untrustworthy, and that is enough. We deconstruct what is told us of the District Commissioner and reconstruct a higher level where we join the author in seeing around the Europeans. But where exactly is this higher level?[24] □

As Kortenaar argues, the implied perspective of the District Commissioner's study is that it will represent the alienness and darkness of Iboland, within a framework which positions the commissioner himself as heroic explorer and pioneer. The directness of style in the rest of Achebe's novel, meanwhile, is intended to establish the opposite: the intelligibility, sophistication and humanity of the Ibo that the colonizer is unable to see.

One of the implications of this strategy, which emerges even more clearly in *Arrow of God*, Kortenaar argues, is that it positions both writer and reader in an attitude of externality and objectivity, where they can see into both cultures and recognize their mutual blindness towards the other. In order to emphasize the separateness of the African and European world, Achebe incorporates untranslated Ibo words, as well as scenes which directly dramatize the characters' lack of understanding of each other. The reader, however, is placed most of the time above such misunderstandings, in a privileged position of overarching knowledge. The problem with this, Kortenaar argues, is that inadvertently, the text thus reproduces one of the key assumptions of colonialism itself:

■ The problem with seeing two cultures as occupying the same world is that they can then be measured against each other and one preferred to another as a reflection of that world. To measure them is to assume a scientific objectivity that allows the observer to stand outside both. But in this case scientific objectivity is a mode of knowledge associated with one of the cultures to be measured. Achebe cannot appeal to the scientific model of knowledge and still be fair to the Igbos about whom he is writing. What Timothy Reiss calls the analytical-referential model of knowledge, the way of knowing associated with science and modern historiography, sees language as a tool that, placed between the observer and the world observed, allows the observer to know the world as it truly is and to manipulate it. It is inseparable from Europe's claim to know fully the world and other societies, in a way that other societies with other modes of knowing are never allowed to know Europe. . . . Achebe is writing of a moment of epistemic rupture, when one mode of knowledge gives way before another. But how can he do justice to both? . . . How then can the Igbo world be made intelligible once it has bowed before another *episteme*?[25] □

Within Achebe's narrative, this problem manifests itself in many ways, Kortenaar suggests. For example, when the novel describes the digging up of the sick child Ezinma's death-dealing *ogbanje* and her subsequent recovery from illness, it does so without obvious irony or scepticism. But, as Kortenaar argues, the reader ends up being placed in an attitude of irony and scepticism nevertheless. In the chapter concerning Ezinma's illness, Okonkwo wakes to the sound of a mosquito buzzing in his ear, and we later hear that his daughter has *iba*, a fever seen as reflecting her *ogbanje* status as a reincarnated spirit, destined to plague its mother by being born and dying many times:

■ Achebe and his reader both know Ezinma's fever would be diagnosed as malaria by a doctor, and the recurring deaths of an *ogbanje* considered a superstitious explanation of a high infant mortality rate more appropriately responded to by modern medicine.
    We cannot say Achebe is exchanging ironic glances with his reader over the heads of his characters. The reader, if at all involved in

Okonkwo's world, is likely to miss the reference to malaria. Yet I believe my reader will agree that the mosquitoes are significant and point to a foreign *episteme* that is otherwise absent.[26] □

A parallel effect of distancing occurs when one of the Christian converts kills the sacred python and dies as a result. As readers, Kortenaar suggests, we are continually privileged to a higher knowledge of events, which disables us from effectively entering the Ibo worldview. When Achebe describes the meeting of the *egwugwu* or ancestral spirits, Kortenaar sees a similar mechanism at play. The narrative informs us that one of the *egwugwu* has Okonkwo's distinctive walk, but that no one ever related that fact to the *egwugwu*'s identity, or saw it as anything less than fearfully authentic. 'Perhaps it was never possible that any reader of the novel should believe that the *egwugwu* were ancestral spirits returned to earth' he argues, 'but it is clear that the narrative itself does not believe'.[27] For Kortenaar such episodes establish a 'double-consciousness' in the reader, who is invited to sympathize with the Ibo, but at the same time to regard them as foolish.

Even beyond this level of representation, moreover, Kortenaar's New Historicist reading of *Things Fall Apart* presents the text as radically problematic. If we consider Achebe as a cultural historian, as Wren, Simola, Ekwe-Ekwe and others do, then how are we to consider Achebe's practice of writing history for a culture which did not frame its experience in written or historical forms? Again, the text's assumption of historical awareness places the reader in a position of assumed superiority to its characters, privy to vast frameworks of understanding that are closed to them:

■ References to time in *Things Fall Apart* are to seasons, to moons, to weeks, and to time that has passed since memorable events occurred. There is no calendar measuring an absolute scale, for such calendars are the product of literate societies. Instead, time is cyclical, observing the recurrence of the seasons and the market days. We can date *Things Fall Apart,* locate Okonkwo's story in relation to events happening elsewhere, because at the end of the book the Europeans appear. In the first two-thirds of the book we are shown a society such as we suppose might have existed at any time in the last three hundred years (they have guns, but have not met Europeans). At the end of the novel, however, when the missionaries arrive, there are references to the queen of the English. Since Victoria died in 1901, the narrative must be set in the late nineteenth century. There is a slight contradiction here. Okoye establishes that the events on which *Things Fall Apart* is based, specifically the killing of a solitary white man on a bicycle and the retribution exacted by British forces, occurred in 1905. That is the year of the large-scale British expedition to subdue Igboland. . . . Of course, what Achebe has written is fiction and does not have to be faithful to the calendar in the same way as history has to be. But in not being faithful to dates he suggests his narrative has come loose from history, as in a way it has. The time frame by which these events can be dated and related to other events – the scramble for Africa . . . or the discovery in 1899 by Sir Ronald Ross that the malaria parasite is transmitted by anopheles mosquitoes – is unknown to Okonkwo.[28] □

Whilst Okonkwo wishes to be the author of his own life, we as readers are allowed to see him as a pawn in a historical struggle he is hardly even aware is taking place. For Kortenaar, this disjunction represents a major problem for *Things Fall Apart*, if it is to be read in any serious sense as an anticolonial novel.

Both Ekwe-Ekwe and Kortenaar, in their different ways, offer quite determinate, positioned readings of *Things Fall Apart*. Richard Begam,[29] on the other hand, presents Achebe's text in a much more open way. He focuses particularly on the novel's ending – or in other words, on Achebe's handling of the problem of 'closure'– in this text of colonialism and resistance. Tied up with the question of closure, he argues, is a whole set of issues about the relationship between postcolonial writing and the past it attempts to narrate:

■ We may begin to appreciate some of the difficulties entailed in this relation by considering a number of connected questions. First, where do postcolonial writers locate their past? Is it to be found in the colonial, precolonial, or postcolonial period? Second, can we neatly separate the different historical strands that traverse and intersect these various epochs? Can we confidently assign to them decisive beginnings and conclusive endings? Third, what historical stance should postcolonial writers assume toward their own history, especially if they wish to forge a sense of national identity after colonization? To what extent does 'critical history', of the sort described by Nietzsche, become a luxury that the postcolonial writer cannot afford?[30] □

Superficially, the narrative structure of *Things Fall Apart* appears simple, following the life and death of one man in the context of his time. Looked at in more detail, however, Begam argues that the novel's attitude to this history is in fact far more complex. Whilst it describes the dissolution of an entire set of social structures and certainties, for example, it simultaneously looks forward to an era of national independence.

The nature of Achebe's approach to historical narration needs to be considered in three ways, Begam suggests. Firstly, we must consider *Things Fall Apart* as a nationalist project of cultural reconstruction. Like many other intellectuals in soon-to-be independent nations in the mid-twentieth century, he is seeking to replace a reductive colonial history with one which does his people more justice. Secondly, Achebe's history must be thought about as an adversarial form of writing: the novel seeks to supplant colonial discourse with a new form of expression which undoes and overwrites its assumptions. Thirdly, Begam suggests, we need to recognize the ways in which Achebe's writing also constitutes a kind of 'meta-history', that is, as a history which 'calls attention to itself as a piece of writing, a narrative construction that depends on principles of selection (what material will be included?), emphasis (what importance will be attached to it?) and shaping (how will it be organized and arranged?)'.[31]

For Begam, much of the critical dispute over *Things Fall Apart*, for example over the nature of the 'tragedy' it embodies, stems from the failure of readers to recognize that Achebe has given the novel three endings, rather than just one. When this is acknowledged, he suggests, it becomes clear that *Things Fall Apart* should be read as a palimpsest, a layered form of history, which invites a kind of reading that is akin to archaeology, a process of gradual uncovering. As Begam argues:

> ■ The first of the novel's three endings centres on Okonkwo's killing of the messenger, his failed attempt to rouse his people to action, and his subsequent suicide. This ending presents the events of the novel largely from an African perspective, equating Okonkwo's demise with the collapse of Igbo culture.[32] □

This first ending corresponds to an important layer of Achebe's novel, in which Okonkwo's narrative is schematically connected to the fate of his entire people. Begam traces this dynamic to the very beginning of the text, in which the protagonist's wrestling match with Amalinze the Cat is framed as the re-enactment of a mystic battle between Umuofia's founder and a 'spirit of the wild'. Whilst Okonkwo does not embody all the characteristics and virtues of the clan (and indeed suffers banishment during the central section of the novel), he is nevertheless cast as a hero who in some way carries the destiny of the whole community on his shoulders. Under the threat of colonial invasion, he stands alone to defend the pride and martial ethos of Umuofia. When he kills the court messenger – a fellow Ibo – and then himself, these twin acts of sacrilege against the earth encapsulate and symbolize the whole community's self-betrayal and ruin. Having set out his first reading, Begam continues:

> ■ The novel's second ending, which I associate with adversarial history, views events from the heavily ironized perspective of the District Commissioner. Igbo culture is now presented not from the inside as vital and autonomous, but from the outside as an object of anthropological curiosity, and its collapse is understood not as an African tragedy but as a European triumph.[33] □

In this layer of his narrative, Begam suggests, Achebe shows the connection between the repressive and the ideological apparatuses of colonialism. The commissioner is both the administrator and the writer of its history, as a bringer of civilization to the 'primitive'. Encoded in the text's handling of the commissioner is the knowledge of his ignorance of Ibo culture, as well as of his self-delusion and complacency. When we learn the title of the commissioner's book, *The Pacification of the Primitive Tribes of the Lower Niger*, the transition between the tragic ending of Okonkwo and the bitterly ironic ending through the eyes of colonialism is complete. The commissioner's 'reasonable paragraph' on Okonkwo is implicitly contrasted with the nuanced and complex account of his life we have just read. With amazing economy, Achebe thus converts his Ibo tragedy into another genre of text entirely – a counter-history of colonialism from the perspective of its victims. For Begam, this second ending to *Things Fall Apart* not only complements the first one, but also works to redefine our understanding of the novel as a whole. As he points out, the text would read quite differently if it ended, for example, with Obierika's account of Okonkwo's death. By ending with the voice of the colonialist, the text implicitly points forward to the legacy of modernization and change of

which the book is itself a product. In important ways, it modi-
fies and complicates the reader's understanding of Okonkwo's and
Umuofia's tragedy.

At this point in Begam's essay, readers will be wondering where
he will find Achebe's third ending for *Things Fall Apart*. Ingeniously,
what he does is to locate it in the second novel, *No Longer at Ease*,
which, in Achebe's first manuscript, formed the second part of a
single larger narrative. Begam argues that *No Longer at Ease* forms a
natural continuity with *Things Fall Apart*, recapitulating, extending
and qualifying Okonkwo's story in important ways. Considering the
second novel as a further layer of *Things Fall Apart*'s palimpsest structure throws the latter, once again, into interesting relief. The specific
scene in *No Longer at Ease* in which Begam identifies the third ending of Okonkwo's story finds his university-educated grandson Obi
being interviewed for a job in the colonial civil service. The conversation turns to the subject of tragedy, as Obi is asked his opinion of
Graham Greene (1904–91):

■ 'You say you're a great admirer of Graham Greene. What do you
think of *The Heart of the Matter?* [1934]'

'The only sensible novel any European has written on West Africa and
one of the best novels I have read'. Obi paused, and then added almost
as an afterthought: 'Only it was nearly ruined by the happy ending'.

The Chairman sat up in his chair.

'Happy ending? Are you sure it's *The Heart of the Matter* you're
thinking about? The European police officer commits suicide'.

'Perhaps happy ending is too strong, but there is no other way I can
put it. The police officer is torn between his love of a woman and his
love of God, and he commits suicide. It's much too simple. Tragedy
isn't like that at all. I remember an old man in my village, a Christian
convert, who suffered one calamity after another. He said life was like
a bowl of wormwood which one sips a little at a time world without end.
He understood the nature of tragedy'.

'You think that suicide ruins a tragedy', said the Chairman.

'Yes. Real tragedy is never resolved. It goes on hopelessly for
ever. Conventional tragedy is too easy. The hero dies and we feel a
purging of the emotions. A real tragedy takes place in a corner, in an
untidy spot, to quote W. H. Auden [1907–73]. The rest of the world
is unaware of it. Like that man in *A Handful of Dust* [1934, by Evelyn
Waugh (1902–66)] who reads Dickens to Mr. Todd. There is no release
for him. When the story ends he is still reading. There is no purging of
the emotions for us because we are not there'.[34] □

For Begam, Obi's account of the relationship between suicide and tragedy helps us to see the final layer of *Things Fall Apart*'s conclusion:

■ Obi draws a distinction in this passage between two kinds of tragedy. In traditional or Aristotelian tragedy, there is a clear resolution, an aesthetic pay-off that comes in the form of *catharsis;* but in modern or ironic tragedy, the tragedy described in Auden's 'Musée des Beaux Arts', the fall from a high place is likened to Brueghel's famous painting of Icarus [*Landscape with the Fall of Icarus* (about 1558) by Pieter Breughel (about 1525–69)]. In the foreground the ploughman ploughs his field; in the background a ship sails on its way. And it is only after careful inspection that we are able to discover the place of tragedy: there in the corner, barely perceptible, we see Icarus's two legs breaking the surface of the water, sole testimony of his personal catastrophe.

   While the point of departure for Obi's discussion of tragedy is Graham Greene's *The Heart of the Matter,* his observations have an obvious application to *Things Fall Apart.* Okonkwo's story as viewed from the Igbo perspective presents history in the form of classical or heroic tragedy. Okonkwo's story as viewed from the District Commissioner's perspective presents history in the form of modern or ironic tragedy. One of Obi's remarks is particularly apposite: there is no purging of the emotions in modern tragedy, because 'we are not there'. These words perfectly describe the situation of the District Commissioner. He 'was not there' in the sense that he was never in a position genuinely to understand Okonkwo, to appreciate who he was and what he represented.[35] □

According to Begam, the significance of Obi Okonkwo's analysis of tragedy is that it offers a direct commentary on his own past and, through it, evokes the entire problematic relationship to history that is implicit in the condition of postcoloniality. Okonkwo in *Things Fall Apart* is both a heroic exemplar of tragedy and an unknowable abstraction of history. As Begam stresses, the novel's strategy is not to invite us to choose between the two, but rather to insist on both possibilities simultaneously. In this double view, moreover, is encoded a third kind of tragedy: that of cultural loss. In the light of Achebe's third ending, we understand Okonkwo's tragedy in a different way: that his world has fallen beyond the reach of anything but speculative reclamation.

CONTEMPORARY CONTEXTS AND DEBATES

In Britain, as we saw in chapter 1, *Things Fall Apart* was treated to a degree of scepticism when it was presented as a manuscript to publishers, as well as by early critics in the British press. Only after a time did the novel begin to be recognized as a defining work of postcolonial fiction. In Nigeria, the novel met with a similar hesitancy when it first appeared. As Ezenwa-Ohaeto notes, even in Enugu, where Achebe was working for the Nigerian Broadcasting Corporation, the novel's circulation was initially small. When the publisher Alan Hill travelled to Nigeria in 1959 on a literary talent-spotting trip for Heinemann, he found that Achebe's growing reputation in the UK was not reflected by equivalent recognition at home:

■ Everywhere I was greeted with total skepticism that a recent student from the University of Ibadan should have written a novel of any significance at all. At the University of Ibadan they didn't take me seriously when I told them that one of their alumni had written a great novel. 'What, Chinua Achebe write a novel! How ridiculous!' they exclaimed.

One of the professors, Molly Mahood, made her students laugh when she said: 'That will be the day when English literature is taught from Chaucer to Achebe'.[36] □

Only gradually, with the support of teachers and writers of Achebe's acquaintance, did the novel begin to find its way onto college curricula and to a wider reading public. In 1961, three years after the its publication, Yeni Lijadu's adaptation of the novel for radio under the title *Okonkwo*[37] was one of the most important developments which helped to raise Nigerian awareness of Achebe and his work. By 1963, the novel was beginning to enjoy mass circulation in Nigeria. Even in Uganda it was listed as a bestseller by Heinemann. By 1969, the publisher was reporting total annual sales of 400,000 copies.[38] Recognition began to flow Achebe's way, allowing him to embark on a tour of the United States and Brazil that was to profoundly affect his own sense of his vocation as a writer.

In the mid-1960s, Achebe began to produce the first of the critical essays that helped to define his politics and aesthetics for a generation of critics. Perhaps the most influential of these critical interventions is his 1965 essay 'The Novelist as Teacher,'[39] in which

Achebe questions conventional European assumptions about the place of literary producers in society: 'We have learnt from Europe that a writer or an artist lives on the fringe of society-wearing a beard and a peculiar dress and generally behaving in a strange, unpredictable way. He is in revolt against society, which in turn looks on him with suspicion if not hostility'.[40]

Importantly, Achebe vigorously defends the right of writers to produce whatever their conscience dictates, without regard to the expectations of their audience. Nevertheless, he does regard it as the duty of African writers to address the historic situation of their societies and, in some sense, to dedicate their craft to the cause of national renewal. Whilst much of the cultural legacy of colonialism may have been banished along with the retreating British, a great deal more work remains to be done:

> ■ Today, things have changed a lot, but it would be foolish to pretend that we have fully recovered from the traumatic effects of our first confrontation with Europe. Three or four weeks ago my wife, who teaches English in a boys' school, asked a pupil why he wrote about winter when he meant the harmattan. He said the other boys would call him a bushman if he did such a thing! Now, you wouldn't have thought, would you, that there was something shameful in your weather? But apparently we do. How can this great blasphemy be purged? I think it is part of my business as a writer to teach that boy that there is nothing disgraceful about the African weather, that the palm tree is a fit subject for poetry.
>
> Here then is an adequate revolution for me to espouse – to help my society regain belief in itself and put away the complexes of the years of denigration and self-abasement. And it is essentially a question of education, in the best sense of that word. Here, I think, my aims and the deepest aspirations of my society meet.[41] □

Writers cannot expect to exempt themselves from the work of national rebuilding that the condition of independence brings with it, Achebe suggests. Indeed, as cultural workers with a unique kind of access to people's thought and feelings, they should be the first to do battle with the negative legacies of the past. As he makes clear elsewhere in his critical writings, by no means is this imagined as an easy or straightforward task:

> ■ Despite the daunting problems of identity that beset our contemporary society, we can see in the horizon the beginnings of a

new relationship between artist and community which will not flourish like the mango-trick in the twinkling of an eye but will rather, in the hard and bitter manner of David Diop's young tree, grow patiently and obstinately to the ultimate victory of liberty and fruition.[42] □

Amongst subsequent critics of Achebe's fiction, the cultural nationalism espoused in such essays as 'The Novelist as Teacher' is recognized as an important influence on his own writing, as well as that of other authors. For some, nevertheless, there remains an important gap between the principles set out by Achebe in theoretical terms and the actual work that is performed by his novels. One of the critics that has been most scathing in his criticisms of *Things Fall Apart* in this regard is the leading critic Ode Ogede, in his study *Achebe and the Politics of Representation*.[43]

At the centre of Ogede's work lies a question – in a postcolonial state, how far is it possible for a writer to 'address his former masters through their own idioms without being complicit in their politics of narration?'[44] If the use of the English language as Achebe's mode of literary expression is not an 'innocent' choice, Ogede argues, then neither is his choice of form. For Ogede, the key literary tools that Achebe uses, satire and tragedy, are far from being neutral in their cultural resonances. Rather, 'they are superstructures that express core Western ideas and attitudes'.[45]

Ogede does acknowledge Achebe's importance as a cultural archaeologist, arguing that his fictions provide important insights into the impact of colonialism on ordinary Africans, illuminating experiences that are elided by many historical and sociological accounts. Nevertheless, this is not enough to prevent him from launching an embittered critique of the author's failings:

■ In his first novel (*Things Fall Apart*), Achebe adopts an uncompromising stance in his criticism of the failings of the indigenous African leadership, while the atrocities of colonization are all too clearly relegated to a secondary focus. Why does he do this? Why does he make excuses for the weaknesses of the colonizers, while spewing undiluted venom at Africans for failing to rule with conscience? Why does he fail to hold the colonizing powers to the same standard of morality, especially since colonialism is initially responsible for creating the majority of the problems with which the indigenous leadership has found itself beset? Could it be that the attempt to exonerate the brutality of the occupation forces issues from a stance Achebe has contrived with deliberation? If so, is he one of those writers who uphold the belief that the moral properties of human beings are genetically determined? Does Achebe present colonialism with such a demonstratively forgiving spirit because he believes its proponents are inherently less capable of moral sentience than the conquered people?[46] □

Here, the novel is seen as revealing a deep complicity with colonialism, and even with the racial theory which underpinned it. For Ogede (to say the least) this represents a major failing in Achebe's work, one that can be directly connected to the issue of form. By adopting the literary idioms of the colonizer, he argues, Achebe's work becomes trapped into reproducing the ideological frameworks which they embody and express:

■ Let us remember the roles British colonial authors bestowed on satire and tragedy in promoting policies of subjugation. Since the tragic mode is inherently a manner of acceptance of imperfection, an acquiescent mode that accepts the status quo (while satire unflinchingly is a mode of rejection of foibles), it should have been clear from the beginning that African writers should employ satire and tragedy with an extreme sense of discretion. That Achebe employs tragedy to depict the activities of the colonizing forces and the immediate African response while utilizing satire to blast the post-independence African leadership shows the misdirection of his early work; he holds himself hostage within colonialist discourses of fiction. An inversion of the direction of their uses would be more appropriate. . . .

It is not only naive but misleading to attach a tragic quality to a situation like colonization. To do so is to give an approving nod to the whole messy affair and to invest it with a false sense of predestination. We do not know why Achebe did not explore an alternative strategy.[47] □

Whilst Achebe's theoretical project for appropriation and reclamation is certainly laudable, his creative practice in *Things Fall Apart* is so problematic as to be rendered a failure, Ogede argues. As a novelist he lacks the radicalism to make a meaningful break with Western liberalism and its modes of literary expression. In his early fiction particularly, Achebe's writing retains too many lines of influence and connection with colonial discourse to be able to seriously challenge it. In *Things Fall Apart*, this problem becomes most acute in Achebe's handling of Okonkwo:

■ In the European novel about Africa, the African character is invariably depicted to show his essential difference from the European norm. Achebe's text can be said to have absorbed this tradition since it juxtaposes such peculiar traits as the 'bushy eyebrows and wide nose' and emotionality commonly associated with the primitive Africans with European reason and logic. Okonkwo is painted as if he lacks the ordinary gift of articulate human speech in a way that is too close to the Conradian image of Africans without a human voice. Thus, predictably, throughout the text, Okonkwo is presented as an overgrown child, whose story details the movement of a typical European pastoral tragedy. . . . The dominant idea in pastoral themes is the inevitable victory of the complex urban civilization over a simple and innocent rural life, with tragic consequences for 'the self-alienated' man. In *Things Fall Apart,* Western influence equates nicely with the complex metropolitan urban life-style that the hero, Okonkwo, standing for simple African ways, resists at his own peril. . . . When he moves from severity toward his children to wife-beating and attempted murder, then cuts down Ikemefuna, his foster child, before he finally commits the homicide that leads him into his suicide, Okonkwo proves unable to conquer this opponent, the enemy within.[48] □

Too often, Ogede argues, the generic problems with Achebe's work have been overlooked by critics, who read his fiction unquestioningly through the lens of his (more radical) critical pronouncements. Rather than reproducing such uncritical readings, he suggests, Achebe's work should be examined for the insights it offers into the difficulties faced by African writers who turn a creative eye to colonialism and its aftermath:

■ Achebe has consistently identified himself as a strategist of decolonization, as one who utilizes literature to further cultural resistance to colonialism. However, the true test of theory is in practice. Achebe has claimed cultural assertion to be the main motivation for his writing, yet he continues to face a problem that confronts every writer from the formerly colonized territory; the problem of how to achieve a novelty of representation and inscribe what is truly revolutionary within forms that were originally meant for retrogressive missions. This is not an easy task to carry out. . . .
    That Achebe never really found a way to get around dealing with the crisis of colonialism does not mean that no writer from the formerly

colonized territory could do so. There is often a discrepancy between an author's intentions and actual achievement. Because this is true, readers of African literature must attend to not only the issue of cultural assertion but also the problems faced by African writers who attempt to work within conventional Western literary forms. These problems are not limited to the 'crisis of representation', the debilitating consciousness of the insufficiency of words, images, symbols, and concepts to capture the true essence of experience. African writers must also grapple with the reality of working with foreign languages – English in the case of Achebe. They also must confront Western forms such as the novel, poetry, drama, tragedy, satire, which have been used to silence indigenous voices.[49] □

If *Things Fall Apart* can be allowed to be a landmark in African writing, for Ogede, its achievement must be found in the way it provided a platform on which later fiction – by Achebe himself and by others – could build. The novel is, he acknowledges, pioneering in the sophistication of its attempt to create a sense of Ibo identity in the late nineteenth century. Politically, it was also important for establishing an agenda of cultural reclamation that shaped the work of many subsequent African writers. If the novel is partially flawed by its enthrallment to Western literary models and values, Ogede concedes therefore, it can still be recognized as an important stepping-stone in the development of modern African literature.

If Ogede ultimately sees *Things Fall Apart* as a text damaged by the ideological ambivalence of its author, this is a theme picked up by other critics in different ways, as we have seen. The final reading of *Things Fall Apart* I want to look at here, by the critic Romanus Okey Muoneke,[50] situates this ambivalence specifically in the context of the Negritude movement, a great influence on Achebe and many other writers around the time of independence.

Originating in the politics and philosophy of the Harlem Renaissance in America and in the Parisian anticolonial movements of the 1930s, Negritude centered on the celebration of black identity and culture, and on wholesale opposition to colonialism. Focusing on the founding influence of the Senegalese activist and politician Leopold Senghor, Muoneke explains:

■ As defined by Senghor, 'Negritude is the consciousness of being Black, the simple recognition of the fact, implying acceptance and responsibility for one's own destiny as a Black man, one's history or one's culture. It is the refusal to assimilate, to see oneself in the "other". Refusal of the other is affirmation of the Self'. This refusal and affirmation gives Negritude its rebellious character. It is not surprising that the movement, which really was a cultural nationalism, coincided with the great nationalist movements sprouting all over the colonies in the 30's and 40's with the principal objective of reclaiming national independence from the colonies. Rejecting negative colonial stereotypes, the Negritude advocates sought for a rehabilitation of the African past, a rediscovery of the goodness in things African. But in this pursuit they beatified and glamorized not only the past but also the present. Leopold Senghor for example, celebrates in *Chants d'Ombré* [1945] respect for the spirit of the ancestors, a longing of an exile in Europe for a return to the land of his birth in Africa, the charm of the African night, the beauty of the Black woman, the need for the Black culture to lend warmth and vitality to the European culture, and other recognitions of the virtues of Blackness.[51] □

One of the problems of Negritude from the beginning, Muoneke suggests, was its ambivalent relationship to the notion of 'race'. Although the movement was centred on resistance to colonial ideology, it also incorporated a kind of reverse racism, often celebrating blackness in explicitly racial terms. Particular qualities, such as an inherently elevated emotionality, were ascribed to blackness in a way which recapitulated (albeit in affirmative ways) the essential ideological framework of colonial racism.

According to Muoneke, Negritude's ideological influence on Achebe is something that should not be ignored. His writings' anti-colonial impulse, their recuperative approach to the African past and their commitment to affirming the dignity of Africans are all features that can be traced in the Negritude movement. On the other hand, Achebe's work can also be distinguished from that of Negritude's proponents in important ways. Most importantly, it illustrates a willingness to balance both positive and negative, beautiful and ugly aspects of the African past. In the case of *Things Fall Apart*, Muoneke detects a realism at the heart of Achebe's novel, which refuses to be limited to the unswerving affirmation of all things African:

■ Such realism underlies Achebe's attitude toward Negritude. As a critic of colonialism, he lauds the role of Negritude in preparing Africans for independence and in helping to restore dignity to Africans.

Negritude's propaganda and art served at a particular period as 'props' fashioned 'to help us get on our feet again'. . . . The other side of Achebe condemns Negritude. In an interview in 1963, Achebe makes the following statement: 'I am against slogans. I don't think, for example, that "Negritude" has any meaning whatsoever. Panafricanism? Maybe. Negritude, no.' To understand this change of attitude, we need to keep in mind that Achebe distinguishes between the early and later Negritude. . . . The later phase of Negritude was defined more in conferences, and became more of empty propaganda and slogans. It was a Negritude that was overtaken by historical realities. The end of colonialism and the failure, to a large extent, of Black politicians and Black rule had reduced Negritude to mere cliché.[52] □

In the novel, as Muoneke points out, Achebe does not attempt to present Umuofia as a new Eden, but instead shows both its strengths and weaknesses as a society. The clan is shown as cohesive and at ease with itself in the early sections of the text, with a developed system of political and judicial institutions. We see how the traditional religion strengthens the collective consciousness of the people. The family, with all its internal tensions, is shown as a key building block of social life. At the same time, however, we are also offered many cruel and disturbing insights:

■ The society in *Things Fall Apart is* lively, prosperous, self-assured, and to some extent, civilized. Yet, it is a society plagued with serious problems. Fear, death, and danger brood over it. There is 'the fear of evil and capricious gods and of magic, the fear of the forest, and the forces of nature, malevolent, red in tooth and claw'. Haunted by her sense of insecurity, often arising from her fear of the gods and the unknown, this society performs some outrageously cruel deeds. Whatever is identified as a threat to Umuofia's security or any possible cause of the wrath of the gods is expeditiously and often ruthlessly disposed of. On the basis of this, twins are abandoned to die in evil forests . . . *Ogbanje* children (who are regarded as viciously plaguing their mothers by their cycle of birth and death) are mutilated at their death to prevent them from coming back. Swelling sickness is regarded as an abomination to the earth goddess and those who suffer from such are tied to trees and left to languish in evil forests and sometimes to be devoured by vultures. Unoka, Okonkwo's father, falls victim to this horrible practice. Nor does Okonkwo escape the fate of abandonment. Suicides are buried by strangers in the evil forest, and Okonkwo who hanged himself is so treated. *Osu* people are denied normal relationships with other citizens, and at death, are buried by their kind in the evil forest. . . . Human sacrifice is practiced. Ikemefuna, the innocent boy, is thus sacrificed for an offence committed by his people.[53] □

In this way, at the same time as celebrating precolonial society, Achebe's novel also asks searching questions about many aspects of traditional culture. For Muoneke, the 'cracks and weaknesses' depicted by the novel prove profound enough to prevent its centre from holding. As he argues, this balanced representation of the past − challenging as well as affirming Nigerians' sense of their historical heritage − is not intended as an easy lesson: 'In this educational role, Achebe seriously departs from Negritude's narrow perspective. Like the sons of the prophets of old, Negritude gives the people only what pleases their ears in order to affirm their pride and dignity. Like Elijah the prophet, Achebe gives them the sweet and bitter truth in order to save them. Achebe's departure from Negritude is not only rebellious but also redemptive'.[54]

In the best sense, *Things Fall Apart* has been a spur to vigorous critical debate, right from the moment of its publication. Whilst many critics have, in different ways, taken issue with the novel's representational strategies and with its politics, few have questioned its significance as a creative intervention in Nigerian culture on the eve of Independence. With the publication of his second novel, *No Longer at Ease*, in 1960, Achebe boldly extended his fictional canvas. In a way, as we will see in chapter 3, his direct address to the culture of the 1950s in that novel was to catch critics by surprise. Only over time did the sequel to *Things Fall Apart* begin to provoke fresh new ways of thinking about the writer and his work.

CHAPTER THREE

No Longer at Ease (1960)

After the publication of *Things Fall Apart* in 1958, it was several years before Achebe became recognized as a major literary figure in Nigeria. During the intervening period, however, his career in the Nigerian media developed very rapidly. In 1961, he was already considered a sufficiently eminent figure to be invited to set up the 'Voice of Nigeria' by the Nigerian Broadcasting Corporation. He was made director of external broadcasting in that year.[1]

Against this background, it might seem surprising that Achebe was able to publish a second novel with Heinemann only two years after the emergence of his first. However, it is important to remember that the novel which Achebe took to England in 1957 comprised the narratives of *Things Fall Apart* and *No Longer at Ease* together. In 1958, when Achebe submitted Okonkwo's story to publishers, the narrative of his grandson Obi was cut in its entirety. With a certain amount of revision, therefore, it was a comparatively easy step for the author to fashion Obi's story as a continuation of *Things Fall Apart* in 1960. Perhaps partly as a result of this history, *No Longer at Ease* has often been overshadowed by its predecessor. Here I will begin by looking at two early responses to the novel, by Arthur Ravenscroft and David Carroll, respectively. The chapter will then explore some of the text's key literary influences, as identified by more recent critics. Finally, I will look at three of the most interesting historical approaches to *No Longer at Ease*, each of which further enhances our sense of the novel's complexity and its strange ambivalence towards Nigeria and her place in the contemporary world.

EARLY CRITICAL RESPONSES

As Arthur Ravenscroft points out in his pioneering early study *Chinua Achebe* (1977),[2] the title of *No Longer at Ease* is drawn, once again, from a canonical literary text, this time 'The Journey of the Magi' [1927, by T. S. Eliot (1888–1965)]. Again, the reference suggests themes of cultural fragmentation and historical change. The novel centres on the figure of Obi Okonkwo, the son of the Christian convert Nwoye in *Things Fall Apart*. As in that text, Achebe's narrative focuses on the struggle of his protagonist to negotiate a world in rapid transition. According to Ravenscroft, nevertheless, it is a mistake to read *No Longer at Ease* too simply as a sequel to *Things Fall Apart*. Though many themes continue from one novel to the next, Achebe's representation of contemporary, urban Nigeria lends a far greyer and more 'austere'[3] texture to the second novel, risking the charge of bleakness:

> ■ Umuofian society still represents values of the past, while the Nigerian capital, Lagos, is the cosmopolitan urban present, where everyone competes, no holds barred, for the meagre perks of incipient affluence. Umuofia is rurally conservative, a hybrid amalgam of pagan and established Christian respectabilities. It still clings to the notion of the ineradicable bonds of clan kinship, and though the liberalized Obi finds these suffocating, the concept does have some value in a confused, disruptive period of rapid change.[4] □

On the level of language, Ravenscroft notes Achebe's subtle handling of different voices and registers, ranging from 'the cliché-ridden English of the popular press'[5] through a local pidgin to Ibo itself. The presence of such constant linguistic shifts forms one of the levels on which the novel establishes a sense of flux and uncertainty in the Lagos of the 1950s. In *Things Fall Apart*, life before the arrival of the colonialist is represented in terms of balance and equilibrium, but this opposition between the old and the new is not reproduced in *No Longer at Ease*. Instead, Achebe paints a less edifying picture in which tradition has been deeply compromised by modernization:

> ■ Though he exposes the slums behind the tinsel glitter of Lagos, though he contrasts humbug and official corruption with the energetic warmth of ordinary life in the city, he does not offer Umuofia as a valid

alternative. On the contrary, despite the humane virtues that still shelter beneath Umuofian solidarity, Achebe more often than not presents the Lagos Umuofians satirically. As in *Things Fall Apart,* we hear again the clan salute *Umuofia Kwenu*! and the choral response *Ya*!, but from the throats of the Umuofia Progressive Union it rings like a comic mockery of the formal opening of a clan assembly that used to thunder across the market place. The UPU has turned Obi into Umuofia's first graduate, and thus into the new Secretary of the government Scholarship Board. Obi becomes Umuofia's 'only palm fruit' in the upper echelons of the civil service, and he is looked to for the influence he will exert on behalf of Umuofians anxious for some crumbs from the national cake, or, as they put it: 'Shall we kill a snake and carry it in our hand, when we have a bag for putting long things in?'[6] □

For Ravenscroft, however, the technique deployed by Achebe in representing such scenes is somewhat problematic. The author's strong satirical style, by means of which he casts a sceptical eye over all echelons of society from the Lagos Umuofians to the colonial school inspector, sits ill, in his view, with the tragic impulse which structures the novel. If this is a 'lesser work'[7] than *Things Fall Apart* (as he believes), then this is partly because of the disjunction between these elements:

■ What one misses is the artistically cohesive tension between chief character and setting that occurs in *Things Fall Apart*. The setting is as economically and convincingly created, but is felt to be almost incidental to the story of Obi. Like one of the magi, Obi returns from abroad, having caught the flavour of a different – an efficient, rational – dispensation. His mind is packed full of elevated notions of public service, and he is determined to play his full part in reinvigorating the Nigerian civil service and stamping out all the old corruption that so ill befits a new nation. The story records his failure. It is an attempt at a tale of muted tragedy, told laconically rather than with detachment.

Achebe's method is clearly hinted at in the account of Obi's interview for his job. During a discussion of Graham Greene's *The Heart of the Matter,* Obi says that life is 'like a bowl of wormwood which one sips a little at a time world without end'. 'A real tragedy', he asserts, 'takes place in a corner, in an untidy spot'. It would seem that Achebe intends Obi's story to be tragic in this sort of Audenesque way, a view confirmed by the very banal level at which Obi's defeat takes place. He succumbs because loans have to be repaid, money sent home, expenses accounted for. For this effect to be produced Obi has to be made so naive and self-deluded that he comes close to appearing merely childish. While his story can also be read partly as a paradigm of a man caught between the irreconcilable values of different ways of life, his enmeshment happens too easily to win our sympathetic involvement.[8] □

According to Ravenscroft, Achebe's protagonist is too naive, too priggish, too sentimental and self-deluding, and the effect of this for the reader is a realization, almost from the outset, that he has no chance of survival. His ethical ideals and opposition to corruption are, similarly, set up as flimsy screens simply waiting to be torn down. If Obi's demise lacks the monumental impact of Okonkwo's, Ravenscroft argues, this is because he is, from the beginning, more of a 'lost child'[9] than a figure of tragedy.

The assumption of the critic David Carroll[10] is that *No Longer at Ease* must be read primarily as a sequel to *Things Fall Apart*. Like Ravenscroft, he sees the world portrayed in Achebe's second novel as a more confused and complex one than that of Okonkwo's Umuofia, but, also like Ravenscroft, he sees the text's attempt to render that world as inferior to its predecessor in most ways.

This overall, rather negative assessment does not of course in itself invalidate Carroll's interpretation of *No Longer at Ease*, and in fact his study makes many perceptive observations about the novel. For the first time in this text, as Carroll points out, Achebe expands his canvas to include the metropolis, a cultural space very different from that of the village. Here, questions of identity and belonging have become much more problematic than 50 years previously, especially for such people as the novel's protagonist, who is the hybrid product of traditional culture and Western education:

■ The Umuofians with characteristic flexibility appreciate the need for modern knowledge in order to defend and extend the gains already secured by their Christian compromise. This is why they want Obi to read law in England, 'so that when he returned he would handle all their land cases against their neighbours'. But what they don't anticipate is that the knowledge which brings power also brings detachment and alienation. . . . We can see that the alignment of forces no longer has the classical simplicity of earlier days. When Obi returns from England and the university, he comes, not to the village, but first to the Afro-European city of Lagos. . . . The city stands midway between Europe and Umuofia and creates its own highly spiced amalgamation of their different cultural ingredients.[11] □

Seen through Obi's eyes, Lagos is far from being a vision of Nigeria's modernity, but instead becomes a picture of decay and dilapidation. By contrast to the fierce tribal loyalty of Okonkwo, Obi's attitude to the Umuofia Progressive Union and to Nigeria more generally is, Carroll argues, one of revulsion. In this way, Achebe positions him as 'a black Englishman whose knowledge of Africa only enables him to discern more clearly the precise nature of its corruption'.[12] On his return from the UK, he is seen as having adopted the voice of a 'colonial describing the natives'.[13] As the narrative progresses, Carroll argues, we then see a gradual softening and change in this attitude as Obi becomes more aware of his position as an African.

As far as Umuofia itself is concerned, meanwhile, the novel depicts a parallel state of ambivalence and a parallel process of development. At the beginning of the text, Umuofia appears to have found a new equilibrium between tradition and Christianity. As the narrative proceeds, however, we become aware of how unstable this equilibrium is. One of the key ways in which this is dramatized is through the lack of consensus about Obi's place and significance as a man who has travelled to learn the white man's knowledge. For the Progressive Union, his education was an investment that is expected to yield material dividends. For the Umuofia Christians, he is an inheritor of the missionary ethos, whose new-found wisdom should be used to spread light among the heathen. In both cases, Carroll suggests, Achebe presents the Umuofians as naive and blind to the historical transitions taking place in their country.

If the Umuofians are seen as a people in transition, Carroll argues that Achebe's portrait of the colonial Mr Green describes a comparable uneasiness and ambivalence. In *Things Fall Apart* the commissioner is unassailable in his ignorance, but the role of Green in *No Longer at Ease* is a much less stable one. His role is to administer the last days of a colonial regime that is soon to be dismantled. He is fiercely loyal to a vision of Africa as a land of primitives being brought to civilization, but this is a mythical Africa that exists nowhere but in the minds of the colonials themselves. Green's response to this looming crisis is to hold more firmly to his 'duty' as an administrator, turning away from the writing on the wall.

With the character of Obi, Carroll suggests, Achebe encapsulates the double-bind experienced by young Nigerians in the 1950s. On the one hand, Obi has absorbed a Western ethos of individualism. The narrative stresses his idea of living according to one's own principles and shows his angry reaction when his personal privacy is invaded, for example over his relationship with Clara. Yet, on the other hand, Obi is also shown as a figure who is tightly bound up with the Umuofian community.

In the novel the tension between Obi's desire for individual freedom and his indebtedness to the clan is most clearly dramatized on the financial level. Obi owes money to the Umuofia Progressive Union for his expensive education and this again gives the clan licence to interfere in various aspects of his life. He believes that when he has paid off the loan, he will be rendered a free agent. However, things turn out to be more complicated than he first imagined. When the clan members hear of his intention to marry an *osu*, or outcast, girl, he is summoned back to the village to face his father Nwoye/Isaac. Despite Isaac's passionate Christianity and the fact that (as we know from *Things Fall Apart*) he was willing to abandon his own father's house for his faith, even he cannot sanction Obi's transgression of fundamental traditional beliefs. Obi argues that the prohibition on the sons and daughters of *osu* is nothing but a pagan superstition, but Isaac nevertheless sees the prospect of the marriage as akin to bringing leprosy into the house. As Carroll argues:

■ In this argument Obi has abandoned his agnosticism and reverted to his earlier Christianity, while his father has abandoned his decades of Christian belief and reverted to the tribal law of his childhood. 'Obi used the very words that his father might have used in talking to his heathen kinsmen'. But we now recognize that this reversal of roles is the characteristic movement of the novel. In times of crisis this regression to earlier beliefs emphatically denies any evolutionary assimilation of cultures which the framework of events might suggest. . . . The implication of this latest reversion is that the basic antinomy of Christian and tribal from which all the previous conflicts and tensions arose is itself in the final resort a false antithesis. Beneath all innovation and modification lies the indestructible and unrelenting solidarity of the tribe.[14] □

When Obi's mother threatens to kill herself if he goes ahead with the marriage, his dilemma deepens. At her death, his failure to attend her funeral accentuates his distance from the clan, but at the same time he is forced to soften his opposition to the custom of 'dash' (or bribery) with which traditional culture is associated in the city.

With Obi's eventual trial for corruption, Achebe completes his diagnosis of the dilemma of cultural contradiction experienced by his protagonist. For Carroll, however, neither the novel's concluding irony nor the drawing of the hero himself is as convincing or powerful as that of *Things Fall Apart*. The novel sees Obi being built up in order to be dismantled, Carroll argues, but he is never sufficiently finished as a character to generate the same response as Okonkwo:

■ Admittedly, this is part of the author's intention: Obi is an alien created out of a miscellany of cultural elements, and the scaffolding of his character is meant to be ramshackle. But it would be a fallacy to accept this as justification for the disturbing void at the centre of the novel. The diagrams of forces, the exemplary episodes, the schematic journeys fail to conceal the absence of any graspable self of the main character. It is not simply that Obi's career is confused, muddled and an anticlimax . . . we still need at the centre of the action an individual we may not only understand but sympathise with. This is especially true of the tragedy of the everyday where the anguish lies in each subtle response to the prosaic and the frequent. No such individual emerges from Obi's relations with his parents – they are simply the two components of his childhood world – nor with Clara – their relationship is conveyed in threadbare romantic cliché. Obi is a thoroughly passive character compelled to act occasionally by the exigencies of his various dilemmas. It might be argued that these dilemmas which arise from his inner contradictions represent Obi's character. But surely this is too deterministic a view. As several of Achebe's minor characters show, one is simply the result of a cultural and hereditary dialectic. But this is what the author seems to believe with regard to his hero. When he has carried out the construction and dismantling of Obi's character there is nothing left, no carry-over from the conflict and alliance of forces to the self of the hero which is their real battleground.[15] □

For Carroll, this weakness at the heart of *No Longer at Ease* fatally limits the novel's impact and reach. Carroll's characteristically liberal humanist demand is that the novel transcend its particular context and speak to the 'universal'. Sadly, he argues, *No Longer at Ease* fails to live up to this expectation. For this reason, he concludes, the text has little resonance beyond the particular time and place that produced it: 'it remains, in a limiting sense, a West African novel'.[16]

KEY INTERTEXTS

In different ways, both Arthur Ravenscroft and David Carroll set out
to judge *No Longer at Ease* against the yardstick of the English literary
canon. From this point of view, by contrast to *Things Fall Apart*, each
of them finds the book to be an inferior product. For Philip Rogers,
however, this equation is reversed. In his essay '*No Longer at Ease*:
Chinua Achebe's "Heart of Whiteness"' (1983),[17] Rogers's approach
is to see Achebe's text as a self-conscious response to the canon and
the cultural values it represents. By bringing out the novel's complex structure of literary reference and allusion, largely overlooked by
Ravenscroft and Carroll, Rogers is able to show *No Longer at Ease* to
be a much more sophisticated work than either of them are willing
to concede:

■ Throughout *No Longer at Ease* Obi is presented both in terms
of his relation to 'book' and to particular books – especially the
canon of literary modernism he studied in England and to which,
as antihero of an ironic and allusive novel, he himself belongs.
Obi's perception of his world and his attempts to make sense of his
experience – 'exegesis' Achebe calls it – are pervasively literary.
Achebe's literary allusions and Obi's literary sensibility combine to
provide a counterpoint of subtle and invariably ironic commentary on
Obi's behaviour. The heart of his action – and more significantly his
inaction – is revealed in the reflected light (or darkness) of several
major antiheros of modern literature: Evelyn Waugh's Tony Last
(*A Handful of Dust*), Joseph Conrad's Mr. Kurtz (*Heart of Darkness*),
Graham Greene's Scobie (*The Heart of the Matter*), W. H. Auden's
Icarus ('Musée des Beaux Arts'), and T. S. Eliot's personae from 'The
Waste Land' [1922], 'The Love Song of J. Alfred Prufrock' [1915],
and, of course, 'The Journey of the Magi', which provides Achebe's
title. These works possess significant common themes and in several
instances allude to one another, creating in *No Longer at Ease* a
substructure of allusion within allusion. *A Handful of Dust* points to
'The Waste Land' [Waugh's novel takes its title from line 30 of Eliot's
poem],' *The Heart of the Matter* to *Heart of Darkness*. Achebe's ironic
annexation of Conrad's imagery of hearts, centres, and emptiness
from 'Heart of Darkness' inevitably brings to mind Eliot's use of
Conrad in 'The Hollow Men' [1925]. 'Musée des Beaux Arts' similarly
parallels 'The Journey of the Magi'; the contrasting attitudes of young
and old toward the nativity in 'Musée' mirror the ambiguous reaction
of Eliot's magi to the same event. The clustered meanings of these
interrelated allusions focus on Obi, revealing more of his nature and

plight – the hollow heart of his whiteness – than Achebe's typically reticent narrative comments.[18] □

For Rogers, this complex metafictional play is central to the novel's dynamics. Again and again, he argues, the text dwells on the power and importance of the printed word. In the case of Obi's father Nwoye/ Isaac Okonkwo, we see an almost religiose veneration of text, 'from obsolete cockroach-eaten translations of the Bible into the Onitsha Dialect to yellowed Scripture Union cards of 1920 and earlier'.[19] In Achebe's narrative this is directly linked to Isaac's unquestioning faith in colonial discourse, a faith which, as Rogers argues, is ominously linked with 'decay and inanity'.[20] The fact that, in his construction of Obi's character, Achebe stresses the young man's infatuation with Western writing, then, is crucial. As Rogers suggests, this obsession is directly related to Obi's own creeping paralysis. Indeed, the fact that Obi identifies 'Easter Hymn' (1936) by A. E. Housman (1859–1936) as his favourite poem is particularly illuminating. As Rogers points out, Housman's text is a prayer to a sleeping or dead Christ who is oblivious to men's calls for aid. The citation of the poem reinforces the sense of Obi's atheism (in contrast to his father's Christianity) but it also foregrounds his unresponsiveness to ethical challenge and his inability to become the author of his own life. Importantly, Rogers argues, the text sets up a direct parallel between Housman's text and Obi's own poem, 'Nigeria':

■ For both Housman's Christ and Obi, personal peace is achieved at a cost of obliviousness or indifference to the lives of others. The failure of Housman's Christ to respond to mankind's prayers also reflects Obi's most distinctive personal failing – his recurring paralysis and inability to act decisively in the major crises of his life, most notably in his failures to prevent Clara's abortion and in accepting (by default) his first bribe. . . . The implied association of Obi's inability to act with the atheist's vision of a dead Christ considerably enhances, I think, the significance of Obi's loss of religious faith as a cause of his fall. In the unfolding of the narrative, Achebe places his allusions to 'Easter Hymn' so as to hint at the poem's relevance to Obi's behavior. The first time he reads the poem is after failing in a typically perfunctory attempt to persuade Clara that he loves her even though she is *osu*. He reads it again in a deliberate attempt to suppress and rationalize his emotions just after he has failed to prevent the abortion.

A further aspect of Achebe's use of 'Easter Hymn' is his juxta-posing it against Obi's own callow poem, 'Nigeria'. Obi has folded his poem into the Housman volume (words within words); here, the naive optimism of Obi's patriotic faith that his 'noble countrymen' will overcome tribalism and achieve national unity ['Forgetting region, tribe or speech/But caring always each for each'] is undercut by Housman's skeptical view that even the death of Christ succeeded only in fanning rather than quenching human hatred. The effect of the juxtaposition of the two poems is to suggest that Obi's faith in his nation is as shallow as his religious faith.[21] □

Likewise, Obi's passion for T. S. Eliot – and especially for 'The Love Song of J. Alfred Prufrock' – helps to underline his quali-ties of paralysis and prissy indecision. If the novel's title refers to Eliot's 'The Journey of the Magi', 'Prufrock' is at least as important an intertext: 'Prufrock frets about his bald spot; Obi imagines his fly to be unzipped. Recoiling in fastidious horror from the dead dogs and night soil smells of Lagos, Obi exclaims, "I have tasted putrid flesh in the spoon", comically echoing Prufrock's "I have measured out my life with coffee spoons". His response to the sober reality of a Lagos slum is to sanitize it in the genteel medium of English literature. By the novel's end Obi himself is "ether-ised" by the formalin of book and can stand aloof from his own emotions'.[22]

Like other critics, Rogers is keen to trace the significance of Obi's reference to Auden and 'Musée de Beaux Arts' (1938) in the civil service interview. In Auden's poem, the fall of Icarus is seen from an outsider's point of view, as the tragedy of an individual boy to which onlookers and passers-by are largely indifferent. Rogers's analysis of Auden's intertextual function in Achebe's novel is a par-ticularly interesting one. As he points out, Obi's own life experience is in marked contrast to that of Auden's Icarus. At each moment in his story, a wide array of family members, clansmen, friends and even strangers show themselves concerned for his well-being. When his car leaves the road and plunges into a ditch, for example, 'the women hold their breasts and weep with joy that he has not been hurt, the men push him out and see him safely on his way'.[23] In Achebe's text, Rogers argues, this incident perfectly illustrates the irrelevance of Auden's European perspective for the understanding of social relationships in Africa. Once again breaking from Ravenscroft and

Carroll, Rogers thus shows how the novel can be read as a new kind
of colonial tragedy:

■ If Obi's experience can be considered tragic at all, it is the tragedy
not of indifference to suffering, but of a perverse denial of human love
and rejection of human sympathy; considered from the perspective
of Obi's preoccupation with western culture, his tragedy may also
be defined as European individualism rejecting African community,
white aloofness denying black love.[24] □

Moving to a further intertextual dynamic in *No Longer at Ease*, Rogers
goes on to suggest that Achebe's self-conscious use of Graham Greene
and *The Heart of the Matter* reinforces this sense of Obi's rootlessness
and inanity. As he argues, the similarity between the name of Greene's
protagonist, Scobie, and Achebe's protagonist, Obi, in this novel is
hard to miss. So too is the similarity in the trials and temptations the
two men face. Scobie is a police captain who tries to act with integrity and according to principles of public service, but who is ultimately corrupted by a conspiracy of events and his own lack of moral
strength. Although Obi is a civil servant rather than a policeman, his
narrative follows the same pattern. For Rogers, however, the clear
parallel between Greene's and Achebe's narratives should not obscure
an important difference between the two. In the end, the downfall
of Scobie is triggered by a particular kind of weakness – that of pity
for others. Indeed, his first key transgression is to destroy evidence
that he believes would implicate an innocent man. Obi, on the other
hand, is propelled towards his demise by a much less sympathetic
weakness – his almost complete loss of religious and cultural values.
    Whilst Eliot, Auden and Greene are important literary coordi-
nates for *No Longer at Ease*, nevertheless, the novel's key intertext
remains Joseph Conrad's *Heart of Darkness*, Rogers argues. As he suggests, Achebe's entire second novel can be read, on one level, as a
parodic reappropriation of Conrad's text, with Obi taking on the role
of a 'black Kurtz'.[25] Like Kurtz, Obi is a 'quasi-literary' man and an
idealist, filled with theoretical, Eurocentric ideas about Africa's need
for civilization. Both men find Africa itself more difficult to navigate
than they anticipated, buckling under the challenges it puts to them.
As Rogers points out, within the framework of his own narrative,
Obi does not of course recognize himself in these terms. Rather, he

sees himself in the writer's role, as a man who will one day set Africa's plight down on paper.

Throughout Achebe's novel, the chiaroscuro of *Heart of Darkness* is reversed, with white becoming black and dark becoming light. In Achebe's depiction of Lagos, for example, it is striking how the funereal ambiance of the white suburb Ikoyi is contrasted with the brightness and life of the rest of the city. Whiteness, meanwhile, is repeatedly associated with decay, corruption and, in Obi's case, emasculation. In his description of Obi's sojourn in England, moreover, Achebe skilfully reverses Conrad's imaginative journey into African darkness. Again, Obi is paralleled with the character of Kurtz. For Obi and especially for the Umuofians, the pilgrimage to England is imagined as much as a metaphysical as a physical journey. Once he is there, Obi, like Kurtz, 'goes native'.[26] Switching from the pragmatic choice of Law, he tries to swallow the culture whole, through the medium of an English degree:

> ■ The significance of this shift of academic interests is suggested in the heavily ironic praise Obi receives when he returns and is numbered among true Umuofians: 'We are not empty men who become white when they see white, and black when they see black'. Achebe suggests that Obi has indeed seen white and become just such an empty man.[27] □

For Rogers, Obi's journey into the heart of whiteness entails more than simply a separation from his family and society. It leads to a hollow utilitarianism that stands in stark contrast to the warmth of Ibo community. Where critics like Ravenscroft see a lack of character development and a failure of empathy, then, Rogers sees a deliberate narrative strategy. For him, the novel concerns, precisely, a hollowed-out man. In this sense, far from being an inferior reprise of *Things Fall Apart*, he shows how to read the novel as a tragedy of quite a different sort.

In his essay entitled '*Things Fall Apart*: the Portrayal of African Identity in Joyce Cary's *Mister Johnson* and Chinua Achebe's *No Longer at Ease*' (1997),[28] the critic Arnd Witte provides a useful complement to Rogers's analysis, by drawing out the negative relationship of influence between Achebe's novel and Joyce Cary's *Mister Johnson*. As he observes, Cary's text was initially greeted with a fanfare of approval amongst (European) Africanists, as the novel which finally 'brought the West African into literary existence'.[29] As the production of a white colonial administrator, however, it is perhaps unsurprising that subsequent literary historians, especially Nigerian ones, have cast doubt on this initial assessment.

Cary's novel is structured around a character opposition between the reserved and 'correct' European Rudbeck and the 'unruly Dionysian' African Johnson, who 'simply lives from day to day, without any sense of duty'.[30] Viewing the novel through a contemporary, postcolonial lens, it is a short step for Witte to reread Cary's novel as a direct product of British imperialism:

> ■ Only European civilisation can promote progress and development, while African savagery is its direct enemy. . . . Cary fails to notice that African life is structured by highly complex social and metaphysical principles which are as incomprehensible for Europeans as their social laws are for Africans at the early stage of 'acculturation'. Against this background Africans do avoid the station, i.e. collaboration with the colonisers, because it stands for fundamental change and loss of power for the traditional African elite. In failing to mention these motives for African opposition to 'development' and by characterising African reservations as a childish fear of ghosts, Cary sticks by his own racist convictions and – whether consciously or not – contributes catastrophically to the cultural misconstruction of 'the others'.[31] □

In Cary's novel, the character of Johnson personifies the emergent, educated black elite in pre-independence Nigeria, a new class resisted by traditional culture because of their frequently questionable social backgrounds, and held at length by white colonials as only 'shoddy imitations of themselves'.[32] For Witte, Cary constructs Johnson as an absurd parody of an Englishman, complete with white helmet and umbrella, a comedic figure who is not even dignified with a full name. In Achebe's text, meanwhile, the character of Obi occupies a comparable social and cultural position. As the literary creation of a young Nigerian rather than a colonial apparatchik, however, it is unsurprising if *No Longer at Ease* offers a perspective on the new Nigerian elite which differs sharply from that of Cary.

Like Johnson, Achebe's protagonist is deeply enamoured of the trappings of European culture, especially after his student experiences

in England. However, Witte suggests, as a result of this extended experience Obi is far more conversant with the intricacies of British culture
than is Johnson, who merely apes colonial manners in an attitude of
awed admiration. Unlike Johnson, too, the cross-cultural vision of
Achebe's protagonist endows him with a profound sense of alienation.
By describing this more complex position, then, *No Longer at Ease* is
able to mount a far more subtle analysis of Obi's Eurocentrism:

■ Obi's alienation becomes evident in many of his actions and
comments, especially on the widespread bribery in Nigeria, which he
sees through the lenses of European values:
  'What an Augean stable!' he muttered to himself. 'Where does one
  begin? With the masses? Educate the masses?' He shook his head.
  'Not a chance there. It would take centuries. [. . .] But what kind
  of democracy can exist side by side with so much corruption and
  ignorance? Perhaps a half-way house – a sort of compromise'.[33] □

As Witte argues, Obi's political judgment here is uncomfortably close
to the logic of colonialism. Change will never come from within
Nigerian society itself; the people cannot be trusted to understand
their own best interests. The European model of development is
assumed to be the only viable possibility. Such attitudes are, Witte
suggests, directly linked in the text to Obi's university experience in
England:

■ [H]is European education alienates Obi even from the more
progressive elements in the traditional society, personified in his
Christian father, who in his time drove his own father to suicide by
being the first person in his village to adopt the Christian faith. Despite
his Christian belief he in turn resists Obi's independent thinking about
the *osu*, and when he runs out of rational arguments, he argues on the
basis of tradition and the 'minds of the people'. Rationally, traditional
society's creation of outcasts cannot be justified, but tradition follows
other rules; the traditional community binds the individual closely
into an organic unit as a member of its social, cultural and religious
network, and operates to a large extent on the basis of metaphysical
principles. The western rational and atomistic view of the individual
is directly opposed to this approach, so that Obi was catapulted by
his European education out of the safety of traditional society. As a
consequence his identity oscillates between the two worlds, as one
of his friends remarks: 'You know book. But book stands for itself and
experience stands by itself'.[34] □

In this way, Witte argues, Achebe's novel uses Obi's own position of ambivalence, paralysis and alienation to illustrate the breadth of the cultural divide between British colonial and Nigerian (especially Ibo) culture. Moreover, an important aspect of Achebe's narrative in this regard is that it *refuses* to offer the reader any kind of ameliatory 'solution' to this impasse. Whilst one might imagine a different ending in which Obi begins to find some kind of reconstructed African consciousness, Achebe's text opts not to embrace such a possibility. Instead, cultural reclamation is represented as an uphill task that is far too challenging for such a weak vessel as Obi. In this sense, the work done by *No Longer at Ease* is less that of providing answers to the problems of postcoloniality, than that of helping to identify the cultural and ideological stumbling blocks that must be negotiated. Whilst the novel goes a long way towards debunking the negative and bogus image of Africans presented by texts like *Mister Johnson*, Witte suggests, it does no more than point the way towards the discovery of a freer, less alienated, less ambivalent African voice.

HISTORICAL CONTEXTS

In Umelo Ojinmah's *Chinua Achebe: New Perspectives* (1991),[35] Achebe's second novel is placed in sharper historical perspective. As Ojinmah begins by pointing out, in terms of historical sequence, *No Longer at Ease* is in fact the third part of Achebe's representation of Nigeria's story. Even though its publication precedes that of *Arrow of God* by two years, he suggests that it is necessary to consider the texts in order of narrative sequence if we are to appreciate the 'progressive sense of disillusionment' that builds in Achebe's fiction as he approaches the present day.

For Ojinmah, an important part of this disillusionment arises from the author's understanding of the cultural legacies bequeathed by colonialism. Historically, the cash economy introduced by the Europeans from the end of the nineteenth century chimed easily with the materialism inherent in Ibo culture and was thus one of the dimensions of colonial culture that was most easy to assimilate. In the society depicted by *Things Fall Apart*, Achebe shows us how such materialistic and acquisitive tendencies were held in check by the balancing power of spirituality, embodied in the earth goddess, Ani. When we move forward in time to the 1950s, however, this balance of values has been largely overtaken. With the character of Obi in *No Longer at Ease*, Ojinmah suggests then, Achebe is partly seeking to show the 'inclination of individuals in contemporary society to repudiate traditional values without acquiring adequate substitutes. . . . Achebe sees this clash of values or more appropriately, lack of values in the post-colonial society as one of the principal causes of the post-colonial tensions in the society. Obi Okonkwo, the protagonist of Achebe's *No Longer at Ease*, illustrates this modern phenomenon as this analysis will prove'.[36]

In the run-up to Nigerian independence, the new black administrative class, of which Obi is a representative, grew immensely in importance, politically and culturally. Amidst the political optimism associated with the nation's impending decolonization, a huge amount of responsibility – and also privilege – was vested in this emergent class, whose members were popularly represented as the natural leaders of Africa into independence. Obi's narrative accurately reflects this process of investment in the young and educated, Ojinmah argues, at the same time as it suggests the crisis of values brought in its wake:

> ■ The society, in Achebe's view, had . . . gone to an extraordinary length to 'create', equip, and set this class apart, as its future leaders through education . . . had 'laboured in sweat and tears to enrol Obi', and by extension his class, 'among the shining élite' . . . in the belief that whatever skills they acquire would be used for the benefit of the society. Achebe's *No Longer at Ease,* therefore, explores how this class discharged their mandate, and what the consequences have been for society of their failure to discharge this obligation honourably.[37] □

In this sense, Achebe's novel represents Obi as a pioneer of national progress, who finds himself both socially and ethically adrift. The position Obi occupies, Ojinmah suggests, is akin to that of a villager encountering the city for the first time, constantly in danger of losing his way or being knocked down by the passing traffic.

For Ojinmah, then, *No Longer at Ease* needs to be read in terms of a metonymic relationship between Obi's narrative and that of Nigeria itself in the 1950s. Nowhere is this clearer than in the novel's satirical ending, in which the judge, the British representative and the elders of Umuofia are united in their inability to comprehend

Obi's weakness and corruption. For Ojinmah, Achebe's decision to foreground this sense of universal confusion and blindness represents a direct commentary on the failure of the new middle class in this period, as well as Nigeria's more general failure to comprehend or address the underlying problems that led to this impasse.

The resolution of such contradictions would require the dedicated commitment of individuals who, like Obi, are positioned to understand something about both traditional and Western cultural values but who, unlike him, also have a deep understanding of the crosscurrents of history. In that sense, Achebe's own work with *No Longer at Ease* and the texts that surround it could be regarded as expressions of precisely the kind of critical intelligence that Obi needs, but lacks.

In Michael Valdez Moses's[38] analysis of *No Longer at Ease* a far vaster frame of historical reference is invoked than we see in Ojinmah's work. As Moses points out, *Things Fall Apart* and *No Longer at Ease* together constitute an attempt to represent a major period of change in West Africa, from the late nineteenth century to the eve of independence. Whilst the first novel shows a specific instance of the colonial encounter, it is only in the second that we begin to be given a full impression of the massive processes of globalization within which Achebe's protagonists' narratives are being played out:

■ Whereas the action of *Things Fall Apart is* largely confined to the small closely knit tribal communities of Umuofia and Mbanta, the drama of *No Longer at Ease* moves from Lagos to London, from Liverpool and the Madeiras to Freetown and Iguedo. The varied international settings of the second novel clearly mark an advanced stage of globalization that has transformed the lives of the provincial Igbo people of the earlier novel. Like Hardy, Achebe records the gradual extinction of local and regional cultural identities. Umuofia – which in Igbo means 'people of the bush' – meets a fate similar to that of [Thomas Hardy's] Casterbridge; it slowly loses its distinctive regional and autonomous character as it is subsumed by a new larger political entity, the emergent nation of Nigeria. The first mention of 'Nigeria' in Achebe's novels thus signals the introduction of one of the central themes of his later work, the not altogether successful attempt to found a new regime, specifically a modern African nation-state, that will take its rightful place in the international community of the postcolonial era.[39] □

In his portrayal of Lagos in particular, Moses argues, Achebe is concerned to explore the emergence of a new kind of cosmopolitan
Nigeria, in which rival indigenous and foreign cultures jostle for
space and prominence. Set down in this context, the character of Obi
is shown as a vulnerable and alienated, even deracinated, figure who
is far from 'at ease' in his world. For Moses, this in itself is symptomatic of the forces of modernization and urbanization of which he is a
product, and which carry their own forms of estrangement:

■ This vast new metropolis sometimes produces in Obi a peculiarly
modern form of discomfort and psychic disequilibrium that is unknown to
members of the clan in Things Fall Apart – anomie. Though he champions
the cause of the new Nigerian nation and thinks of himself as an exemplary
representative of a sophisticated rising generation in Nigeria, a member
of the new African elite, Obi sometimes feels lost, alienated, and alone
amidst the multiethnic crowds of modern Lagos. . . . Though there are
many reasons for his eventually accepting the bribe that brings his career
in the civil service to an end, his succumbing to political corruption is
made easier by his moral and physical isolation in Lagos, where he is
increasingly cut off from his family and clan. His acceptance of the fateful
bribe occurs in the privacy of his apartment, where his fellow clan
members can no longer watch him and therefore no longer reproach him
for his misconduct. Much like Conrad's hero aboard the Patna [in *Lord
Jim* (1900)], Obi finds that his social isolation in a cosmopolitan setting
helps to subvert his heroic resolution and to undermine his faith in an
exacting and high-minded ethical code.[40] □

Obi is constructed (like Achebe) in the mould of a cultural nationalist,
by direct contrast to the *clan* loyalties of his grandfather and his fellow
Umuofians. For Okonkwo, the integrity of the clan was something
to be defended to the death against the invasive force of Christianity.
By the 1950s, however, these ideological coordinates have shifted.
As Moses says, in Obi's story, Christianity itself 'seems nearly as ves-
tigial and anachronistic as do many of the precolonial tribal traditions'.[41] The fundamental opposition is no longer Christianity versus
traditional culture, but rather traditional culture versus a more-or-less
postreligious model of capitalistic modernity. For Moses, then, the
historical transitions represented by the novel are at least as much economic as ideological in nature:

■ By themselves neither European Christianity nor imperial British rule
are sufficient to create modern Lagos. The growth of the city depends

upon increased commerce. Achebe is clear about the reasons that Igbo villagers leave Iguedo to come to the capital. At a meeting of the Umuofia Progressive Union (U.P.U), the president of the organization naively suggests that it is 'work' that brings so many of his clan from the countryside to Lagos; he is corrected by one of the group's members: 'It is money, not work. . . . We left plenty of work at home'. The widespread desire of the villagers for the greater prosperity available in the modern city draws them from their ancestral homes. *No Longer at Ease* provides a critique of a market economy, but it is a cultural rather than an economic one. In Achebe's view, economic liberalization transforms Nigeria precisely because it answers the material needs of its inhabitants, not because it materially exploits them. Achebe finds fault with a market economy not because it does not work well enough, but because it often works too well.[42] □

In the case of the Umuofia Progressive Union, Moses argues, Achebe shows us how a collectivity founded to defend the cultural identity of the clan becomes transformed, in practice, into an organization focussed chiefly on the financial interests of its members. Whilst the Umuofians are certainly not represented as embracing the ideology of consumer capitalism, he suggests, they are nevertheless shown as strongly motivated by a materialism which seems far less prominent in *Things Fall Apart*. The notion of 'greatness' to which Okonkwo aspired has been replaced by a distinctively European ethic of material acquisition. Likewise, in such practices as the negotiation of the 'bride price', we see a parallel transformation. Whilst *Things Fall Apart* stresses the ceremonial and rhetorical nature of such exchanges, in *No Longer at Ease* the same process has become 'a serious business pursued openly for the financial benefits it brings to the family of the bride; efforts of the Nigerian government to control the practice have merely pushed up the already exorbitant price of marriage'.[43] As we see with Obi's loosening relationship to his family, this developing commercial ethos is accompanied by a corresponding ethos of individualism. Although he has the means and the opportunity to do so, for example, the previously unthinkable option of not attending his mother's funeral becomes a comparatively easy choice for Obi.

Against this theme of capitalist modernization in the novel is the counterbalancing question of corruption. Referring to the author's later texts as well as his political writings, Moses is justified in his contention that for Achebe, corruption is one of the most damaging and fundamental obstacles to advancement in the new Nigeria.

In *No Longer at Ease*, however, the theme of corruption is also powerfully linked to tribalism. That is not to say that corruption is seen as an old tribal practice which should be abolished by modernization: rather, it is seen as a product of the intermixture of elements of traditional culture with the capitalist ethos introduced by colonialism:

> ■ For a great many Nigerians, including Obi's Igbo friend Christopher (educated at the London School of Economics), bribery is merely the modern equivalent of 'kola'. The gradual transition from the giving of kola nuts as an Igbo ritual that provides a ceremonial means to encourage neighborly relations among clan members to 'kola' as the popular term for bribery is one key to what is happening in *No Longer at Ease*. . . . In Okonkwo's time, 'bribing' a man with kola nuts would be absurd, not to say impossible. In Obi's day, the accumulation of 'kola' is the mark of the great man who has made it in the new Nigeria.[44] □

For Moses, in this way, the corruption of the symbolic function of kola in traditional society can be read as a representation in miniature of the most negative effects of cultural hybridization in Nigeria. Whilst, as we see in *Things Fall Apart*, traditional practices were powerfully orientated around an ethic of communal harmony, in the modern context such checks and balances no longer assert themselves in the same way. The new culture of corruption and graft is thus neither a traditional nor a modern evil, but rather a result of the specific circumstances of cultural intermixture that produced the new nation:

> ■ The U.P.U. . . . lends moral legitimacy to the lavish and wasteful behaviour of government officials that makes bribery and graft all the more likely, even necessary. A market economy unleashes the acquisitiveness already inherent in traditional Igbo culture; the vestigial elements of tribal culture in turn undermine the modern legal and moral imperatives that serve to regulate and channel acquisitiveness so that truly free markets, unhampered by governmental interference or economic privilege, might flourish.[45] □

In the character of Obi, Moses argues, Achebe embodies precisely these tensions and contradictions. If his fall from grace is at once less tragic and socially significant than that of his grandfather, then this is

symptomatic of the profoundly unheroic nature of African modernization in the 1950s.

For the critic Simon Gikandi,[46] as for Michael Moses, *No Longer
at Ease* is fundamentally an exploration of marginality and cultural
transition. After Achebe's celebrated representation of colonization
in *Things Fall Apart*, Gikandi, like Moses, sees the novel as a brave
attempt by the author to extend his historical canvas, in order to
narrate the transition from colonialism to nationhood. In so doing,
Achebe is forced to move away from the established narrative techniques he uses to such effect in *Things Fall Apart*, and to pioneer
a different and less comfortable aesthetic. As Gikandi points out,
drafted as it was in the run-up to independence, the subject matter of
Achebe's novel is almost contemporaneous with his own act of writing. This in itself implies a host of problems and challenges. In these
senses Gikandi takes issue with earlier commentators, who criticize
the novel for failing to provide the deep aesthetic unities offered by
the earlier novel:

> ■ By the time the novel was published in 1960, the year of Nigerian
> independence, the discourse of national identity was still seeking
> forms through which to express itself; writing about the cultural and
> social pressures which young Nigerians encountered at the dawn
> of independence required multiple forms of experimentation with
> narrative techniques. Critics who have rushed to compare *No Longer
> at Ease* with *Things Fall Apart* have found the former wanting in
> 'depth', 'coherence', or 'vision' precisely because they have not paid
> enough attention to its contemporaneous and experimental nature, to
> the improvisorial element in its modes of representation.[47] □

What appear, for critics like Ravenscroft and Carroll, to be problems
with Achebe's text are seen by Gikandi as directly reflective of his
subject matter itself. In *Things Fall Apart* a unified and harmonious
literary language is used to evoke an (initially) unified and harmonious cultural milieu. In *No Longer at Ease*, however, such a writing
strategy becomes impossible:

> ■ [T]he more he tries to evoke Nigerian realities as a referent for his
> text, the more the new nation resists domestication in the text and
> hence recuperation by the reader. For when everything is said and

done, Achebe's generation is trying to invent a Nigerian nation and a Nigerian national consciousness from amorphous and unstable entities arbitrarily yoked together by the colonizer. Certainly the ways in which Nigeria is invented by the colonizer and reinvented by the African nationalists will be a major theme in the novel. But Nigeria will henceforth remain a central problem in Achebe's quest for a stable historical referent.[48] □

On the personal level, if Okonkwo's identification with Umuofia seemed unproblematic in *Things Fall Apart*, his grandson's equivalent attempt to identify himself as 'Nigerian' is fraught with far more difficulty. For all the goodwill and well-placed ambition associated with Achebe's cultural nationalism, Nigeria's transition from arbitrary colonial construct to coherent national identity is very far from complete in the late 1950s. Gikandi argues, therefore, that Achebe's novel can be read in one sense as a performative act – an attempt to give narrative form to a national entity that is still in the process of gestation. The novel's repeated sense of 'incompleteness and incoherence'[49] is precisely symptomatic of its project.

For Gikandi, Achebe's second novel is profoundly influenced by the political leader (and later President) Nnamdi Azikiwe (1904–96; President of Nigeria 1963–66), and in particular by his insistence on the centrality of young educated Nigerians in forging the nation's future. Obi, Gikandi argues, is in one sense a prototypical nationalist, especially in his dismissal of clan loyalties and of the authority of his elders. However, Achebe's narrative as a whole clearly cannot be seen as simply 'aligned' with Obi's own point of view. Rather, the novel enables us to see, at the same time, the shallowness and problematic nature of Obi's 'national' consciousness. For Gikandi, 'Nigeria' is represented by the novel almost as an idle fantasy of Obi's. In his lack of serious reflection on the meaning of cultural and political reconstruction, as well as his final failure to resist the 'national disease' of corruption, Obi is ultimately shown as a poor representative of Nigerian youth and as an ineffectual agent of change.

In its wider invocation of Nigeria in the 1950s, Gikandi suggests moreover, Achebe's text is frequently 'geared towards creating incongruence rather than clarity'.[50] Whilst Obi is an alienated, confused protagonist, the world he inhabits is shown as threateningly empty. From the opening of the novel, the reader is made aware of Obi's general insufficiency as well as the manner of his demise, and the narrative as a whole progresses as much through ellipses and detours as through conventional structures of suspense. As Gikandi suggests, 'the tone adopted by the narrator . . . is one of boredom or cynicism'.[51] For Gikandi, these narrative features are far from accidental (much less simply aesthetic 'flaws', as some critics have suggested). Rather, the narrative of *No Longer at Ease* is plotted very deliberately to subvert 'the logic of promise and destiny which underlies Obi's quest'.[52] Instead of representing the fulfilment of Obi's nationalist aspirations, the effect of Achebe's novel is to show their 'disappointment and reversal'.[53]

Placed between the force fields of a declining colonial power and a not-yet-realized Nigerian nationhood, Obi is comprehensively disabled by ideological confusion and ambivalence. He is sent to England by the Umuofians to learn how to enrich the clan and returns with a shallow nationalist sensibility. Once installed in the national civil service amidst the modernity (but also alienation) of Lagos, he struggles to locate himself. In stark contrast to the author's handling of Okonkwo, Achebe places his second protagonist in a liminal space, in which he finds it difficult to formulate a coherent sense either of himself or his community. If the novel documents the corruption of a promising young Nigerian, then it is the corruption of a man who never quite knows who he is or what he stands for in the first place. Obi's revelation at the end of the novel is precisely that 'the self he thought was unique and original, not to mention moral, was a projection of others' desire – the union, his parents, the colonial culture, the nationalist movement, the collective desire for a new Nigeria'.[54]

Gikandi's reading of the novel in these terms is, certainly, both persuasive and provocative. Viewed as a text of Nigerian independence, written by a young Chinua Achebe, who, in the 1950s, can himself be considered a cultural nationalist, *No Longer at Ease* is shown to be an extraordinarily uncompromising work. The novel may indeed have started life as the second half of *Things Fall Apart*, but in 1960 it must have read very differently from that first novel. Both in terms of its narrative technique and its political-historical address, *No Longer at Ease* feels like the work of a different, more troubled Achebe.

As we have seen in this chapter, then, it was some time before critics of Achebe's work began to recognize *No Longer at Ease* as a novel of comparable complexity and interest to *Things Fall Apart*.

92 THE FICTION OF CHINUA ACHEBE

Certainly, its form is more fractured and its narrative sweep less magisterial; in lots of ways, it is very different from its predecessor. In the decades to come, the novel's representations of colonial ambivalence and its intimations of political corruption would become more familiar fare for readers of African fiction. In 1966, Achebe himself was to develop these themes further with *A Man of the People*. In his third novel, however, he chose to return to an earlier historical period, in the immediate aftermath of Nigeria's formal colonization by the British. Chapter 4 explores the critical response to *Arrow of God*, its sources, intertexts, politics and narrative strategies.

CHAPTER FOUR

Arrow of God (1964)

In a seminar organized in 1973 by the University of Missouri,[1] Chinua Achebe characterized *Arrow of God* as a novel motivated by the desire to 'revaluate my culture'.[2] He encouraged readers to approach the text as an attempt – like *Things Fall Apart* -- to counter colonial representations of Iboland and Nigeria as a cultural void. Although intended to be read by the widest possible audience, Achebe also saw *Arrow of God* as a text written especially for his own people. In that sense the novel's representation of diminishing confidence and self-determination amongst the Ibo, under the influence of colonialism, might come as a surprise. According to the writer, however, it is also important that we recognize the threads of resilience and heroism caught up in that larger narrative of decline. The novel is intended in part as a testament to those things, so often obscured by history:

■ I do not know whether I am obsessed by failure, but that makes a better story than success. Really, I mean. I mean that failure is much more interesting; it is deeper and more moving, especially if one fails with dignity. This is important, and I tend to be drawn to it. Of course, one could write a comedy about failure, but one has to respond to one's leanings. Mine may be macabre, yet there is much interest when people die. To take a man like Ezeulu, for example, the important thing is not whether he really succeeded but his failure itself, the way it happens. That is much more important than any success.

Ezeulu was struggling with the white man, and his return, we could hope, would compensate for his struggle. But his people turned against him, and so the white man had it all his way. I was not saying, of course, that the white man is therefore right. What I was saying is that, in such kind of extreme situation, the important thing was that Ezeulu was able to fight and to cope, as best as he could, with the circumstances. Even when he failed, he failed as a man, you see. That is very important in our culture. The recent experience we had, in Nigeria, of the civil war, had this exemplified. There were leaders who showed up complete cowards and others, a few, of whom people could say, 'This is a man'.[3] □

Given a historical situation in which a fundamentally negotiative and democratic culture comes into collision with an aggressive invasive force, Achebe seeks to show how an exceptional man reacts to an extreme situation. In Ezeulu's case, this response is characterized by the very traits of sophisticated, pragmatic intellectualism that colonialism deemed impossible for a 'native' to attain. By reframing the colonial encounter as a meeting between African sophistication and European naivety, indeed, Achebe's novel deliberately attempts to effect a reversal of colonialism's pretensions as a 'civilizing mission'. In his narrative, this is most graphically dramatized by Ezeulu's meeting with the young British administrator Clarke, who in the former's eyes appears as a young, inexperienced 'puppy'. As Achebe says:

■ Now, this reversal itself is tied up with the colonial situation. There is no other situation in the world where power resides with inexperience and young people. A young male would not approach the seat of power in England, but in a colonial situation he is given power and can order a chief around. In a very deep sense this reversal is the quintessence of colonialism. It is a loss of independence. These are some of the ideas that are implied at the end of the novel.[4] □

INTERTEXTS AND INFLUENCES

As Robert Wren shows in his study *Achebe's World* (1980),[5] amid the general praise for *Things Fall Apart*, one of the most repeated criticisms levelled against the novel concerned the way it seemed to present Ibo culture as static and unchanging. In one sense, such a view accords with the perspective of colonialism, which frequently represented Africa as unhistorical – even primeval – and untouched by development. In fact, Wren suggests, Iboland in the nineteenth century was subject to extensive historical change, much of which is elided by the first novel:

■ [B]ut for peculiar stabilizing mechanisms, especially ozo, the stateless societies of which Umuofia is an example would have been radically transformed as a result of pressures and circumstances unnoticed in *Things Fall Apart*. The rise of trading cities on the coast, the scarcity of forest in the hinterland, the power of the Aro and their Abam mercenaries, the development of industries such as iron working at Awka, the installation of rulers along the fringes of Igboland (as happened at Onitsha), the change in the flow of trade, with the introduction of cloth and metal objects from Europe and new crops from America, the decline of the ancestral priesthood of Nri – all these and more changed life in the Igbo hinterland to produce the apparently changeless society Achebe described.[6] □

In *Arrow of God*, Wren suggests however, the entire question of historical change is addressed in a far more subtle and concerted way. The fact that the six clans have been forced to become one and that a new, more powerful deity has been created are only the most visible of the historical adaptations suggested by the novel.

For many critics, Achebe's fiction is often seen in a sense as a breaking of silence, a fictional surrogate for more systematic analyses of the colonial past. Wren, however, takes a slightly different point of view. As he points out, the years before independence saw extensive reorientation and development of academic perspectives on Nigerian identity and history amongst scholars in many areas. As talks producer for the Nigerian Broadcasting Corporation (NBC), Achebe would have been closely familiar with these debates. Alongside research conducted in university departments, there was a widespread culture of amateur scholarship, in which educated Nigerians collected and documented their own local histories, as well as recording the proverbs and fables of the oral tradition.

In Achebe's own case, as Wren suggests, material for *Arrow of God* was gathered in a wide variety of places, ranging from stories told by his mother and other family members through existing local histories to records of legal petitions and land disputes. In seeking to understand the novel's historical engagements, it is important to grasp its relationship to these intertexts.

Amongst the academic studies that parallel *Arrow of God*, the work cited by Wren as most important is A. E. Afigbo's *The Warrant Chiefs*,[7] published in 1972. Although it is unlikely that Achebe himself read Afigbo's work before the publication of his novel, it is useful to note that the two men's research was conducted simultaneously. Indeed Afigbo submitted a PhD thesis based on his work in

1964, the year that *Arrow of God* was published. Afigbo's research is based upon a specific historical case featuring the chief priest of six villages, named Ezeagu Uchu, whose position closely resembles that of Ezeulu in *Arrow of God*. According to Colonial Office records, Ezeagu was first imprisoned by the District Officer of his region, before being released and offered the position of Warrant Chief — a local ruler under the control of the colonial authority.

As talks producer for the NBC, Wren argues, it is highly possible that Achebe had an exchange on this case with Afigbo, during the period in which the latter was working for his PhD. As Wren says, in subsequent interviews 'Achebe denies that he researched the novel, yet he was well aware of details of the Warrant Chieftaincy dispute that only a successful worker in colonial archives could discover'.[8] Whether or not the Ezeulu story was directly drawn by Achebe from conversations with Afigbo, *The Warrant Chiefs* undoubtedly offers an interesting intertext for *Arrow of God*, with its academic analysis of Britain's attempt to impose the system of indirect rule on the Ibo.

As Wren argues, perhaps the most important exponent of the philosophy of indirect rule in this period was the British colonial entrepreneur Frederick (later Lord) Lugard (1858–1945). Lugard's efforts to subdue a multiplicity of peoples led directly to the establishment of the protectorates of Northern and Southern Nigeria and their subsequent unification as a single British colony. In the Northern Region, the practice of governing through local leaders was comparatively unproblematic for the British because of the pre-existence of a network of regional Islamic rulers. In the South East, however, the policy was frustrated by the democratic culture of the Ibo:

> ■ [T]he Native Councils exacerbated conflict; the kings and chiefs the colonial officers confidently looked for did not appear. Nevertheless, as Afigbo shows, the British determinedly forced towns to produce chiefs who were then required, under penalties, to demand of their peoples an obedience which the 'chiefs' had neither the strength nor traditional authority to enforce. Worse, a chief would certainly be required to do things that tradition absolutely forbade him to do. For this reason, the villagers might nominate as chiefs people whom neither custom nor ability recommended to the job. The result was often very bad indeed.[9] □

As a result of this forced, unsatisfactory compromise, the exercise of regional authority, especially in the administration of local law

courts, was frequently problematic. As Wren reports, *The Diaries
of Lord Lugard* (1959–63) reveal the depth of Lugard's own frustration with the situation in the East, which he calls a 'thrice accursed
place'.[10]

Lugard's favoured measures for the enforcement of authority in
the region are several times reflected in Achebe's novel, as Wren
shows. First, Lugard recommended a blanket policy of creating chiefs
in place of councils of elders. Secondly, he prescribed a system of pris-
ons under the control of local authorities, to punish both offenders
and those resistant to colonial authority. Thirdly, he proposed direct
taxation of villages, collectable by the chiefs themselves. Fourthly, he
called for a hereditary system of authority, whereby the sons of chiefs
would be groomed to assume authority on the deaths of their fathers.
In practice, these policies were implemented by stages over a period
of 20 years from the turn of the century. By the 1920s, there was a
substantial body of resistance to both the principle and the detail of
Lugard's colonial philosophy. By that time also, however, the dam-
age wrought by colonial maladministration, based on ignorance and
mistaken assumption, was already extensive.

Given Nigeria's very recent emergence as an independent nation,
by the mid-1960s there had still been little specific historical analysis
of such policies and their effects. In this sense, for Wren, *Arrow of God*
helped to fill an important gap of understanding about the complex
interaction between British colonial rule and traditional Ibo culture
at the turn of the twentieth century.

For critics such as Wren, the parallel between *Arrow of God* and
Afigbo's *The Warrant Chiefs* raises important questions about Achebe's
research methods. However, these questions are radically intensified
in the controversy over the novelist's use of another historical source.
Indeed, the allegation made by Charles Nnolim in the leading jour-
nal *Research in African Literatures* in 1977[11] was that the entirety of
Arrow of God is 'shackled' to one single source text, Simon Alagbogu
Nnolim's 1953 pamphlet *The History of Umuchu*.[12]

If this source had not been identified hitherto, Charles Nnolim
argues, then this is attributable simply to the complacency of
academics, who tend to assume that material simply 'comes naturally'
to African authors 'like leaves to a tree'.[13] *The History of Umuchu* is
an account of his own home village in Akwa, Nigeria, written by a

retired corporal of the Nigerian police force. According to Charles Nnolim, the major events detailed in *Arrow of God* are lifted directly from the pamphlet:

■ It was while I was preparing a second, enlarged edition of this booklet (published by Ochumba Press, Ltd., Enugu, Nigeria, 1976) that certain passages began to remind me of *Arrow of God*. One such passage was the story of the priest who refused chieftaincy, was imprisoned, and stubbornly refused to roast the sacred yams. As it turned out, this happened in my own village, Umuchu, in Awka Division, Nigeria, in 1913. The District Commissioner who is called Winterbottom by Achebe in his fictional work was, in history, J. G. Lotain. The High Priest called Ezeulu by Achebe was, in the history of Umuchu, Ezeagu, the High Priest of Uchu. He was actually imprisoned for two months at Awka by J. G. Lotain; and the Seed Yam Festival (changed to New Yam Festival by Achebe), which usually fell during the harvest months of November and December, began to fall – and still falls to this day – in February and March, because he refused to roast two sacred yams in one month. As I began to collate the two texts, I found out to my amazement that Achebe did not merely take the story of the High Priest and blow life into it, as Shakespeare did when borrowing material for *Julius Caesar* from Plutarch's *Lives of the Noble Grecians and the Romans;* Achebe went much further. He lifted *everything* in *The History of Umuchu* and simply transferred it to *Arrow of God* without embellishment.[14] □

Clearly, the implication of Nnolim's essay is that Achebe's use of the identified source falls well outside the boundaries of fair dealing, even for a novelist. He goes on to describe how, armed with this information, he was determined to confront Achebe at an African Literature conference in Texas in 1975. Faced with his questioning, Nnolim reports, Achebe admitted to knowing the former policeman and indeed to interviewing him for the Eastern Nigeria Broadcasting Service in 1957. Achebe had stayed in Umuchu for three nights in that year, researching the performance of its Night Masks. Although Achebe did not remember having read *The History of Umuchu*, Nnolim claims that 'the internal evidence is overwhelming that he had the book before him as he wrote *Arrow of God*'.[15] Nnolim's essay is dedicated entirely to laying out this textual evidence, citing detailed parallels between sections from the pamphlet and passages from Achebe's novel:

■ [I]t is surely more than coincidence that Achebe's Umuaro is Nnolim's Umuchu; that Achebe's Ezeulu is Nnolim's Ezeagu; that Achebe's

god, Ulu, is Nnolim's Uchu; that Achebe's six villages which sought
amalgamation are Nnolim's six villages in Umuchu; that Achebe's New
Yam Festival is Nnolim's Seed Yam Festival; that Achebe's missionary,
'Hargreaves', is no more than Nnolim's anthropologist, 'Hargroves';
that Achebe's story of Umuama and the sacred python is Nnolim's
Umunama and the sacred short snake; that Nnolim's Gun Breaker,
J. G. Lotain, is Achebe's Gun Breaker, Winterbottom; that Achebe's
'The Festival of the Pumpkin Leaves' is Nnolim's 'The Feast of Throwing
First Tender Pumpkin Leaves'; that Achebe's ceremony of Coverture is
Nnolim's ceremony of *Nkpu;* that the main market in Achebe's Umuaro
and Nnolim's Umuchu is Nkwo, where the Ikoro and the amalgamation
fetish in both sources are located.[16] □

Here, Nnolim cites a series of linkages between historical figures
and events detailed in *The History of Umuchu* and those depicted in
Achebe's text. However, his claim is that the novel's parasitic relationship to the pamphlet goes further. According to Nnolim, even
the paragraph-to-paragraph drafting of *Arrow of God* shows evidence
of direct lifting from the earlier text. Nnolim's quotations from both
publications are quite extensive: here I will reproduce one small
example, in which each author discusses the creation of a new medi-
cine/deity. In *The History of Umuchu*, first, we read:

■ They met and agreed to unite; to do this effectively they invited a
strong team of qualified native Doctors who prepared a medicine
known as 'Ichu' meaning Antidote, in other words to render null and
void the attempt of any aggressors to cause them more harm by means
or by violence. Though the legendary 'Ichu', meaning antidote was
supposed to be the goddess, after the medicine had been prepared,
the united towns dedicated themselves to and called themselves the
children of 'Ichu' (Umu-Ichu); the medicine was parcelled in two; one
buried in the heart of the meeting place now called Nkwo Uchu, the
other parcel was buried into a lake formerly known as Odere; the lake's
name automatically became Ichu Stream; the meeting place became
the seat of the goddess protectoress of the town.[17] □

The equivalent passage in *Arrow of God* picked out by Nnolim certainly does suggest a relationship of influence:

■ Things were so bad for the six villages that their leaders came
together to save themselves. They hired a strong team of medicine-
men to install a common deity for them. This deity which the fathers of

the six villages made was called Ulu. Half of the medicine was buried at a place which became the Nkwo market and the other half thrown into the stream which became Mill Ulu. The six villages then took the name of Umuaro, and the priest of Ulu became their Chief Priest.[18] □

Elsewhere, cultural practices which Nnolim claims are unique to Umuchu, such as the feast of the Pumpkin Leaves, are directly reproduced in *Arrow of God*, together with details such as costume and body decoration which accord with the historical account.

The tone of Nnolim's argument, for the majority of his essay, is somewhat reminiscent of a university plagiarism hearing. In his conclusion, however, he attempts to strike a slightly more ameliatory note, stressing that it is not his intention to deny the significance of *Arrow of God* as a work of historical fiction. What the comparison of *Arrow of God* with *The History of Umuchu* does teach us, he argues however, is that Achebe's own account of his research methods should be taken with a 'grain of salt'.[19] Far from basing his novels solely on his own observations and on memories of oral tales told by his father and grandfather, Nnolim argues, Achebe's work draws deeply on historical scholarship of a more formal kind. In that context, it is appropriate that the scholarship of Simon A. Nnolim be recognized by critics, notwithstanding Achebe's own refusal to acknowledge his debt of influence.

Such was the fallout from Nnolim's claims in the article just discussed, that an academic riposte by the critic Catherine Innes was forthcoming in the very next issue of *Research in African Literatures*.[20] As Innes admits, she read Nnolim's argument in 1977 with 'some concern for the reputation of Achebe, against whom these accusations of artlessness, lack of creativity, and failure to "admit sources publicly" were being leveled'.[21] Having considered Nnolim's claims in some detail, however, she finds his argument 'far from "overwhelming"'.[22]

As Innes acknowledges, the pamphlet and the novel do address common cultural practices. A careful examination of their points of overlap, however, is very instructive. A particular example she picks out in this regard is the Sacrifice of Coverture. Here, close scrutiny of the two writers' translations from Ibo reveals that Achebe's account – not Simon Nnolim's – is truer to the historical evidence. The clear implication of this, as she suggests, is that Achebe's work cannot be seen as simply parasitic on Nnolim's. From such specific examples as this one Innes moves to a more general critique of Nnolim's case:

■ This comparison between Charles Nnolim's translation and Achebe's might seem more telling if one wasn't aware that such a ritual prayer would be widely known and also that Charles Nnolim has considerably altered his original's translation in order to make his point. . . . On the evidence of Nnolim's article alone, then, the charges of faithfulness to sources and of 'lifting *everything* . . . without embellishment', were clearly disproved by the very examples compared. In general, the passages placed side by side did not 'defy commentary', but rather suggested a whole range of comments on the degree to which Achebe's skill as a writer was underlined by contrast with Nnolim's accounts of the ceremonies described and also on Achebe's concern with the *significance* of the ceremonies in contrast to Nnolim's bare descriptions of the ritual movements. Nor were those passages similar enough to prove conclusively that *The History of Umuchu* must have been even one source, although they do suggest it as a possibility.[23] □

Rising to the challenge set out by Nnolim's article, Innes proceeds to mount her own comparison of the two texts. The conclusion she draws from this exercise is that the story of the head priest of Umuchu and his rejection of the role of Warrant Chief in 1913 is almost certainly an important historical source for *Arrow of God*. As she points out, however, this fact in itself does nothing to place the integrity of the novelist in question, especially given Achebe's free acknowledgement that the novel was based on actual events.

Simon Nnolim's pamphlet may certainly have been one of the influences on Achebe when he was planning and composing his novel, but the implied charge that he simply plagiarized the earlier text is far from being justified:

■ [T]hinking that Charles Nnolim's apparent ignorance of the meaning of 'verbatim', his inability to think of comments on passages to be compared, and his failure to notice that Achebe's Ulu is a masculine deity might be indicative of a more general failure to communicate his case clearly, I read *The History of Umuchu* in both the original (1953) and revised (1976) versions. It is a fascinating history, full of details which one feels would have been of great interest to Achebe and which he might well have included in his novel had he known about them – the story of the six sons of Echu and the founding and history of the original six villages prior to amalgamation, an account which takes up a good half (about 17 pages) of Nnolim's *History;* various power names and stories attached to them; the salutations expected between husband and wife; ceremonies such as 'The Risky Feast' preceding marriage; the foods forbidden women and certain men; the burial ceremony and mourning customs; the New Yam Festival. *Only* those passages quoted by Charles Nnolim – a total of 5 pages – have any relevance to the rituals and events described in the 230 pages of *Arrow of God.* That simple fact alone makes nonsense of the claim that Achebe 'lifted *everything* in *The History of Umuchu* and simply transferred it to *Arrow of God* without embellishment'.[24] □

Whilst Achebe was clearly interested in the cultural history of Umuchu when he visited the village in 1957, the notes of his conversations with Simon Nnolim in that year are likely to have provided only one of a great many threads out of which the novel was ultimately woven, four years later. To suggest that *Arrow of God* is copied in some crude sense from *The History of Umuchu* exclusively is therefore, Innes argues, 'unconvincing and irresponsible'.[25]

THREE CRITICAL READINGS

Like Achebe's first two novels, *Arrow of God* has been subject to a fascinating range of critical readings. In this section, I will focus on three contrasting treatments of the text, by three important critics of his work.

As we have already seen, the central action of the novel almost certainly represents a fictionalization of actual incidents which occurred in the village of Umuchu in 1913. As Simon Nnolim's 1953 history describes, the chief priest of that village, Ezeagu, was imprisoned by the colonial administration for refusing to take on the role of Warrant Chief. One of the priest's responses to his incarceration was to refuse to eat the ritual meal of yams that traditionally signalled the start of the harvest festival. As K. Indrasena Reddy argues in his book *The Novels of Achebe and Ngũgĩ* (1994),[26] it is useful to consider this historical incident as a starting point for Achebe's exploration of the political and religious dynamics of Ibo culture at the beginning of the twentieth century. As we see in both *Things Fall Apart* and *Arrow of God,* Achebe's fiction seems keen to establish the democratic credentials of the Ibo, especially by contrast to colonialism's autocratic tendencies. As Reddy points out, however, *Arrow of God* also offers a balancing insight, representing as it does the enormity of the powers wielded by key ceremonial figures like Ezeulu:

■ The functions of Ezeulu as the chief priest are, in the main, religious – to perform the rituals periodically, offer prayers and sacrifices to the deity on behalf of Umuaro. Besides, he also enjoys the privilege of keeping the agricultural calendar of the community. In this capacity, he names and conducts two important events of Umuaro: namely, the festival of Pumpkin Leaves – a ceremony of Purification before plantation and the New Yam Festival or the Harvest Festival which marks the end of the old year and heralds the new year. Ezeulu is also the guardian and custodian of the community in matters affecting the security and other secular problems of the people.[27] □

Within the political and religious structure of Umuaro, Ezeulu's power is importantly held in check by the council of elders. Where any question of significance concerning the governance and security of the clan comes to light, it is the council's responsibility to meet and negotiate a response. Here Ezeulu's voice is only one amongst many, even if he continues to be respected as closer to the divine than other clan members.

As Reddy argues, the tension implicit in this arrangement runs to the heart of *Arrow of God*'s concerns. Despite his comparative wisdom, like Okonkwo in *Things Fall Apart* Ezeulu is presented as powerfully egocentric. Invested with extensive powers, but prevented by tradition from properly exercising them, the novel shows the priest in a position of ambivalence and crisis:

■ That his role is no more than of 'a watchman' is unacceptable to Ezeulu. The word 'dare' hurled at him as though by an 'enemy' is in the nature of a challenge to the ambitious and egocentric priest. He indulges in a sort of internal monologue as to the nature and reality of power vested in him. He wonders what use is power if it is only superficial, elusive and cannot be exercised. If this is what power means, he would rather not have it at all. Ezeulu is caught up in this dilemma and tension arising out of the limitations and the absoluteness of power.[28] □

As Reddy points out, the godhead Ezeulu represents, *Ulu*, is not a deity who precedes human existence, but is instead a recent historical creation arising from a conscious decision of the clan. In this, *Ulu* contrasts significantly with pre-existing deities such as *Idemili*, who have 'been there from the beginning'.[29] In the dialectic between Ezeulu and Nwaka, the contingency of the former's position, as priest of a created god, is immensely important. If, under the threat of the colonizer, *Ulu* is shown to be ineffective, Nwaka argues, then he should be destroyed. As the chief mediator between human and divine, Ezeulu's significance in the clan is far-reaching, but so too on another level is his rival's: 'Nwaka is very wealthy, influential and he has won the highest number of titles in Umuaro. He is a famous wrestler and an impressive speaker called "the owner of words". Besides, he has his "flute-player" in Ezedemili. Ezeulu cannot boast of such advantages'.[30]

Whenever Ezeulu's authority is challenged by the secular forces represented by Nwaka, Reddy argues, his strategy is to appeal to his 'unknowable' nature as a divine witness. At the same time, he seeks new forms of connection with the colonizers, including sending his son to learn their obscure wisdom. In these senses, he is shown as supremely flexible and inventive, politically. However, this clever and pragmatic streak is fatally undermined by egocentrism, Reddy suggests. Instead of guiding his son more carefully in his encounter with the white man, Ezeulu tacitly uses him as an agent in the battle with Nwaka and Ezedemili. When Oduche catches the Royal Python they worship, his father's complex motives begin to be revealed:

■ Both Akuebue and Edogo disapprove the action of Ezeulu in sending Oduche to the white man's religion. Edogo complains to Akuebue about his father's intentions and says: 'A man should hold his compound together, not plant dissension among his children.' He suspects that his father seems to be grooming Nwafo for the priesthood.

Ezeulu seems to be guided by more than one reason in sending Oduche to the white man's school. In the first place, he hopes that Oduche will be his 'eye' there and report to him about the secrets and wisdom of the white man. This is how he plans to 'confront danger before it reached his people' and [believes] that 'a man must dance the dance prevalent in his time'. On being pressed by Akuebue why he has sent his son to the white man's religion, Ezeulu interprets it in terms of 'a sacrifice' just as their ancestors had sacrificed a kinsman to make 'the great medicine which they called Ulu'. Aluebue is stunned at this revelation which Ezeulu shares with him in confidence.[31] □

When Ezeulu is imprisoned by Captain Winterbottom later on in the novel, these warring impulses again skew his actions. In refusing to eat the ceremonial yams, he aligns himself very literally as the upholder of divinity and tradition, but in a way that, at the same time, furthers his own personal struggle for influence in the clan. By styling himself as a helpless arrow in the bow of his god, in other words, he allows the clan to be wounded rather than forego one pound of possible leverage in the direction of its affairs.

In this way, Reddy is led to an interesting and distinctive reading of the central political event of *Arrow of God* – Ezeulu's refusal to accept the role of Warrant Chief. For many critics, Ezeulu's refusal to eat the yams, as well as his refusal to accept the position of chief, are seen in terms of the contradictory demands of religion and clan he faces, complicated as they are by his desire for personal revenge. Reddy, on the other hand, shows how a different political reading of the novel is possible, in which Ezeulu appears as an even more complex and ambivalent figure:

> ■ Ezeulu is haunted by his temptation to test his power throughout the novel. It is part of his subconscious to experience what it is in real terms. He is not the one to be satisfied with indirect power just as Captain Winterbottom is disgusted with the kind of Indirect Rule imposed on him from above by those at the Headquarters. Both Ezeulu and Winterbottom make a mockery of the Indirect Rule as envisaged by Lord Lugard for Nigeria. They seek to enjoy power in absolute terms and refuse to share it with others. What Ezeulu attempts is to superimpose his own sense of authority on his deity Ulu so as to lend a greater credibility and authenticity to Ulu's voice.[32] □

Behind Ezeulu's desire to style himself as an 'arrow of god', Reddy suggests, lies a deeper will to power. As the messenger of *Ulu*, by the end of the novel Ezeulu has virtually constituted himself *as* the god. His thirst for power is so great that he is willing to expose the clan to ruin rather than compromise his own pride. Only in this way, Reddy argues, can we understand why the foremost representative of the clan's traditional religion becomes the instrument of its capitulation to colonial Christianity.

Reddy's reading of *Arrow of God*, hinging as it does on the theme of Ezeulu's egotism and intransigence, contrasts interestingly with that of

David Carroll in his book *Chinua Achebe: Novelist, Poet, Critic* (1990).[33] As Carroll recognizes, the novel depicts a much later stage in the colonial encounter than does *Things Fall Apart*. At the beginning of *Arrow of God*, he argues, Achebe is still concerned to impart a sense of the harmony and equilibrium of traditional Ibo culture, characterized by an 'effortless interaction of individual and community'.[34]

Nowhere is this sense of balance better represented than in the twin festivals of the Pumpkin Leaves and the New Yam, with their symbolic buildup of dramatic tension leading to release and renewal. Ezeulu is a pivotal figure in each of these ceremonies and thus stands on one level as the epitome of the clan's spiritual and cultural balance. Like Reddy, however, Carroll is keen to point out the ways in which, through Ezeulu himself, Achebe begins to show us the spreading fracture lines in the clan's conception of itself:

> ■ He has begun to question the crucial role he plays in the life of the six villages. What kind of power does he really wield? . . . As his ceremonial appearance indicates, Ezeulu is half man, half spirit; in the world of man he is very powerful, in the world of spirits he is a servant. What is the true relationship between his two roles? Where does his primary duty lie, with the god or the tribe? These are some of the questions the events of the novel will seek to answer.[35] □

As Carroll points out, by the end of *Things Fall Apart* the reader has already been offered an intimation of the growing importance of such questions, especially as mediated by the new challenges posed by the white man and his religion. In *Arrow of God*, Achebe makes them central, choosing for his protagonist a figure in whom religious and political power are combined. As the clan's chief priest, Ezeulu is placed in a position which is, in a sense, even more intimately tied to the *status quo* than was Okonkwo in the earlier novel. In terms of the ideological challenge posed by Christianity to the traditional religion, on the one hand, and the political challenge posed by colonialism to the democratic structures of Ibo self-governance, on the other, Ezeulu is directly in the firing line.

At first, Carroll argues, we see these challenges in terms of a personal crisis in Ezeulu's own life. As the novel widens out, however, we begin to recognize the ways in which his story is symptomatic of much wider processes of transition. Within the structure of the text,

Ezeulu's perspective begins to be balanced by the rival viewpoints of Nwaka and Ezidemili, and then by that of Captain Winterbottom, the British District Commissioner. For Carroll, indeed, the introduction of the latter establishes a crucial parallel with the figure of Ezeulu. As we begin to understand as the novel proceeds, both men are struggling to negotiate their role and mission in the context of complicated, changed cultural parameters. If the worlds of George Allen and Okonkwo in *Things Fall Apart* were comparatively black and white, for Winterbottom and Ezeulu alike, such clarity would seem a relative luxury:

> ■ Like Ezeulu, [Winterbottom] is principally concerned with the problem of power. A strongminded, authoritarian person, he finds himself being forced to implement the British Government's policy of Indirect Rule which he strongly disapproves of. . . . Like the Chief Priest of Ulu he rebels against the idea of becoming simply an intermediary of power, between, in his case, the British Government and the native chiefs. . . . He recalls the time of *Things Fall Apart* when his friend George Allen was in Umuofia and wrote his book, *The Pacification of the Primitive Tribes of the Lower Niger*. In this way, Achebe employs his first novel to give an added historical perspective to the problems of colonial policy in this novel.[36] □

If Okonkwo's policy of aggressive resistance and stubborn adherence to tradition no longer seems feasible to Ezeulu, Clarke's over-simple view of 'civilizing the savages' now also seems ridiculously naive to Winterbottom. Both are forced to enter a process of negotiation and accommodation which each finds profoundly unsatisfactory. Both men look back with nostalgia to the days when a simpler, more authoritarian approach to the handling of power still seemed possible, and, partly through that commonality of perspective, Achebe begins to show us how alike the two men are. Both recognize the necessity of pragmatic interaction with the other. For Winterbottom, there is a growing recognition that the '"impressive looking fetish priest" who seems to understand the white man's justice'[37] might indeed be a useful conduit of power. For Ezeulu, meanwhile, cooperation with the colonial authority appears to offer an opportunity to further his private struggle to establish the supremacy of *Ulu*.

Against this background of accommodation, between resistance and compromise, the introduction of a third, missionary perspective, in the person of Oduche, complicates the dynamics of the novel still further. With the figures of Mr Brown and Mr Smith in *Things Fall Apart*, Carroll argues, Achebe has already suggested two alternative models of religious insurgence – negotiation and accommodation versus authoritarian imposition. In *Arrow of God* this opposition repeats itself in the crisis of the New Yam festival. Ezeulu's implacable adherence to the letter of tradition is set against the more pragmatic view of the other elders. As importantly, it also repeats itself in the contrast between the missionary zeal of Oduche and the spirit of accommodation we see in the closing pages of the novel, as the clan enlists the power of Jesus to defend against the vengeance of the abandoned *Ulu*.

Through these oppositions, Carroll argues, Achebe seeks to dramatize the massive cultural transition from early colonialism to the (in many ways, far more intimately invasive) phase of indirect rule in the early decades of the twentieth century. As we see in the novel, this is a period in which the interests and ideological orientation of colonizer and colonized were becoming, at the same time, more fractured and less separable than in the world depicted by *Things Fall Apart*. Almost without exception, all parties are revealed as troubled and self-divided. If the novel ultimately leaves us with an awkward sense of ambiguity, then, this is a direct function of the complexity and uncertainty of the power relations which characterized this transitional period in the history of colonialism.

As we saw earlier in this chapter, in Achebe's eyes, the project of *Arrow of God* is at least as strongly tied to the politics of the 1960s – to the post-independence drive for cultural reconstruction – as to the politics of the turn of the century. This way of considering the novel, as a text doubly located in the present and past, is picked up by a number of critics. As Tejumola Olaniyan[38] points out, indeed, this distinctive political/historical orientation is characteristic of many African writers around the time of independence. In the efforts of such writers to counter the racist and orientalist representations fostered by colonialism, Olaniyan concurs with the political scientist Patrick Chabal in his contention that 'African writers did more to reveal the reality of postcolonial Africa than most African Scholars'.[39]

On the whole, he argues, social-scientific analyses of the problems faced by newly independent African states focussed on maladministration by Africans, without questioning the structure or appropriateness of the governmental apparatus bequeathed by colonialism. Writers of fiction, on the other hand, have been far bolder in their willingness to question 'the foundational issue of institutions and their legitimacy'.[40] Amongst such writers, Chinua Achebe emerges as a figure of outstanding subtlety and insight, with the novel *Arrow of God* standing as an exceptional creative analysis of the emergent crisis of legitimacy that was to affect the developing state.

As Olaniyan acknowledges, the specific action of *Arrow of God* is at some historical distance from the problems of postcoloniality. What the novel shows very clearly, however, are the historical and political roots of the problems that Nigeria was to suffer more than half a century later:

■ It is set at the turn of twentieth-century Igboland, Nigeria, and dramatizes the penetration and ultimate consolidation of British colonial authority over the indigenous societies. In other words, it is set about seven or so decades *before* independence, decades described by the historian Basil Davidson as 'wasted' in terms of crucial 'political and structural development' of the continent. '[I]n every crucial field of life', writes Davidson, 'the British had frozen the indigenous institutions while at the same time robbed colonized peoples of every scope and freedom for self-development'. This arrest and devastation of the indigenous society's *general* capacity for self-directed evolution is the drama enacted by *Arrow of God,* while the resulting wasteland is the central focus of the later *A Man of the People* (1966), Achebe's now classic merciless excoriation of the new postcolonial state.[41] □

As Olaniyan says, the precolonial society depicted by Achebe's novel is not, in fact, shown as enjoying an unproblematic equilibrium. At the time when the action begins, the villages of Umuaro have already formed a coalition against invasive forces, creating a powerful new deity, *Ulu*, as the spiritual expression of their union. In the novel, however, this arrangement is continually contested by representatives of other rival gods. Thus, at the time of colonialism's appearance, we are shown a society which is already unstable and divided. With the clan in a weakened position that makes it ripe for conquest, only comparatively minor interventions are required to trigger its internal self-destruction:

■ The novel opens at a moment of stress on the Umuaro political arrangement. The pre-eminence of Ulu is under regular but furtive challenge from the priests of the older deities who never quite got used to their secondary role. One of such is Ezidemili, the priest of the goddess Idemili. But it is the titled elder Nwaka, Ezidemili's friend and mentee, who forcefully carries on Ezidemili's fight in the open. What this challenge threatens and promises is a complete reconfiguration of the delicate power relations in the union. Nwaka is brasher, richer, more flamboyant, and fits the profile of one with the kind of ambition the union was designed to discourage. Ezeulu, on the other hand, is profound and reserved; he appears to be the one for whom the saying was invented that genuine power needs no advertisement, and carries himself with majestic gravity. Ezeulu could deal with Nwaka's provocations, but not when the other elders are consistently won over by his (Nwaka's) demagoguery on important council decisions. Enter into this volatile atmosphere the Colonial Factor. Ezeulu was imprisoned for two months by the white District Officer for refusing to be a chief (in furtherance of the colonial policy of 'indirect rule'), and the resulting disruption of his duties to the community, coupled with his own miscalculations, breaks the society apart.[42] □

As Olaniyan argues, the fact that Umuaro is depicted as being in a period of crisis and change does not, of course, in any way relieve British colonialism of the responsibility for its work of cultural destruction in West Africa. Read as a historical analysis of the background to the subsequent problems of Nigeria as a postcolonial state, however, this fact certainly does warrant attention. At the centre of the novel, Olaniyan suggests, lies the ongoing dialectic between Ezeulu and Nwaka, as representatives of alternate impulses in Ibo society. Within the dialogic culture of the clan, this opposition has the capacity to be productive and developmental, helping the community to rationalize and negotiate the challenges it faces. The introduction of Captain Winterbottom and the District Office into the locality, however, radically changes the dynamics of argument within the clan. Winterbottom, with his own quite separate agenda of easing colonial dominance through the installation of a local puppet leader, radically destabilizes the relationship between Ezeulu, Nwaka and the clan as a whole. Instead of continuing to debate, develop and redefine the nature of the governing values and institutions, the clan is driven into a condition of democratic paralysis.

This is perhaps most graphically illustrated in Ezeulu's refusal to announce the beginning of the harvest festival. As the senior priest of Umuaro, it is Ezeulu's role to uphold and epitomise the clan's ethos of 'contingency and a discountenance of all extremes'. Whilst resisting the white man's most direct threat to the clan's political balance – his own installation as chief – the novel shows the way in which Ezeulu ends up by engendering a conflict between the community's traditions and its basic material survival, thereby destroying the very ideal of equilibrium it is his purpose to uphold.

By contrast to Christianity, as Olaniyan suggests, Ibo culture is founded on a symbiosis between human and divine and on a symbolic balance between authoritarian, aggressive and nurturing principles:

■ The narrative of *Arrow* is itself immersed in this Igbo philosophy. It is predicated on the figure of the dancing mask, which is repeatedly deployed at significant moments. The mask is as treacherous and enabling as any text, for it says everything and says nothing. 'The world is like a Mask dancing', Ezeulu justifies his sending Oduche to the Christian mission. 'If you want to see it well you do not stand in one place'. But to 'see it well' will still be humbled by the fact that we can never have all meanings completely within our grasp. This becomes in Achebe's hands a most potent tool of narrating historical instability. Though we are dealing with an omniscient narrator, this all-seeing eye is many times unsure of what to believe out of all the possibilities that constantly assail him or her. . . . The dispersal of narrative meaning so central to the text aptly captures the dispersal of social authority among competing groups. To a large extent, the crisis in the text results from attempts to unduly tame a delicately structured contingency, to force a monologue upon a polyvocal terrain. *This is the meaning of Nwaka's challenge, and also of Ezeulu's almost inexplicable reciprocation; both without distinction are consumed by colonialism and its Christianity whose main distinguishing feature is systemic parochialism* [italics in original]. Here, finally, is the vacuum into which is inscribed, simultaneously, the fall of the indigenous, and the rise of the colonial, episteme.[43] □

In the wake of Ezeulu's – and the clan's – failure of self-preservation, we see nonentities installed as local governors, with authority derived from nowhere but the colonial power itself. As Olaniyan suggests, corruption and despotism are the almost immediate result, with figures like James Ikedi developing an extensive apparatus of extortion, using all available levers of power including false imprisonment and abduction. For Olaniyan, Achebe's representation of the breakdown of Umuaro under the pressure of these processes represents a powerful description of the actual historical conditions which characterized the early period of formal colonization and which also set the mould for subsequent political developments. In this sense, he suggests, *Arrow of God* must continue to be respected for the incisiveness and continued relevancy of its political insights:

> ■ The postcolonial state was determined by, and is an expression of, the political superstructure elaborated by colonial power, and not an outgrowth of the autonomous evolution of the people. . . . Is it shocking then that this state has never productively served the people? Maybe it need not be, but all we know is that the postcolonial state has been unable to escape the logic of its origin in the colonial state: absence of legitimacy with the governed, dependence on coercion, lack of political accountability, a bureaucracy with an extroverted mentality, disregard for the cultivation of a responsive civic community, uneven horizontal integration into the political community such that the government is most felt in the cities, extraction of surplus from the interior to overfeed the capital, and many more! Maybe this fact is clearer today than ever and we have finally began [*sic*] to listen, but we have been warned all along by our distinguished writers, led by the indefatigable and visionary Chinua Achebe.[44] □

With *Things Fall Apart, No Longer at Ease* and *Arrow of God*, Achebe explores three crucial moments in the colonial history of Nigeria: the incursion of the British into Iboland in the late nineteenth century, the aftermath of formal colonization and the run-up to independence in the mid-1950s. With his fourth novel, he turned to the contemporary Nigerian scene. Even before it arrived at the booksellers, *A Man of the People* was surrounded by political controversy. Chapter 5 explores its reception, from the furore that surrounded it in 1966 to some of the most recent critical interpretations. If each of Achebe's previous fictions had shown him as a writer capable of innovation and surprise, *A Man of the People* proved to be a further milestone in his political and imaginative development.

CHAPTER FIVE

A Man of the People (1966) and *Girls at War* (1972)

By 1966, Achebe's reputation, both in Nigeria and internationally, had risen to a level that was incomparable to that of any other African writer. His fourth novel, *A Man of the People*, seemed to flow from his pen with the poise and assurance of an author at the height of his powers. After the crisis which greeted its publication, however, Achebe would not produce another novel for 20 years. This chapter examines the background to *A Man of the People* and looks at some of the main critical responses to it. The final section explores some of the short fiction written during the Biafran struggle, collected in *Girls at War and Other Stories* (1972).

In understanding the context to *A Man of the People*, as well as the controversy it generated, one of the most useful and reliable sources is the critical biography written by the Nigerian scholar and short-story writer Ezenwa-Ohaeto, *Chinua Achebe*.[1] A former student of Achebe's at the University of Nigeria and a fellow member of the executive of the Society of Nigerian Authors, Ezenwa-Ohaeto offers a sympathetic portrait, stressing the democratic and patriotic commitments which shaped Achebe's work as director of external broadcasting for the Nigerian Broadcasting Corporation (NBC) in the mid-1960s. Frequently, Ezenwa-Ohaeto suggests, this involved Achebe in disseminating a far-from-flattering image of Nigerian public life around the world.

The NBC's international coverage of the treason trial of the Yoruba leader Obafemi Awolowo (1909–87) in 1963 was one of many moments in which Achebe's broadcasting work placed him in a tense relationship with the Nigerian establishment. From 1964, public expectations of his fourth novel, trailed as a book which would bring the writer's critical engagement with Nigerian history and politics 'up to date', were mounting. In the same year, his address to the inaugural Commonwealth Literature Conference at Leeds University, later published as 'The Novelist as Teacher',[2] further reaffirmed Achebe's commitment to political critique and social action. Both as a professional observer of the Nigerian political scene, and as a pioneering writer of African fiction, then, Ezenwa-Ohaeto shows Achebe as a figure who is both quite powerful and quite vulnerable in the years preceding *A Man of the People*'s emergence.

In 1964, a population census was carried out nationwide, as preparation for fresh elections. The results revealed widespread corruption, with preposterously inflated population figures reported in many regions, as the leaders of rival ethnic communities jostled for influence. The December elections of that year were boycotted by Lagos, the East and the Mid-West after Prime Minister Balewa (Abubakar Tafawa Balewa 1912–66; Prime Minister 1957–66) refused to allow United Nations monitors to observe the electoral process. In February 1965, the nationwide ballot was finally completed, but political unrest continued.

As Ezenwa-Ohaeto argues, it is during this period of political crisis that Achebe completed the final drafts of *A Man of the People*. However, a much more serious crisis was to greet the novel's publication. In October 1965, regional elections were held in the Western Region, including in the capital, Lagos, where Achebe lived with his wife and two young children. As Ezenwa-Ohaeto describes, political rivalries had now reached such a pitch that the election quickly turned very sour indeed:

■ [C]ontestants were beaten and detained, and ballot papers destroyed. . . . In Ibadan and Lagos many people were subjected to violence; houses were burnt and hundreds of people fled their homes. That state of anarchy continued into the new year of 1966 with barricades erected by opposing factions and many commuters killed or spared according to the answers they gave to the roving political thugs.[3] □

Clearly, one of the salient features of Achebe's novel is its commentary on the themes of corruption and electoral violence in postcolonial

Africa. Looking at its scenes of political manipulation and intimidation, it certainly would have been easy for readers of Achebe's final drafts to see parallels between the novel's action and the contemporary Nigerian situation in 1965, and also to see in it a bold call for regime change. What was much less expected, however, was that the novel's prediction of a military coup would turn out to be so accurate. On Friday, 14 January 1966, the Society of Nigerian Authors held an evening at the Lagos Exhibition Centre, partly to mark the imminent arrival of *A Man of the People*. As president of the Society as well as author of the novel, Achebe was an enthusiastic participant in the celebrations, which went on well into the night. As Ezenwa-Ohaeto describes, however, it was not until his arrival for work at the NBC on the morning of Saturday the 15th that he learned what had happened during the night. In an uncanny recapitulation of the novel, the midday radio pronouncement by the coup's leader, Major Chukwama Kaduna Nzeogwu, declared that the radical action taken by army officers over the preceding hours had been a patriotically necessary act – as much an ethical as a political purge of the Nigerian establishment:

■ Our enemies are the political profiteers, swindlers, men in high and low places that seek bribes and demand ten per cent, those that seek to keep the country permanently divided so that they can remain in office as Ministers and VIPs of waste, the tribalists, the nepotists, those that make the country look big for nothing before international circles.[4] □

Styling himself the leader of the 'Supreme Council of the Revolution of the Nigerian Armed Forces', Nzeogwu proceeded to implement martial law in the North, suspending the constitution, dissolving all elected assemblies and banning all political, cultural, tribal and trade union activities. Across Nigeria, though, the coup was far from an unambiguous success. Although the prime minister, the finance minister and the governor of the Western Region had all been killed, the commander of the Nigerian army, Major General Aguiyu Ironsi, had survived. In a short time Ironsi was able to wrest control back to the establishment and to arrest Nzeogwu and several of his co-conspirators, assuming for himself the role of Nigerian Head of State.

Ezenwa-Ohaeto's narrative of these momentous happenings around Achebe's novel illustrates the escalating sense of danger surrounding the writer in 1966. This soon intensified even further, with anti-Eastern pogroms in the North, in which an estimated 3000 of his fellow Ibos were massacred. The targets of the violence were not only army officers of Eastern descent, but also doctors, civil servants, teachers and others. As the killings spread across Nigeria to Lagos, the position of Achebe and his family became increasingly dangerous. When soldiers arrived at Broadcasting House, it became desperate. 'It transpired that the soldiers were looking for Achebe. The sheer co-incidence that *a Man of the People* had been published in January 1966, had convinced them that he must have been privy to the coup of Nigerian majors.'[5] For two weeks the family stayed in hiding at the residence of the British Council representative, Frank Cawson, before attempting the dangerous journey back to Achebe's home in the East. When the governor of the Eastern Region, Emeke Ojukwu, announced its secession from the Nigerian Federation in January 1967, Achebe saw little choice but to throw in his lot with the new rebel Republic of Biafra.

EARLY RESPONSES TO *A MAN OF THE PEOPLE*

In his essay 'Achebe's African Parable' (1968), published only two years after the novel itself, Bernth Lindfors[6] addresses the scandalous reputation of *A Man of the People* head on. As he confirms, there are certainly close correspondences between the political developments of the mid-1960s in Nigeria and those that are depicted in the novel. Achebe's account of the military takeover at the end of his text, in particular, comes remarkably close to describing the actual events that followed. However, it is Lindfors's purpose to argue that despite the clairvoyant appearance of certain passages in the novel, it is inappropriate to read *A Man of the People* as prophetic:

■ Indeed, given the circumstances in Nigeria during the time Achebe was writing, *A Man of the People* should be recognized as a devastating satire in which Achebe heaped scorn on independent Africa by picturing one part of it just as it was. I believe Achebe ended the novel with a military coup in order to enlarge the picture to include Nigeria's neighbours, many of which had experienced coups. By universalizing the story in this way, Achebe could suggest to his countrymen that what had happened in other unstable independent African countries might easily have happened in Nigeria too. The coup was meant as an African parable, not a Nigerian prophecy.[7] □

As Lindfors suggests, first of all, it is instructive to observe the dates of submission of Achebe's third and fourth novels. Since *Arrow of God* was delivered to the publishers in February 1963, it is unlikely that Achebe began *A Man of the People* until that time. The manuscript of *A Man of the People* itself was submitted in February 1965. Thus, it is fair to assume that the novel was largely written in the course of 1963 and 1964. During this period, Achebe would have been well aware, through his work at the NBC, of the developing political crisis. A series of national leaders were arrested and charged with treason and conspiracy in 1962 and 1963, whilst the national electoral census held in the same period was surrounded by suggestions of corruption. Public demonstrations were widespread. In 1964, the federal election itself took place amid a rising tide of violence and disorder. Towards the end of that year, Lindfors suggests, the entire nation already seemed on the brink of chaos:

■ It should be remembered that Achebe's publisher received the manuscript of *A Man of the People* one month after this period of crisis and compromise. Achebe must have been working on the last chapters of the novel, which dramatize the turbulence and violence of an election campaign, during the months just preceding the Nigerian election. He was obviously drawing much of his inspiration from daily news reports. The last pages of the novel, those which describe the coup, must have been written very close to the time of the five-day crisis following the election.[8] □

If there is a clear parallel to be drawn between contemporary events in Nigeria and the background of the novel itself, Lindfors argues moreover, it is also important to understand the position of the military in this context:

■ Before the campaign, they had been used to restore civil order both at home and abroad. In December, 1960 Nigerian troops had been sent to the newly-independent Republic of the Congo (Leopoldville) to help United Nations forces keep order, and in April, 1964 they had been dispatched to Tanganyika to relieve British troops who had put down a Tanganyika Army mutiny. In Nigeria, Army troops had quelled a Tiv riot in 1960 and had maintained order in the Western Region during the 1962 state of emergency. During the 1964 election campaign they were ordered to put down another Tiv riot and did so at the cost of 700 lives. Throughout the campaign, large squads of riot police were deployed to battle the thugs and hooligans hired by political candidates to terrorize their opposition. During the post-election crisis, troops were called out to safeguard the residences of Azikiwe and Balewa in Lagos and the cell of Awolowo in Calabar. Thus, before, during and after the 1964 election campaign the Nigerian Army played a prominent role as a peace-keeping force in Nigeria and abroad.[9] □

This peacekeeping role contrasted sharply with the disruptive effects of the military in other African states in this period, Lindfors observes. Togo, Liberia, Uganda, Kenya and Zanzibar were only some of the nations which witnessed violent coups or revolutions led by the army in the mid–1960s. In Nigeria, however, the army was viewed primarily as a stabilizing rather than revolutionary force. In this context, Lindfors argues, calls for the army to restore order and to cleanse the political system of corruption and/or incompetence were widespread:

■ The people themselves expressed their discontent with politicians in no uncertain terms. During the election crisis, Lazarus Okeke wrote a letter to the Lagos *Daily Express* asserting that

. . . no well-wisher of Nigeria would recommend a blow-up of the country just because certain politicians cannot have their demand [*sic*] met. The welfare of the people as a nation definitely supersedes [*sic*] in importance the various vain and sectional claims of erring politicians.

An unsigned article in the Lagos *Sunday Express* of January 3, 1965, went a step further:

Democracy has bred corruption in our society on a scale hitherto unknown in human history. Nigeria needs a strong man with a strong hand. By this I mean, that Nigeria needs to be disciplined. Nigeria needs to be drilled. The leadership we want is the leadership of a benevolent dictator who gets things done; not that of 'democratic administrators' who drag their feet.

It is clear that a number of Nigerians would have welcomed a military coup in January, 1965. Indeed, several days after Azikiwe and Balewa had worked out their compromise, one disgruntled Easterner writing in Enugu's *Nigerian Outlook* expressed regret that the compromise had not been forestalled by military intervention:

If civil strife had broken out on December 30, the armed forces might have gone into action as a last resort, and the President and the Prime Minister might never have had an opportunity for negotiations.[10] □

Read against this background, Lindfors suggests, Achebe's novel appears much less 'prophetic' and more simply reflective of a powerful mood in Nigerian public life in late 1964 and early 1965. Furthermore, to limit interpretation of the novel merely to its relationship with the January coup of 1966 is, Lindfors argues, to do an injustice to its wider representative reach. Far from applying to Nigeria alone, the drama of Achebe's text can be read as a commentary on the situation of many of the newly independent states of Africa in the 1960s. It is for this reason that Lindfors characterizes the novel as 'Achebe's African parable' rather than as simply his 'Nigerian prophecy'.[11]

Amongst the contemporary responses to Achebe's novel, Ngũgĩ wa Thiong'o's 1966 essay 'Chinua Achebe's *A Man of the People*'[12] provides an interesting complement to that of Lindfors. Although he too is concerned to explore its political dynamics, Ngũgĩ's reading places the text much more firmly in the context of the author's previous novels. For him, *A Man of the People* can be seen as a direct continuation of the project of those earlier narratives, each of which seeks to 'look back and try to find out what went wrong, where the rain began to beat us'.[13]

In his fourth novel, Ngũgĩ suggests, what we see first of all is a confirmation of Achebe's control and technical skill as a novelist, his characteristic economy with language and seemingly effortless ability to establish a 'relaxed warm flow'.[14] On the historical level, on the other hand, Ngũgĩ sees the novel as marking a break with the earlier texts, in the sense that this is the first time Achebe completely turns his back on the colonizers. In *A Man of the People*, his anger is directed with full force at his countrymen for their corruption, indifference and cynicism:

■ Everybody is caught up in this complicity with evil: the masses with their cynicism – 'Tell them that this man had used his position to enrich himself and they would ask you if you thought a sensible man would spit out the juicy morsel that good fortune had placed in his mouth' – and hardened indifference; and the elite – even people like

Odili are shown as being perilously close to Nanga – with their greed, lack of creativity and pitiable dependence on their former colonial rulers. It is left to the army, in the novel, to halt what has become an intolerable position.[15] □

For Ngũgĩ, Achebe's choice to end the novel with a military coup is a deeply problematic solution to the problems he depicts, however. Most importantly, Ngũgĩ argues, the coup leaves too many of the questions posed by the novel unanswered. Its effect is to leave the reader wondering whether (in the absence of military intervention) any of the actors in the national drama – including politicians and intellectuals – have even the potential to find a workable solution. Even at their most radical, characters such as Odili or Max imagine little more than the possibility of tinkering with and extending the existing social and political structures. Truly meaningful change is never on the agenda.

On one level, then, *A Man of the People* fails to become the narrative of political transformation that Ngũgĩ would like to see. On another level, however, Ngũgĩ argues that the novel still deserves serious recognition, inasmuch as it does insist on placing such concerns at the heart of the cultural agenda. Achebe might not be able to offer a complete set of answers in *A Man of the People*, but in his self-designated role as novelist-teacher, he still compels us to attend to the questions that matter:

■ The pupils, and the teachers as well, must define their attitude – and find solutions – to these questions. What Achebe has done in *A Man of the People* is to make it impossible or inexcusable for other African writers to do other than address themselves directly to their audiences in Africa – not in a comforting spirit – and tell them that such problems are their concern. The teacher no longer stands apart to contemplate. He has moved with a whip among the pupils, flagellating himself as well as them. He is now the true man of the people.[16] □

ALTERNATIVE READINGS OF *A MAN OF THE PEOPLE*

As critics like Lindfors and Ngũgĩ show, in different ways, *A Man of the People* is undoubtedly a politically engaged novel. The question raised by Joe Obi in his essay 'A Critical Reading of the Disillusionment Novel' (1990),[17] however, is how this political engagement might match up to the doctrine of 'commitment' set out repeatedly in Achebe's critical writings. By way of illustration of this notion of commitment, which Achebe shares with many other African writers, Obi quotes O. Chinweize and I. Madubuike's well-known essay 'Towards the decolonization of African Literature' (1975):

■ The function of the artist in Africa, in keeping with our traditions and needs, demands that the writer, as a public voice, assume a responsibility to reflect public concerns in his writings, and not preoccupy himself with his puny ego. Because in Africa we recognize that art is in the public domain, a sense of social commitment is mandatory for the artist. That commitment demands that the writer pay attention to his craft, that he not burden the public with unfinished or undecipherable works. It also demands that his theme be germane to the concerns of his community.[18] □

For Obi, the key purpose of critically analyzing the novels of Achebe and others is to delineate their ideological 'vectors'[19] and interests. Following the Marxist theorist Pierre Macherey (b. 1938), he is concerned to draw out both the explicit ideological content and the implicit or 'unsaid' of the literary text, in order to understand its relationship to dominant and oppositional ideologies.

For Obi, *A Man of the People* fits into a body of African novels written in the mid-1960s which explore their authors' disillusionment with the fruits of independence:

■ Prior to the mid-1960s, the bulk of African literature concerned itself with racial affirmation and reclamation. The virtues of blackness were extolled, and Africa became a bucolic haven in the works of the period. This moment in African literature saw the fructification of the influential literary and psychopolitical movement, Negritude, which was soldered onto some countries' attempts at decolonization at the time.

By the middle of the sixties, the bubble had burst as the onus of exploitation and political strife shifted onto African shoulders. The indigenous ruling elite that had come to power on the crest of a powerful nationalist conflation of popular forces (and, of course, the various collusive retreating colonizers) soon effected a volteface that left the bulk of their countrymen *as well as the literati* [italics in the original] disillusioned. In Nigeria, the change in gear from literature of affirmation to that of critical realism did not take long in arriving.[20] □

According to Obi, *A Man of the People*, like many other texts of its time, is 'critical of all and sundry'.[21] Politicians and the common people fall, alike, under its disapproving gaze. Indeed, he argues, the only group to escape the novel's critique is Achebe's own, that of the intellectuals and literati. Certainly, the novel does depict anti-intellectualism as a phenomenon, but it does so only through the eyes of 'pompous and insecure politicians'[22] whose viewpoints are far from being endorsed by the novel. In this way, Obi reads Achebe and other 'disillusionment' novelists as adopting a very specific position in relation to the politics of independence:

> ■ Much has been written on the overt political tendency of the disillusionment novel, and it is not our intention to traverse well trodden ground. Nevertheless a point bears emphasis: The postindependence fiasco in Africa resulted in an intraelite split, that is, between the political elite and the literati. The handful of nationalist politicians who articulated the demands for self-government (and whose claims were buttressed by earlier novels of identity like *Things Fall Apart*) joined their not-so-educated colleagues (i.e., the commercial elite as well as traditional rulers) to wield power. This arrangement excluded the writers and the bulk of the intellectual class from real power to direct their societies other than as subservient civil servants.[23] □

For Obi, in this context, the profound anxiety and fear articulated by novels like *A Man of the People* does not spring from any truly revolutionary impulse. The ire of the literati arises rather out of the frustration attendant on their own exclusion from the centre of power. On a political level, it is this frustrated ambition that drives the narrative of *A Man of the People*, and which also prevents it from becoming a more radically challenging text:

> ■ In Achebe's *A Man of the People*, Odili is the David that Chief Nanga, the Goliath, slays. Odili and his equally idealistic friends venture into a world, the world of politics, where integrity and honesty are dead. At the end of the story, both hero and antagonist are supplanted by a new force – the military – whose posture the reader can only guess at. Odili Samalu fails as a hero: He does not inspire us precisely because he represents the ineffective plight of idealism in a rotten environment.
>
> If the heroes of the novels of disillusion are 'hooked, hogtied, and collared', what about those on whose behalf progressive individuals claim to speak – the common people? The common people in the disillusionment novels are depicted as passive and cynical; unable to

help themselves, as already observed, they are unwilling to challenge the status quo.[24] □

In Achebe's novel, as in those of many of his contemporaries, Obi observes, change will never come from below, since the people themselves are considered as 'inert and ignorant'.[25] In this sense, the novel lacks the ability even to imagine the kind of radical, popular, political upheaval that might seriously address Nigeria's ills. Instead, Achebe opts for military intervention as the 'answer' to the nation's crisis, a solution which 'represents the triumph of neither democracy nor the electorate'.[26] Such an analysis leads Obi to a clear conclusion:

> ■ The foregoing analysis serves to underscore a contention that we may now state succinctly: The novels of disillusion are pessimistic and lack a vision for the future. *Vision* in this context refers not only to the writer's ability to depict antagonisms within society but also to *reveal the possibility of change through these antagonisms*. Thus realistic literature that is visionary will necessarily come into conflict with the status quo that presides over and legitimates these antagonisms. There is an uncomfortable anticlimactic void at the end of these disillusionment novels – a void that suggests an impasse in the writer's consciousness or, alternately, *a junction* that requires explicit ideological commitment. Unfortunately, the novels end their broadsides at just this critical point. (italics in the original)[27] □

Whilst novels such as *A Man of the People* try (in some ways admirably) to force society towards the recognition of its blindness and hypocrisy, Obi argues, their own imprisonment within ideological vested interests prevents that critique from achieving either depth or true radicalism. In searching for the causes of Nigeria's national crisis, *A Man of the People* is ultimately unable to show us anything more than its symptoms.

If the analysis presented by Obi's essay is generally scathing of both *A Man of the People* and its author, Onyemaechi Udumukwu's 'Achebe and the Negation of Independence' (1991)[28] represents a very different approach to both. Indeed, Udumukwu argues that Achebe's contribution to the emergence and survival of the Nigerian novel has been a crucial one, and it is in this context that we should approach *A Man of the People* itself. For Udumukwu, the major achievement of

Achebe's fiction, far from espousing some easy ideological mantra, is that it succeeds in conveying the actual, complex texture of national life at various stages in Nigeria's history. In addressing the aftermath of independence in his fourth novel, the author captures an authentic sense of desperation at the failure of the nation to live up to its own hopes, including its failure to decisively slough off the negative effects of foreign domination. For Achebe such problems, however intractable, cannot simply be left to fester, but must be met with political and intellectual courage, Udumukwu argues:

■ Achebe's creative endeavours in postindependence reveal a specific consciousness oriented toward an attempt to inspire a genuine form of leadership and political activism for his country. Consequently, the problem of leadership and its correlative abuse of power constitute a major thematic preoccupation in Achebe's postindependence writing. . . . [T]he negation of independence in Nigeria has been occasioned by the failure of the leaders to rise up to the challenge of leadership.[29] □

Achebe's novel is primarily designed to draw attention to the failure of Nigeria's leaders to have 'a plan, a blueprint, or a direction for the new nation at independence',[30] Udumukwu suggests. Furthermore, the novel seeks to foreground the basic lack of contact between the new ruling class and the ordinary people they aspire to rule.

As we are aware, the national political impasse is 'solved' in *A Man of the People* by means of a military takeover: importantly, Udumukwu argues, the novel seems to give this solution a kind of 'subtle applause'.[31] On the level of Odili's personal narrative, it clears the way for a resolution of the narrative's central romantic conflict, since with Nanga out of the picture Odili is now free to marry Edna. On a broader level, moreover, the coup is also represented in a positive light, since it is seen as ending the violence and disorder that were dominating national life.

When we consider Achebe's depiction of ordinary Nigerians in the novel, Udumukwu argues however, the picture becomes much more complex. Indeed, if Nanga and Odili are seen as equally careless and ignorant of the public good, the people too are represented as paralyzed by false consciousness:

■ In *A Man of the People* the people are portrayed as disillusioned with the prevailing violence . . . they seem to be unaware of the condition of their jaded existence. In other words they have a distorted perception of their condition. For them this distortion and life in postindependence are one and the same. Thus, they seem to perceive independence as their leaders do, in terms of a huge national cake. They do not see any evil in engaging in a scramble for chunks from this cake . . . the language of Nanga has been accepted as the all-inclusive language. . . . What is happening here is that the people have been entangled in the false notion that such consciousness is the norm.

In a sense then, we can argue that the people of Anata and Urua suffer from a condition of false consciousness. They are neither dejected by nor indifferent to the prevailing asphyxiating morality secreted by the Nangas. These states – that is, of indifference and dejection – are implicated in a condition of awareness. At least to be indifferent toward a condition, one has to know what has precipitated one's indifference; indifference is in itself a reaction against what one recognizes as being in existence whether it has negative or positive implications. But the people of Urua and Anata are not aware; hence they lack a true knowledge of the essence of their condition. They live in the world and fail to recognize the truth of this world. Thus, they are not only ignorant, but they suffer from the worst kind of ideological blindness.[32] □

In an interview for the Kenyan *Sunday Nation* in January 1967,[33] Achebe admits his awareness that *A Man of the People* would be controversial and that its publication might lead to some negative personal consequences. It is clear, though, that the extent of the personal fallout from the novel's publication came as a very unpleasant surprise: 'Well, I was quite determined that the thing had to be said. I felt that the worst that might have happened would be losing my job.'[34] Recorded before the descent to civil war, before what he saw as the genocidal campaign against his native Eastern Region, this interview also captures a sense of ambivalence about the benefits and dangers of military intervention in the state:

■ [M]ilitary takeovers are not always bad in themselves. You see, the Nigerian situation left no political solution. The political machine had been so abused that whatever measures were taken, it could only produce the same results. We had got to a point where some other force had to come in.

When I was writing A *Man of the People*, it wasn't clear to me what that force was going to be – whether it would be the army, or even civil war. In fact, civil war was already developing in Western Nigeria. So I don't think one can say a military takeover is never worth it. Now the fact that it has sort of soured was rather due to a second stage.

I don't think it was inevitable from the first stage. We should not ignore the idealistic character of the first revolution because it has been overtaken by a counter-revolution that has no basis other than tribalism.[35] □

That he intends Chief Nanga as a representation of the Nigerian leadership before 1966 is made explicit. The fictional coup with which the novel ends is cast as a blow against both political corruption and neocolonialism. Though it represents Nigerian public life in the 1960s in terms of a rotten body politic, then, the novel clearly appears, through the lens of this interview, as an expression of the kind of soft nationalism that we see reflected in *Things Fall Apart*, *No Longer at Ease* and *Arrow of God*.

In my own critical reading of the novel in the book *Scandalous Fictions: The Twentieth Century Novel in the Public Sphere* (2006),[36] the development of this nationalism in *A Man of the People* and Achebe's subsequent writing is further explored. As I point out, in early 1967 Achebe was still working on the draft of a fifth novel which, like *A Man of the People*, was to combine political commitment with an interest in representing the contemporary. As he says in the 1967 interview for the *Sunday Nation* cited earlier, '*A Man of the People* wasn't a flash in the pan. This is the beginning of a phase for me, in which I intend to take a hard look at what we in Africa are making of our independence.'[37] Within months of Achebe's statement, however, the situation for Easterners was to turn drastically for the worse. Armed with massive supplies of military hardware from the British government, the Nigerian Federation launched a campaign against the rebel East which was to cost three million lives. As an international spokesman for the secessionist cause, as well as a cultural figurehead for Biafrans, Achebe became intimately involved in the civil war. Although he continued to write poetry and produced the short story collection *Girls at War* in 1972, the new novel did not appear. Rather than heralding the beginning of a new phase in Achebe's experiments with the novel, therefore, *A Man of the People* turned out to be the end of an era in his writing.

Even before the publication of *A Man of the People*, as we have already seen, Achebe's own personal and political position was undergoing a series of radical transformations. In order to understand the significance of this, as I suggest, it is important first of all to recognize the incredible popular status that Achebe enjoyed in

Nigeria in the mid–1960s. As the nation's most celebrated novelist and at the same time director of external broadcasting for the NBC, he enjoyed an almost unrivalled position of authority in cultural matters. His novels were already permanent landmarks in the high school curriculum, and his role as an international cultural ambassador for Nigeria was a growing one.

This is the context, I argue, within which we need to consider the novel's scathing critique of Nigerian society, and in particular to view its problematic, politically extreme 'happy ending'. Although it is true that the nation depicted in *A Man of the People* does not match Nigeria in every respect, the political circumstances it evokes closely mirror the scene of Lagos in 1964/5. In the narrative, Odili is seen as welcoming the army's intervention at the end of the novel; as we have seen, this also seems to reflect Achebe's own view at the time:

> ■ Interviewed in early 1967, certainly, Achebe is far from condemnatory of the January coup. At least for the moment, in the interregnum before the descent to civil war, it appears that the coup's undesirable effects – including the curtailment of individual freedoms and suspension of democratic rights – is a price he feels is worth paying, if it promises a cleanup of Nigerian public life.[38] □

In one sense, this willingness to countenance martial intervention as the only means of redemption for Nigeria could be seen as an expression of nationalism. However, to read Achebe's fiction as nationalist in any simple sense is, I argue, difficult to sustain. Far more of his oeuvre is given over to the reclamation of Ibo (tribal) heritage than in seeking to 'narrate the nation', for example. Similarly, Achebe's protagonists are, almost without exception, more problematic and self-destructive than inspirational. Rather than seeing *A Man of the People* as a 'nationalist' work in an ideological sense, I argue then, it is perhaps more useful to think of the text as a *provocation to debate* about the future of the Nigerian state. If Odili and Nanga are, each in their own way, profoundly unsatisfactory agents of national development, then this in itself can be read as one of the challenges Achebe's novel lays down to its readers:

> ■ Certainly, the text seems at least as concerned to flagellate Odili for his failings as it is to punish Chief Nanga. The latter is shown as

corrupt, yes, but this is directly linked in the novel to the structures of clannish loyalty associated with traditional culture. To borrow the language of the text, Nanga is 'eating', but his extended family and the people of his district are also 'eating'. In the minds of his electorate, Nanga is in a position to ensure that Anata gets its share of the 'national cake', and if he is taking a portion for himself, then this is both reasonable and natural: 'Tell them that this man had used his position to enrich himself and they would ask you – as my father did – if you thought a sensible man would spit out the juicy morsel that good fortune had placed in his mouth'. In other words, I would suggest that the effect of Achebe's text is to present Nanga's corruption as an organic extension of traditional mores into modern national culture. If Nanga is shown as a retrograde figure whose weddedness to the past stifles both political and economic development, however, Odili is shown as an equally poor progenitor of change. Vain, pompous, misogynistic and elitist, even as a candidate for the Common People's Convention he remains disdainful of the 'silly ignorant villagers' and the city's 'contemptible' masses. A far greater proportion of Odili's narrative is taken up with his dubious seductions of women than with any kind of political or social reflection, and he is ultimately revealed as a figure who is as impotent as he is self-regarding.[39] □

Certainly, the narrative choices Achebe makes in this regard are interesting. At the same time that, in his critical writings, we see the author calling for a more socially responsible, politically engaged form of literature, his own novel chooses to present us with two alternate 'men of the people' who are united in their inadequacy to fulfil the historic tasks that lie before them.

For critics such as Joe Obi (whose Marxist analysis we encountered earlier in this chapter) *A Man of the People* is read as typical of the 'disillusionment novels' of the 1960s, in which writers allegedly abandon their political ideals and turn to a more scathing and bitter representation of the postcolonial state. For Obi, the problem with Achebe's fourth novel is its ultimate failure to provide a more radical critique, especially of the role of intellectuals. Instead of providing a redemptive social analysis, he argues, *A Man of the People* leaves us with 'an uncomfortable anticlimactic void'.[40] For me, however, the problem with Obi's reading is that it seriously misconstrues the political character of Achebe's narrative, missing the important ways in which it *does* critique the status quo:

■ Where [Obi's] reading of Achebe's text falls short, I would argue, is in its overdetermined focus on an ideological panacea which *A Man of the People* very deliberately refuses to offer. This is not, as I have suggested, a novel of political solutions, and neither is it easy on the new middle class. Rather, I would argue that the concern of *A Man of the People* is to represent the failure of the educated bourgeoisie to constitute a functioning 'public sphere' in post-independence Nigeria, which might have checked and supervised the political establishment more effectively. The story of Odili as a representative of this class is a story of ethical and political inadequacy.[41] □

On a political level, I suggest, the political theorist Frantz Fanon (1925–61) is once again a profound influence on Achebe in this novel. Indeed, as a character, Obi himself can be read as enacting precisely the warning articulated in Fanon's *The Wretched of the Earth* (1961), of the failures of the new middle class in newly independent African states. Instead of dedicating its intellectual and technical resources to the service of the people as a whole, Fanon argues, all too often this new bourgeoisie backslides into cynicism and corruption. Read in this light, like Obi in *No Longer at Ease*, Odili's failure to rise to the task of national renewal has implications and reverberations far beyond his individual story. His narrative might not offer the kind of class analysis which Joe Obi would like to see, but it does suggest one kind of class analysis nevertheless. Far from shying away from the unpleasant, wider implications of Obi's inadequacy – within which, by extension, Achebe himself would be implicated – one can argue that the effect of *A Man of the People* is precisely to confront its middle-class Nigerian readership with the immanence of their own failure.

Conventionally, the public 'scandal' of Achebe's novel has usually been seen in terms of its prediction of the January coup of 1966, and the shockwaves that followed when Achebe was identified as a possible conspirator. What *A Man of the People*'s 'prophetic' reputation often works to obscure, I argue however, is the scandalous nature of the novel's address to its readers. In order to understand *A Man of the People* as a text of its time, we need to recognize the force with which Achebe confronts his middle-class Nigerian readership here, demanding whether this is a future they are prepared to see unfold:

■ If *A Man of the People* was read as evidence of conspiracy by the Nigerian Military government in 1966, the novel's portrait, through Odili, of a self-regarding and impotent middle class must have made equally discomfiting reading for much of its liberal audience. Even as it

describes the dissolution of the Nigerian public sphere, and predicts the
end of liberal democracy itself, it is a novel which demands a response,
challenges a different ending. In and through its very scandalousness,
in other words, its effect is to assert the novel's survival as a space of
public debate.[42] □

GIRLS AT WAR AND OTHER STORIES

Between the publication of *A Man of the People* and *Anthills of the
Savannah* stretches a gap of 20 years in which Achebe found himself
unable to produce another extended work of fiction. Arguably, the
Biafran War experience was a large part of the reason for this long
period of writer's block. As he says in the 1969 essay 'The African
Writer and the Biafran Cause,' he had been struck by a realization
that 'one had been operating on a false – but perhaps naïve – basis
all along. The problems of the Nigerian Federation were always well
known, but one somehow felt that perhaps this was part of growing
up and given time all this would be over and we would solve our
problems. . . . Suddenly you realise that the only valid basis for existence is one that gives security to you and your people'.[43] In 1972,
however, Achebe did publish a collection of short stories, *Girls at
War*, dealing partly with the Biafran experience. Although these have
excited much less critical attention than his novels, interesting work
has been done on them. Here, I discuss three critical approaches to
the collection, offered by C. L. Innes, Umelo Ojinmah and Ode
Ogede, respectively.

As Innes points out in her study *Chinua Achebe*,[44] although the stories
of *Girls at War* are often taken to be a complete unit, they actually
span a period of 13 years in Achebe's writing, from 'The Sacrificial
Egg', which first appeared in 1959 to 'Sugar Baby', first published in
1972. They differ considerably in tone and technique. In some of the
stories, what we seem to see are alternative sketches of characters and
events which figure in the novels. 'Chike's School Days', for example,
deals with the question of marriage to an *osu* – a theme explored more
fully in *No Longer at Ease* – and also plays with the figure of a colonial
preacher, Mr Brown, who recalls the character of that name in *Things
Fall Apart*. In stories like 'Uncle Ben's Choice' and 'the Voter', both
written around the same time as *A Man of the People*, we see reflections

of the contemporary political concerns which structure that novel. Like Odili's, Uncle Ben's narrative revolves around the dilemmas of the new middle class, balancing the claims of tradition against new-found privileges and freedoms. 'The Voter', meanwhile, includes a sketch for a different aspect of the novel, a prototype of a corrupt minister of culture who trades in 'votes for cash'.

In other stories, however, Achebe deals with people and perspectives which we see only in the margins of the longer fiction:

■ Although the themes and techniques of Achebe's short stories are often closely related to those found in the novels, the characters are those who appear only in the background or in the margins of his major works. Here, in *Girls at War and Other Stories* he brings those marginalized characters into the foreground – the women, the children, the clerks, the poor traders and craftsmen – and also focuses a much harsher light on those who exploit or ignore them, the complacent middle-class professionals like Mrs. Emenike and Reginald Nwankwo.[45] □

As Innes says, whilst the novels deal primarily with figures of ambition who seek defining roles in their communities, stories such as 'The Sacrificial Egg', 'Akueke' and 'Girls at War' concern themselves with other kinds of experiences, especially those of women living in difficult circumstances, negotiating for their very survival, such as Gladys in the collection's title story. Throughout the collection, there is a concern with issues of gender, which seems to be relegated to a position of lesser importance in the first four novels. In 'Akuke', for example, Achebe explores the position of women in traditional Ibo society. The story depicts – through the eyes of the victim – the plight of those afflicted with the 'swelling disease', who in traditional Ibo practice were carried out into the bush to die. Like *Things Fall Apart*, the story brings an unsentimental eye to such problematic traditional practices. At the same time, however, it also explores how Ibo attitudes to disease are tied up with attitudes about the role of women, as we see the main character save herself and go on to fulfil the role of marriageable daughter.

In 'Vengeful Creditor' we see a very different kind of Nigerian woman, confident in her wealth and modernity. Here, as Innes observes, Achebe's eye is turned to the ambivalent reactions that attended the introduction of free state education in the East and

West just before independence. The story centres on the conflict between Mrs Emenike, a married woman and social worker, and her ten-year-old servant, Veronica, who wishes to be released from her duties to take advantage of the new free education. When Veronica tries to kill Mrs Emenike's baby (for whom she is employed as a nurse), the story dramatically exposes the class and gender dynamics tied up in the building of the new Nigeria.

In the story 'Girls at War', Achebe addresses the specific experience of women in the Nigerian Civil War. Gladys, initially a promising schoolgirl, becomes progressively embroiled with Reginald Nwankwo, an official from the Ministry of Justice, as her options for survival in the war-torn region contract. When Reginald finally seduces the girl, Achebe confronts the reader with the bitter irony of her position, through the eyes of her unlovely seducer:

> ■ He had his pleasure but wrote the girl off. He might just as well have slept with a prostitute, he thought. It was clear as daylight to him now that she was kept by some army officer. What a terrible transformation in the short period of less than two years! Wasn't it a miracle that she still had memories of the other life, that she even remembered her name? If the affair of the drunken Red Cross man should happen again now, he said to himself, he would stand up beside the fellow and tell the party that here was a man of truth. What a terrible fate to befall a whole generation! The mothers of tomorrow![46] □

In its 'swift and terrible'[47] ending, Innes argues, in which we see Gladys killed trying to save an injured soldier, Achebe completes his bitter commentary on contemporary gender relations and the devastation of war.

Amongst other critics of *Girls at War*, Umelo Ojinmah[48] is amongst those who see the collection as a much more coherent unit, especially in its portrayal of the civil war experience. For Ojinmah, the whole of Achebe's writing can be viewed through the prism of his powerful social consciousness, especially his desire to comment on the corruption and maladministration of the new Nigerian state. If Achebe's vision in novels like *A Man of the People* is a bleak one in political terms, then this tendency was entirely justified by Nigeria's subsequent history, Ojinmah argues, and especially by the experience of the Biafran war:

> ■ That civil war finally eventuated was both a vindication of the seer's prophetic vision, and his realistic analysis of contemporary political trends which he says was evident as far back as 1964. 'And the indication of how politics was going to develop in Nigeria was there already. If you cared to look, I think the signs were everywhere'. Achebe sees the death of democracy as being a consequence of the lack of responsibility already highlighted and believed that the Biafran revolution (1967–1970) provided a chance for Africans to lay a political foundation that is authentically egalitarian and based on philosophies 'which took into account their present conditions'. Achebe in an interview in 1969, saw the Biafran issue as, 'a revolution that aims toward true independence, that moves toward the creation of modern states in place of the new colonial enclaves we have today, a revolution that is informed with African ideologies'.[49] □

If the Biafran dream turned out to be a failure, Ojinmah argues, then the collection *Girls at War* represents Achebe's disillusioned response to that failure. With stories like 'Vengeful Creditor' and 'Girls at War', he looks deep into the private and public corruption that poisoned Biafra, as much as it had done the Nigerian Federation.

The story 'Civil Peace' similarly reflects this anger and disillusionment. In the story, Jonathan Iwegbu rejoices to find that he, his wife and children have all survived the war. When the family are attacked by robbers, however, we see that the war has taken away more than the lives of others: in their moment of need, the traditional Ibo ethic of community is nowhere to be seen:

> ■ As in his earlier fictions, Achebe indicts the society for its apathy. The comic charade of the robbers, from their cool announcement of their presence and who they are, to their helping Jonathan and his family raise the alarm of their presence, once more demonstrates the 'spinelessness' of the society (neighbours). While Achebe highlights the heartlessness of the robbers, in depriving this poor family of their 'egg-rasher', he criticises the society in which no one raised a finger to help a fellow in need of assistance – a society in which robbers have the boldness and audacity to raise an alarm of their own presence, knowing that no one would have the guts to do anything.[50] □

In 'Girls at War', Achebe explores the breakdown of Biafra's revolutionary ideals. The story tracks its heroine Gladys from the early days of her youthful idealism to her sexual exploitation and death. Through the twin figures of Gladys and Reginald, Ojinmah argues, the story illustrates the rottenness of Biafran society. Reginald's treatment of Gladys powerfully illustrates the corrupting influence of power, as he appropriates food relief intended for the starving masses for his family's private enjoyment, and exploits his position to force sexual favours out of desperate young girls. For Ojinmah, 'Girls at War', like the collection as a whole, reflects the profound bitterness of a writer whose political and artistic aspirations had been radically undermined, but who remains committed and willing to confront society with the ills it must address, even in the most difficult of circumstances.

Whilst Ojinmah's focus is on the social and political engagements of *Girls at War*, the critic Ode Ogede[51] offers a different approach. Ogede's aim is to draw out the aesthetic inventiveness and originality of the stories as works of short fiction. Whilst he does not claim that Achebe's skill with the short story matches up to the form's most celebrated practitioners, such as Edgar Allan Poe (1809–49) or Alex la Guma (1925–85), he sees the collection *Girls at War* as, in itself, a significant literary achievement. As Ogede argues, critics of Achebe's work have often neglected to pay sufficient attention to the stylistics of his short fiction and especially its debt to the Ibo oral tradition:

■ Oral tradition in this essay refers to the body of tales told both in the home by the fireside and in the wider community in African villages. Achebe heard these tales during his childhood. While he was growing up in the village of Ogidi in Eastern Nigeria in the 1930s, traditional storytelling flourished in the home as well as in the schools. As noted by Isidore Okpewho in his important book *African Oral Literature* [1992], though different storytellers have different performance styles, there are certain resources that all performers have in their repertoire. Among these are repetition, tonal variation, parallelism, piling and association, the direct address, ideophones, digression, imagery, hyperbole, allusion, and symbolism. In addition, traditional tales tend to conclude with an appended moral that often confirms the norms of the society in which they are performed. Of these resources, the direct address (which ensures interaction with the audience), digression, exaggeration, and didacticism are the features most prominently deployed by Achebe in his short stories.[52] □

In stories like 'The Madman', Ogede argues, Achebe deploys the same traditions of storytelling – based on traditional oral culture – that we see used in *Things Fall Apart*. The story revolves around the destruction of a middle-aged villager, Nwibe, when he decides to take a rejuvenating bath in the local stream. When a naked madman steals his loincloth, Nwibe chases him to a marketplace, where his own nudity and inexplicable antics convince onlookers that he himself is the lunatic. In this way, the story enacts the kind of ironic reversal, as well as the didactic ethos, that characterizes much of the Ibo storytelling tradition.

In stories like 'Chike's School Days', similar techniques are used, with a clear, declarative style further suggesting the oral aesthetic:

■ Chike's School Days' is especially remarkable for the economical, but effective, way in which it invokes the reversals of fortune brought about by colonialism. The story depends for its effect on the use of digression, rumour or hearsay, summary recapitulation, and authorial commentary, all of which are devices favoured in oral storytelling, as they lend liveliness and a sense of immediacy to the events depicted.[53] □

Across the collection as a whole, Ogede argues, traditional mores are stressed. Indeed, many of the stories focus specifically on the threat to such values posed by colonialism and the very different social attitudes associated with 'modernity'. 'The Voter', 'Vengeful Creditor' and 'Girls at War' are selected as particular examples. In these fictions, Ogede suggests, the reader is offered an unusual insight into the growing culture of political corruption, through the eyes of ordinary people:

■ Though not written in the language of the people, ['Girls at War''s] accessibility is bound to appeal to those ordinary Africans who have neither the leisure nor the skill to read elongated prose narratives. 'Vengeful Creditor' achieves several goals simultaneously: it exposes the ostentatious lifestyle of the elite and shows that it can be sustained only by corruption; it documents the failure of African governments' social policies; it explores the vested interests of powerful commercial concerns, revealing how they discourage genuine involvement; and it uncovers the hypocrisy of greedy political leaders, who take undue advantage of the masses.[54] □

Through their many perspectives, Ogede suggests, the stories of *Girls at War* engage the reader in a social and political conversation, establishing multiple thematic connections with his longer fiction. Through a multiplicity of different viewpoints, the problems and complexities of the larger social scene are brought into view. Set against his five novels, he suggests, these stories powerfully enrich Achebe's representation of colonization, war and their mutually devastating effects on society and its people.

If Achebe's first three novels have attracted a number of conflicting responses, this is equally true of his fourth. Perhaps because of the directness of its political engagements, *A Man of the People* has continued to excite fierce differences of opinion amongst critics. Whilst the collection *Girls at War* is sometimes overlooked in assessments of Achebe's writing, it too provides much food for thought, especially about the writer's changing perspective on the future and meaning of the Nigerian nation, and his developing commitment to exploring gender relations and the role of women. In Achebe's fifth novel *Anthills of the Savannah*, as we will see in chapter 6, both of these concerns are again pushed strongly to the fore.

CHAPTER SIX

Anthills of the Savannah (1987)

With *Anthills of the Savannah*, Achebe ended a 20-year gap in his career as a novelist, producing what many would judge to be his most subtle and sophisticated work of fiction. As I suggested in the discussion of *A Man of the People*, the events of the late 1960s, especially the Biafran war, seem to have led to profound changes in Achebe's conception of the writer's role and were certainly a step back from the optimistic cultural nationalism of the independence years. Speaking to Jane Wilkinson soon after the publication of *Anthills* in 1987,[1] Achebe distances himself from the earlier stance of novelist-as-teacher. In its place, the mode he seeks to establish in the new novel is a more tentative one of 'drawing out . . . helping the reader to discover . . . to explore'.[2]

If this represents a significant redefinition of his 'teacher' function, Achebe is also keen to recast the notion of 'commitment' so often associated with his writing. By the late 1980s, commitment seems to relate less to the political than to the personal and the aesthetic – a writer's willingness to hold firm to the truth of his vision, the authenticity of his language and to his own artistic integrity. Writers who allow themselves to be distracted from these core values are guilty of betraying not their country or their people's right to self-determination, but 'the nature of art'.[3] By contrast to the interviews and critical writings of the 1960s, there is a marked turn away from any kind of political orthodoxy:

■ This is why it is so difficult for me to accept legislation from some kinds of people who cannot see the world in its complexity: the

> fanatics of all kinds, of right or left, the fundamentalists of all kinds. . . .
> That is not what I had in mind. It is not what I mean by commitment:
> not commitment to a narrow definition of the world, to a narrow
> perception of reality. . . . The same goes for politics. What [writers]
> are committed to is bigger, something of infinitely greater value than
> what church you go to, what race you belong to, what language you
> speak.[4] □

As Achebe clearly acknowledges, an important reason for this
retrenchment from the political commitments associated with his
earlier writings is the experience of the civil war. In the composition
of the first four novels, that event was simply not part of the cultural
and historical complex that the author needed to assimilate. In the
wake of the deaths of three million of his fellow Easterners – even
after 20 years – it simply was not possible for him to write as if Biafra
had not happened, Achebe suggests. This is not to say that *Anthills
of the Savannah* can be regarded as simply 'inspired' by the civil war.
What does seem clear, however, is that the civil war did force Achebe
into a long rethink of his earlier positions, and ultimately into a new
mode of writing. *Anthills of the Savannah* took many false starts and
many rewritings before it was able to reach completion.

In an important way – as its title suggests – the novel concerns the
business of managing to survive in a difficult and inhospitable environment. During a drought in the savannah, Achebe explains, bush
fires typically consume all vegetation, so that the principal remaining
signs of life are the marks made by the few survivors: termites working the earth. When the grass grows again, the work of these small
creatures is dwarfed and obscured. Thus although the novel clearly
does deal with the political crisis of Nigeria (and other African states)
in the present day, it is also intended to resonate with small struggles
for survival that are, in a sense, timeless.

As well as showing a renewed concern with the earth and with survival, Achebe also attempts in this text to avoid presenting a monologic
view of Africa or Nigeria. Very deliberately, this is a novel of multiple
points of view:

> ■ It's like the masquerade I talked about in *Arrow of God* . . . you just
> have to keep circling the arena in order to catch the various glimpses
> which you need in order to approach anything like a complete image
> of its formidable presence. If you stand in one place, you see one

view, and it's not enough. That's what I try to do . . . to tell as complete a story as possible. And of course our situation itself is not standing still; it's adding to itself all the time – and subtracting from it![5] □

THREE POLITICAL READINGS

Recognizing this new breadth of vision in Achebe's text, Simon Gikandi[6] is an important example amongst critics who read *Anthills of the Savannah* as a sweeping meditation on the meaning and failure of nationhood. As Gikandi points out, the long period of the novel's gestation was one of repeated political turmoil, including a succession of military coups, the civil war itself and a series of corrupt dictatorships during the 1970s and 1980s. Whilst the novel's mood partly reflects this context, however, it also points towards an impulse of rejuvenation and renewal, particularly in its conclusion:

■ The way narrative recreates history and memory, and how this recreation gives meaning to moments of crisis and then transcends them to point out new vistas for the future, is a crucial theme in *Anthills*. In this novel, says Achebe, 'there is more of looking into the future, not just for women but for society generally; how, for example, we can use our past creatively'.[7] □

In each of his previous four novels, Achebe is centrally concerned with the evolution of social and national consciousness in the context of oppression and corruption. Whilst *Anthills of the Savannah* continues these themes, what sets it apart from the earlier texts, Gikandi argues, is that it expresses the perspective of a much later period, when the contours and character of the Nigerian nation have become well established. Thus, if *No Longer at Ease* or *A Man of the People* look back on the past in order to illuminate the troubles of Nigeria's emerging polity, *Anthills of the Savannah* looks back with a rather different gaze, asking what responsibilities Africans themselves might bear, and seeking to understand where the processes of nation-building went wrong:

■ For narrative to dramatize and provide imaginary answers and resolutions to such questions and problems, for narrative to map a terrain in which diverse groups of Africans can speak about their condition and its problematics, it must clearly go beyond what

> [Edward] Said [1935–2003] calls a politics and rhetoric of blame, to come to grips and hence rethink the process of decolonization as the condition that has established the postcolonial society Achebe deals with in *Anthills*.[8] □

Of the four protagonists, Ikem and Chris, in particular, continually meditate on the past, seeking to reinterpret it in the light of present circumstances, and to rethink the political and personal choices they have made.

For Gikandi, the influence of the theorist Frantz Fanon on Achebe's earlier novels – and the Fanonian insistence on narrative's role in imagining and articulating national liberation – cannot be underestimated. In *Anthills of the Savannah*, however, he sees Fanon's influence as dramatically reduced. Far from embodying the people's freedom from oppression, in this novel, the new nation has become the instrument of that oppression. As a result, the role of narrative and its relation to the nation must be radically rethought. For Gikandi, this meditation runs powerfully through Achebe's novel. Resisting the lure of quietism or relativism, he argues, the text shows a strong continuing commitment to the powers of narrative:

> ■ Achebe will not succumb to the postmodernist seduction which expresses its disappointment with the politics of liberation; he will not share the now common belief that narrative is 'no longer an adequate figure for plotting the human trajectory in society. . . . On the contrary, Achebe is seeking ways of establishing new forms of narration that might have the power to liberate us from the circle of our postcolonial moment; he seeks a narrative that speaks about, but also transcends its historical imperatives.[9] □

In a world where truth and ideology are difficult to disentangle, Gikandi suggests, the novel bespeaks a continuing commitment to narration – now in a much more democratic and polyvocal form – as a way of bringing new vision and insight to the nation and its problems.

In the opening sections of *Anthills of the Savannah*, we see a particular kind of historical excavation, as Chris tries to document the transition from a restorative to a repressive form of nationalism. In the course of the text, however, we are offered a diversity of attempts to articulate 'the contradictions that inform the nation'.[10]

The novel's three key narrators, Ikem, Chris and Beatrice, are all ideologues, Gikandi argues, but ideologues of quite different kinds. The testimony of each of them is grounded, firstly, in a claim of witness – each presenting itself as an authentic account of contemporary historical events. Secondly, each of them expresses a persuasive sense of the narrating 'I', claiming the reader's attention in a directly personal way. Thirdly, the richness of narration which characterizes each of their accounts represents an attempt to recreate, for the reader, a sense of relived, authentic experience. In the case of Chris's narrative, we are given a sense of distance and detachment. In Ikem's narrative, we are offered something far more personally and ideologically mediated, with a sense of *presentation* which sometimes verges on the spectacular or surreal. In Beatrice's narrative, Gikandi argues, Achebe frames a discourse that is essentially 'salvational'.[11]

The fact that Beatrice is Achebe's first fully developed female protagonist is, he suggests, especially significant in this regard. For much of the novel, her character is mediated through the perceptions and desires of the men that surround her. Towards its conclusion, however, it is Beatrice who is chosen to signal the possibility of rebirth. Unlike her male counterparts, Beatrice refuses a monologic account of the nation or its future. Instead, her narrative calls attention to its own disjunctures and unanswered questions. Beatrice's account is symbolically surrounded by discarded pages, suffused with doubt about her own right to narrate. In this sense, she begins from the recognition that the writing 'I' must itself be rethought, before the question of the collective or the national can be addressed:

■ The last chapter of the novel suggests that the new dispensation depends not only on a radical rethinking of the past but also a redesigning of the forms in which our cultures are represented. The naming of Elewa's new baby is a narrative (imaginary) resolution to the paradoxes and problems of 'an alienated history'; it is a symbolic gesture 'to appease an embittered history'. Significantly, history is not appeased by any return to a mythical tradition, but by a radical questioning of tradition itself; the new dispensation includes the license to name and rename differently, hence the boy's name given to Elewa's baby. Clearly, the narratives of our postcolonial future must reconceive all the doctrines which have fixed Africans in alienated histories. Such narratives are needed 'to ensure that Africa and the rest of the Black world step into the next century with dignity and a rekindled optimism'.[12] □

For Gikandi, then, *Anthills of the Savannah* can be read as an act of radical rethinking, especially on the level of politics. Not all critics are in agreement with this interpretation, however. According to Supriya Nair,[13] for example, the novel can ultimately be seen, for all Achebe's reservations and caveats, as a reasonably straightforward extension of the project of his earlier fiction:

■ Chinua Achebe has always insisted that an African writer cannot afford the luxury of ignoring social issues when so much remains to be done after independence. [His essays] proclaim the writer's functions of guidance and even leadership in his society. Achebe also disclaims the notion of individualist art since, by his definition, art is both functional and communal and therefore has to meet the needs and demands of the people.

Achebe's fiction has been equally insistent on a connection to his specific political situation. His novels, short stories, and poems have kept pace with the unfolding developments of Nigerian history. His latest novel, *Anthills of the Savannah,* which was published in 1987, is perhaps his most explicit comment on the place and function of literature in the modern Nigerian context. The novel includes various types of literature, ranging from autobiographical accounts and poems to communiqués, graffiti, folktales, lectures, and the cryptic sign-writing on buses. All these literary forms speak in different ways to the specific social predicament in Kangan (a fictional military state in Africa that closely resembles modern Nigeria).[14] □

For Nair, there is an especially close relationship between *A Man of the People* and *Anthills of the Savannah*. The former novel concludes with a military coup, whilst in the latter we see how the state is faring under its dictatorial new leadership. As in the earlier novels − and essays − there is a deep concern with the political function of literature, as well as with the role of intellectuals, who are striving to sustain themselves in the face of a profoundly anti–intellectual leadership.

Anthills of the Savannah, then, shows just how wrong the project of Nigerian (or African) democracy has gone, as the gap between the privileged classes and the ordinary populace yawns ever wider:

■ Their position as privileged members of a clique, looking out, as Odili puts it in *A Man of the People,* at the people who have been unable to come in from the rain, is reflected in the stand of the 'First Witness' in *Anthills,* Christopher Oriko, Commissioner for Information: 'pure, unadulterated disinterest'. This cynical and powerless perspective coming from a man who is in charge of national communication speaks for the disenfranchised populace of Kangan. The people's revolution anticipated in the celebrated coups both in Achebe's fiction and Nigerian history has quite unmistakably failed. This failure is reinforced in the novel by the President's refusal to meet the delegation from Abazon and hear their testimony. The story the elders from the northern province have come to tell about the drought in Abazon and their struggle to survive is apparently not important enough for His Excellency's ears. Even the Commissioner for Information does not get to hear it.[15] □

Against this backdrop, the position of Ikem in Achebe's narrative, as the only one to actually meet the people's delegation, as well as the only one to articulate public opposition to the regime, is crucial. At his public lecture, Nair argues, Ikem is positioned as a storyteller who is willing to turn the tables on his listeners, confronting them with an unfamiliar and radical new understanding of their own position. In his role as editor of the *National Gazette*, meanwhile, he is equally articulate in his silence over the issue of the drought in Abazon:

■ The condition of drought has been aggravated by the President's order to stop boring wells in this recalcitrant 'natural guerrilla country', in retaliation for the insult to his position: Abazon alone refuses to 'say yes' to the President-for-Life referendum and defeats His Excellency's bid for unlimited authority. The writer's relevance to the power struggle between the periphery and the centre is proved by the elder's acknowledgement that Ikem's silence on the issue had guided their suspicion of the referendum. Not having the approval of the editor, himself a native of Abazon, the villagers realize that Ikem's refusal to speak is a political act conveying his views silently in a state where all speech is carefully monitored.[16] □

After Ikem's death at the hands of the security forces, it is Chris who takes over the task of counter-narration, wielding the 'Voice of Rumour', the scourge of totalitarian regimes. As Nair argues, this resort – by the Commissioner for Information – to underground channels of communication in itself implies an ironic comment on the relationship between writers, government and the people. In each of these instances, she suggests, it is easy to see how *Anthills of the Savannah* seeks to sustain the notion of writing as a politically charged act. Such writing refuses to be held hostage either by power, or by an elitist, purely aesthetic concept of itself:

> ■ Given the urgency of the correct message and its delivery into the right hands, Achebe's continual emphasis on the writer's political stance gains significance. In military dictatorships and one-party states, the writer's separation from social realities and distance from his/her particular community would be a blessing to neocolonial hegemony. As seen in the case of Abazon, the writer can actually influence public opinion and check unlimited authority. The writer's refusal, then, to relate to current political issues in the interests of a 'universal' literature and a 'pure' art results in an aesthetically appealing but functionally sterile 'work', an alienated and useless piece of 'labour'. Achebe's choice is clearly in favour of an unabashedly functional literature, responsible to the writer's community and what he calls 'right and just causes', regardless of the interests of those in power.[17] □

In this context, Nair argues, the growing importance of Beatrice in *Anthills of the Savannah* signals a recognition by Achebe of the need for Africa to re-empower its women. In the novel, Beatrice is shown as tired of women's traditional role – that of picking up the pieces once the men's battles have been fought out. At the end of the novel, she has successfully repositioned herself 'at the head of the struggle'.[18] She rejects the collective arrogance of Sam, Chris and Ikem, who imagine that the nation's history is essentially the story of themselves alone. In building the character of Beatrice in this way, Nair suggests, Achebe once again draws on traditional cosmology, especially the daughter of the Sun, *Idemili*. In the Ibo myth, *Idemili's* role is to clothe the body of power, showing him control and respect for the moral responsibilities that come with authority. In her own narrative, similarly, it is Beatrice's role to point to a more ethical and grounded model of governance than the three male protagonists could grasp:

> ■ The 'return of utterance' to Beatrice is a triumph of the people's struggle, in spite of failed leadership and betrayed hopes. . . . Beatrice's own separation from the marketwomen and taxidrivers and her superior attitude to her maid Agatha are reworked through the crisis in her life caused by the deaths of both Chris and Ikem. Her isolated home becomes the refuge of Emmanuel the student leader, Braimoh the taxi driver, and Adamma, the nurse. This breakdown of class and

gender barriers and the potential for such an alliance is underlined by the naming ritual usually performed by men but which is now taken over by the women. Elewa's child is given a boy's name, Amaechina, 'may-the-path-never-close'. Amaechina's birth in a period of social unrest through a union between a middle-class male intellectual and an illiterate working class woman suggests the emergent bonding between classes and the unlimited possibilities that such a 'path' opens up. The toast at the end of the ritual is to 'People and Ideas'.[19] □

For Nair, then, what Achebe seeks to offer through the character of Beatrice is not only a different model of power but also a different model of community. In the new dialogue that must take place, writing will once again occupy a privileged position. Literature is identified as the medium that must mediate social and political questions between rulers and the ruled, pointing out injustice and empowering the people. The novelist resumes his role as teacher, 'not necessarily to lead the people in their confrontation with unjust power structures, but to point out the legitimacy of their cause and their capacity to triumph'.[20]

Complementing the two readings offered by Gikandi and Nair, Neil ten Kortenaar's essay '"Only connect": *Anthills of the Savannah* and Achebe's Trouble with Nigeria' (1993)[21] marks an interesting third way to read Achebe's text. Kortenaar's focus is on the interplay of identities in the novel – each cutting across the others – of village, ethnicity, nationhood and race. As he points out, Achebe's own identity position could be regarded as multiple and conflicted, associated as he is, in different ways, with his home village of Ogidi, with the traditions of the Ibo people, with early Nigerian nationalism and with the shaping of African culture as a whole. For Kortenaar, indeed, the long silence in Achebe's fiction-writing career between the early 1970s and the late 1980s can be directly ascribed to the tensions between these warring identity claims. In *Anthills of the Savannah*, he dramatizes the ongoing political debates over class, ethnicity, region and nation in Africa, trying to imagine the conditions under which these divisive demarcations might be swept away:

■ Christopher Miller has forcefully made the case for the centrality of ethnicity to an understanding of African literature. According to him, the nation-states into which Africa is divided can be dismissed as arbitrary divisions that were imposed by the colonizers and that have little impact on the identity of the colonized. Kwame Anthony Appiah shares Miller's opinion of Africa's nation-states: he argues that a second wave of African fiction has abandoned realism, as well as the nationalist legitimation associated with realism, because nation-states have been hopelessly compromised by the African bourgeoisie. Novelists now are Pan-African in their vision, he concludes, and they open their texts to the suffering of the continent. My essay assumes that the nation-state, the ethnic culture, and the continent are configured differently in the imagination and that Achebe's conflation of them is a utopian strategy.[22] □

In the narrative, Kortenaar suggests, Sam represents the principle of central, dictatorial rule, whilst the journalist Ikem argues for a more meaningful linkage between power and the people. In that sense, the novel begins by opposing two paradigms of national governance. At the same time, however, it also sets out two models of community. On the one hand, the state of Kangan is shown as a state in crisis, paralyzed by the paranoia of its leader. On the other hand, the idea of Abazon is offered as an alternative political possibility:

■ All that we readers ever see of drought-stricken Abazon are the six representatives who come to the capital to beg an audience with His Excellency, but we understand that their appearance is enough: when they speak, Abazon speaks. Information in the tribal model does not come from the top down; not does it travel from the bottom up to the leaders. Instead, the leadership embodies the will of its citizens. and information is always shared because it is never divided.

At times in *Anthills of the Savannah* Abazon expands to include all the hinterland outside the capital, and at times it contracts to become a mere village, like Umuofia in Achebe's *Things Fall Apart or* Umuaro in *Arrow of God*. The Abazonians have a legend of their origin. In flight from a terrible drought that occurred in the distant past, the Abazonians descended from the North and dispossessed those whom they found living in 'the tiny village of Ose'. Chris, when speaking of Abazon to the long-time Kangan resident, the Mad Medico, reminds him, as if he might have forgotten, 'you know the drought place'. Depending upon the context, Abazon is either one of four regions into which the country is divided or merely a remote village that someone might not have heard of. This contraction of the province into a village is explicable if one recalls the portrait of pre-colonization Igboland in *Things Fall Apart*: as depicted in that novel the community with which Igbos identified prior to colonization was not the ethnic group but the village or Clan. Abazon is a community in which everyone knows everyone else, if only potentially or as the son or wife of someone who is known. Abazon exists in the imagination of its members.[23]□

Through this schematic comparison between the failed state and the organic unity of Abazon, Kortenaar suggests, Achebe's text opens up an important debate about the proper nature of nationhood. In the novel, both Chris and Sam believe that a nation state can be constructed 'from the top down',[24] starting with an abstract model of power which is then implemented on the ground, as the dictatorial leaders of Mogul India might have done. For Ikem, on the other hand, such a project of nation–building is quickly recognized as redundant:

■ He now believes that the true nation-state is not built but rather grows from below, starting from the nation and not from the state. Ikem finds a nation-in-itself already in existence, not in Abazon, but in the community that includes his woman friend Elewa (the daughter of a market woman) and the taxi drivers that he meets on the street. He envies their 'artless integrity, a stubborn sense of community which can enable Elewa to establish so spontaneously with the driver a teasing affectionateness beyond the powers of Ikem'. Ikem's search is for a way in which he too can 'partake of this source of stability and social meaning'.[25] □

Through the novel's action, both Chris and Ikem begin to understand the importance of the ordinary populace in the shaping of a better future. In Chris's case, this realization is most dramatically illustrated by means of his forced pilgrimage into the Abazonian hinterland, where his perspective finally evolves free from the capital's political machinations.

Nevertheless, Achebe is far from implying that the nation state *per se* must be swept away, Kortenaar argues. Instead, the novel suggests that the nation's philosophical foundations must be rebuilt out of a dialogue between modern literacy and education, on the one hand, and a shared sense of tradition and collective memory, on the other. On both sides of the equation, as before, the role of the writer is crucial. For Kortenaar, therefore, *Anthills of the Savannah* must be read as an expression of this desire: to imagine the conditions within which a new and redemptive national consciousness might be born:

■ At the end of the novel, a 'born-again' nation is ratified by the blood of two sacrifices: that of Ikem (a victim of Sam's political repression) and that of Chris (killed as he tries to prevent a rape). The two deaths bring together the friends of the slain, who come from different classes and speak different African languages. The two men's sacrifices are then commemorated in communion rites that involve the breaking and sharing of a kolanut. Hope literally assumes the form of a new birth, for the occasion of the gathering is the christening of Ikem's posthumous daughter, in whom the blood of an intellectual and that of a market woman are mingled. Chris's death also creates a legacy that can be passed on. Emmanuel, the student leader who accompanies him on his journey, adopts Chris as a father. Emmanuel's own father had died disgracefully, and Chris had taught him how one can die with dignity. Thus, consent and descent reinforce each other as the nation-to-be acquires a myth of origin that is based on blood in the dual sense of paternity and sacrifice.[26] □

As Kortenaar points out, Kangan is not quite Nigeria, just as Abazon is not quite Iboland (it is located in the northwest, rather than the southeast and its savannah landscape also recalls that of Nigeria's northern provinces). Nevertheless, he argues, *Anthills of the Savannah* can certainly be read as a fictional treatment of Nigeria's history during the 1970s and 1980s. However, it can also be read as a wider commentary on the redundancy – and need for renewal – of a number of African nation states in the postcolonial period. The text does not offer a complete 'solution' to Nigeria's woes or those of her neighbours. It does not present us with anything like a finished vision of the nations that they might become. What it does do, Kortenaar argues, is to say 'Here's what a solution would look like if one could be imagined'.[27]

ANTHILLS OF THE SAVANNAH AND GENDER

As the novel in Achebe's oeuvre which deals most extensively with issues of gender, *Anthills of the Savannah* is also the text which has attracted most concentrated attention from feminist scholars. This section examines three contrasting readings of the novel which focus in different ways on its handling of gender, especially in relation to class and nation.

Perhaps the most provocative feminist treatment of Achebe's fifth novel is provided by Ifi Amadiume in her essay 'Class and Gender in *Anthills of the Savannah*: A Critique' (1990).[28] For Amadiume, early critical readings of *Anthills* were, in general, either so concerned to congratulate the 'master storyteller' or else so steeped in their old quarrels with him, that they were unable to look at the novel with any objectivity. The aim of her own piece is to remedy this, as well as to bring particular attention to Achebe's socialist and feminist 'commitment'.

As Amadiume argues, Achebe's critical writings and interviews in the 1980s make clear that he embarked on the fifth novel with a commitment to exploring the ambivalent attitude to women in African writing. In the novel itself, correspondingly, she finds a host of negative representations of masculinity, from the petty dictator Sam to the 'boot-licking and crawling' intellectuals who surround him. In its opening chapters particularly, she argues, Achebe ruthlessly exposes the inadequacies of such men. Here, the novel exposes the paranoia and impotency of the entire male establishment, which with all its military muscle remains fearful of the unarmed populace. Despite these early appearances, Amadiume argues however, the novel as a whole remains far from convincing, either as a revolutionary or as a feminist text:

■ If this was going to be a book about 'the people' or giving women power, we would have expected to encounter the main characters in their capacities as leaders or representatives of these interest groups. It does not take long before we find out that the book is not about 'the people', but the elite classes and their individualism. Opposition to the corrupt President comes from two intellectual elites in the persons of the main characters Chris Oriko and Ikem Oshodi, poet and editor of the *National Gazette.* The important political dialogues and debates are between these two individualistic men.

As for the author's commitment to feminism, we find that the story has already taken shape before the female characters are introduced. The females in fact come in as 'subordinates' or in 'service relationship' to the men. We meet a first female in chapter 3. She is secretary to a main character, Ikem. Then we meet Ikem's girlfriend, Elewa. She is not very schooled but ordinary, solid and sensible.[29] □

With both Beatrice and Elewa, Amadiume argues, Achebe presents us with female characters whose primary role is to service men. On the level of class, meanwhile, Elewa is the only major figure in the text who is not a member of the elite. Her 'shop girl' simplicity is presented as refreshing. However, Amadiume is fair to ask 'why

Achebe did not cast her as the main female character, since she has amazing potentials for linkage with the grassroots, which Achebe's favourite female, Beatrice, does not have'.[30] Although Achebe does have Elewa raising questions about the subordinate role of women, she is also presented as ignorant and uncomprehending of the business of the intellectual elite. Here Amadiume diagnoses an interesting ambivalence on the author's part, on levels of both class and gender, which somewhat undermines his socialist and feminist credentials.

With Beatrice, we are offered a woman who is the intellectual equal of her male companions. She too, however, is featured more in sections on sexual and relationship matters than in passages which deal with questions of history or politics. At the President's party, it is her sexuality that Beatrice must use to defend national pride against the threat posed by Lou, his American companion. Once again, Achebe's novel seems to promise more in terms of feminist analysis than it actually carries through:

■ Because Beatrice is a so-called 'strong' woman, she acquires an undeserved reputation as using 'bottom-power', as being ambitious. She is even called 'the latter-day Madame Pompadour'.
   It is significant that there is no disguise in Beatrice's origin. She is Igbo like Achebe himself: Through her, Achebe states his own position on the woman question. Criticizing Ikem's lack of clear role for women in his political thought, Beatrice says, 'But the way I see it is that giving women today the same role which traditional society gave them of intervening only when everything else has failed is not enough . . . It is not enough that women should be the court of last resort because that last resort is a damn sight too far and too late'. This is exactly what Achebe has had women do in this novel – pick up the pieces after the three green bottles get shattered.[31]□

As soon as the male protagonists, Chris and Ikem, begin to discourse on matters of national importance, Beatrice seems to fall silent, Amadiume observes. Achebe must be given his due for at least attempting to approach issues of sexuality, which have often been taboo in African writing. In the passages where sex is described in detail, however, the only sexual feelings described are those of men. He does include two women amongst his cast of key characters, but the main drivers of suspense in the narrative remain the careers and ultimate ruin of the men. The relationships between the three male protagonists are developed in considerable detail, whilst Beatrice does not even know Elewa well enough to know where she lives. Only in relation to the deaths of their partners, Chris and Ikem, are the women propelled into a more supportive union.

More importantly, for Amadiume, the overall framework of the novel is, despite Achebe's pronouncements, decisively organized around the male:

■ Achebe's paradigm is masculine. The skeleton of the story is power relations between men. Even when introducing the concept of divinity in chapter 8, which he titles 'Daughters, Idemili', he makes God a 'he' and a 'man'. I do not know any direct translation from Igbo which would render God a 'he' and a 'man'. Achebe subordinates the all powerful divine goddess Idemili to this he-God by making her his daughter. Again, I do not find any cultural prescription for this subordination. I know that she is usually given a husband, but not a father.

Achebe yet again assumes that the first Power was male, hence he writes, 'wrapping around Power's rude waist a loincloth of peace and modesty'. Only men ever wore loincloth. There is also a contradictory use of the royal python as sexual in the incident of the President's encounter with Beatrice, where the python conjures up the image of erection. Yet, the royal python is a sacred symbol of the goddess Idemili as Achebe writes on page 105 [edition not specified]. It is the messenger of the goddess.[32] □

Only at the end of the novel does our focus move significantly outside the orbit of the elite, as Chris begins to recognize both the oppression and the resourcefulness of the common people. In its conclusion, Amadiume argues, *Anthills of the Savannah* does seem to offer a prescription for radical change – based on a union between intellectuals, women, youth and the grass roots. However, as she suggests, this prescription never amounts to more than an imagined ideal: 'at no point in the book does Achebe deal with the material basis for that social transformation'.[33] If the novelist wants to continue as teacher, addressing gender and class with any degree of seriousness, she argues, he himself first needs to take a few lessons.

By no means have all feminist critics concurred with Amadiume's evaluation of *Anthills of the Savannah*, however. Indeed, for Rose Acholonu,[34] Achebe's achievement in the novel, including its handling of gender, deserves a much more positive assessment. All of

Achebe's fiction, Acholonu argues, is concerned with the evolution of a redemptive vision of Africa, and *Anthills* represents a further development of his thinking in this respect. In the early novels, the author's representation of women's roles is quite limited, accurately reflecting the gender inequality of Ibo and Nigerian society in earlier eras. In *A Man of the People*, the move towards creating women characters of strength and intelligence had begun with Eunice. In *Anthills of the Savannah*, the representation of women has developed much further:

■ In both Elewa, the illiterate but 'solid sensible' woman and the intellectually oriented Beatrice, we get divergent but highly complementary facets of the ideal modern women. These women, rather than being presented as mere on-lookers or outsiders in the vital incidents and happenings in their world, are depicted as being at the very centre of the drama, always ready to please, advise, support and initiate actions.

   In this novel, while the women are presented as individuals whose solidarity directly results in their success, in contrast, the men emerge as self-conceited, individualistic eccentrics, whose inability to work out a compromise and accommodate one another's views yields failure. By means of vivid characterization, and a complex web of narrative techniques, Achebe contrasts the female world of solidarity and practical commonsense, with the masculine one remarkable for the men's deadly jealousy, self-conceit, betrayal, absolute lack of mutual trust, and insensitivity.[35] □

Amidst the stew of corruption, apathy, oppression and discontent depicted by the novel, Acholonu argues, Beatrice seems to embody the opposite qualities – those of nobility, dignity and clear-sighted intelligence. Almost immediately, Beatrice is able to mediate between the male protagonists, each of whom inhabits a much more closed mental world. The 'strength' so valued by each of the men is also shown as brittleness, arising directly from social isolation and conceit. Beatrice, however, counterbalances these traits:

■ Beatrice is humanism personified. Apart from her heroic efforts to reform the men – Chris and Ikem – she also proves by her own life-style the positiveness of the human qualities of understanding, tolerance and forbearance. Her easy accommodation of both the highly placed as well as the less fortunate members of her society (housemaid, chauffeurs, taxi-driver; illiterate shop assistant, in the person of Elewa), bears eloquent testimony to her nobility of heart and solid humanistic personality. Through authorial commentary, we get a better insight into the philosophy that guides our heroine. Thus, we see her forbearing attitude towards her maid Agatha, the fanatical 'born again':

> Who was so free with leaflets dripping with the saving blood of Jesus, and yet had no single drop of charity in her own anaemic blood.

Yet, Beatrice realizes the fact that

> being a servant could not be fun. Beatrice knew that she had never belittled the problem or consciously looked down on anyone because she was a servant . . . For she was sensitive enough and intelligent enough to understand.

She understands the role of 'blind luck' in the determination of one's social status in society, where man's struggle for survival is a mere gamble in absurdity.
     However, Beatrice's character as portrayed in the story emphasizes her sterling human qualities and potentials as a capable, lovable, and loving friend, counsellor, master planner and executor.[36] □

Beatrice is then, in Acholonu's reading, a paragon of positive qualities, and Elewa too is characterized in an unabashedly positive light. Although she is an illiterate shop worker, she still possesses a broad and incisive vision, particularly on the universality of women's subordination, as well as on women's own complicity in sustaining it. Like Beatrice, Acholonu argues, she takes advantage of all opportunities to improve the lot of women in general:

> ■ If Beatrice is tough and strong, Elewa is even tougher. Generally, the men are no match for the women in terms of positive thinking or even moral courage: Chris 'was trembling' and had to be driven by Beatrice when the news of Ikem's abduction was received. In the dramatic scene where Beatrice and Elewa were confronted by the military men hunting for Ikem, we watch the two friends in action;

> She (Beatrice) took the bunch of keys from the sideboard and began to unchain the iron grills. Her hands were shaking so violently she couldn't get the key into the keyhole. Elewa snatched the bunch from her, turned the padlock and unchained the heavy grill. Beatrice

shocked into calmness by this action snatched back the keys [Heinemann 1988 edn, p. 176].

At the climatic [*sic*] moment of the story, with Ikem dead and Chris in hiding, the three women – Beatrice, Elewa and Agatha – are able to strike an accord, which provides them the needed solace and feeling of emotional security.[37] □

In the novel as a whole, Acholonu argues, we see unambiguous evidence of positive development in Achebe's representations of women. From the role of outsider they often occupy in the earlier works, they have moved in *Anthills of the Savannah*, if not to the centre of power, then at least to a position of narrative centrality.

For the critic Elleke Boehmer,[38] *Anthills of the Savannah* represents an undoubted development from Achebe's novels of the 1960s. This text is, she argues, at once less compromising than his previous works and at the same time more finely attuned to the complexities of gender and class. If *A Man of the People* ended with power's attempt to redeem itself – in the form of the military coup – we can expect no such 'miracle' in the later text. The book is a call for new ideas, she argues, not only from the elite, but also from those previously excluded, including the urban working class and, crucially, women:

■ In creating a 'populist inclusiveness', Achebe may to some extent be suspected of deliberate design. This impression is reinforced by the rather determined development of the novel's two main heroes: Ikem Osodi, the poet-journalist, comes to realise the importance of establishing 'vital inner links with the poor and dispossessed . . . the bruised heart that throbs painfully at the core of the nation's being', and Chris Oriko, carrying Ikem's light, forges contacts outside his elite group. The charge of deliberateness, however, should not disparage what is Achebe's obvious commitment to imagining a reformed national politics. Expressing at once mature disillusionment and heavily-qualified fresh hope, his tentative new vision is manifested in the strategic gender configurations of his central characters.[39] □

At the beginning of the novel, we witness the machinations of a male elite. At its ending, we are offered a sisterly celebration, as a newborn baby is named. This transition is crucial, Boehmer suggests, inasmuch as it signals a 'new conception of rulership'[40] in the novel and possibly, a new future for the nation.

In *The Trouble with Nigeria* (1983), Achebe complains bitterly of the selfishness and indifference of the powerful, who are responsible – by example and by influence – for a general malaise in national life. As Boehmer points out, the author's conception of power here very clearly implies a 'top-down' analysis, in which leaders stand as 'role-models' for the nation, defining its ethical standards as well as administering its affairs. In *Anthills of the Savannah*, she argues, this analysis is again implicit: even after the demise of the male triumvirate of Ikem, Chris and Sam, 'a highly exclusive elite "we" will still remain in place and in force',[41] that of Beatrice and her tiny new alliance. For Boehmer, this reformulation of an already familiar structure leaves important questions unanswered, even whilst it speaks of greater (gender) inclusiveness:

■ The group that coheres around Beatrice is to be the catalyst of the future, or, as Achebe has remarked *a propos* of the novel: 'the ultimate responsibility for getting us out of this bad patch is with the small group of people who, in one way or another, find themselves in positions of leadership'. In this small group, the tendencies to nepotism and corruption which have compromised elite rulers in the past, will presumably be mitigated by the advent of women's salubrious force. Yet their anticipated beneficent influence does not eliminate other significant paradoxes. If woman is to be included in the new elite because she is uncorrupted by power, once included, how is she to retain that force for good? And again, if the faith in an alternative female rule depends on the stereotypical image of woman as inspirer and spiritual guide, does that idea, whether as stereotype or as ideal, have much hope of practical application?[42] □

For Boehmer, the paradox here, which runs to the heart of Achebe's novel, stems from a fundamental contradiction between two equally powerful tendencies in the author's work: cynicism or pessimism, on the one hand, versus a redemptive or even revolutionary impulse, on the other. In important ways, this contradiction is made manifest by the structure of the novel itself, especially through the central antagonism between Chris and Ikem.

The compromise solution to this contradiction which *Anthills of the Savannah* embodies, Boehmer argues, lies in its presentation of an altered model of leadership – one which still relies on the presence of a ruling elite, but which endows that elite with an enlightenment based on deep and broad contact with the ordinary people. As she suggests nevertheless, from a theoretical and political point of view, this too is far from unproblematic:

■ A question which remains unanswered . . . however, is how the broadened, non-sectional elite is to maintain its structural integrity, as well as its identity as elite, following the broadening process. Then, too, it seems unlikely that this process is always to be as conveniently *ad hoc* as is the formation of the group around Beatrice. How to avoid the appearance of tokenism? Where are likely elite candidates – women, 'people' – to be found? How might an exclusive Idemili cult be adopted by the mass? At this point, where questions of political identification and structuration arise, Achebe as it were purposively intervenes in his narrative, transposing such difficulties into the medium of the imaginary rather than trying for some sort of practical resolution. Just as story transmits the visions of the past into the future, so *Anthills,* the African story as novel, carries its own vision of the future in appropriately figural terms. Achebe's 'transposition' is in a number of ways, quite clearly, an avoidance technique, literally, a displacement of the problem.[43] □

According to Boehmer, Beatrice's symbolic elevation to the role of goddess at the end of *Anthills of the Savannah* can be seen, in itself, as an important moment in the literary representation of women in the African novel. However, the novel's overall commentary on issues of gender contains too many echoes of traditional assumptions to be thought of as a major step forward, from a feminist point of view. Women, especially those who lack 'book', continue to exert influence principally through sex, whilst men wield power through intellect and/or force of personality. Beatrice's promotion to the role of earth mother – whilst definitely an upgrade on the role of secretary – does not radically depart from existing categories of gender representation.

The novel does spare an eye for the interlocking, oppressive structures of class and gender, Boehmer concedes, for example, through such characters as Beatrice's house girl Agatha. Although it proposes no really fully developed, practical solutions to the problems of inequality it raises, moreover, the novel must at least be credited with its attempt to address questions of social justice and collective self-determination on a symbolic level. Through Achebe's act of narrative imagining, *Anthills of the Savannah* does, at a minimum, point a way forward and upward, out of the bleak landscape of the contemporary:

> ■ So, just as a relatively ordinary woman may become, through her spiritual understanding, an example or 'shining path' to her companions, in the same way an ordinary stick in the sand is transformed through ritual into a pillar of Idemili, the connection with 'earth and earth's people'. The real functions as index to the beautiful. In this way, too, a random collection of individuals can come to represent the ritual passage into the future of another Kangan. In 'serious' politics, symbols and supernatural signs such as these might seem superficial and, certainly from a gender point of view, compromising. Yet, where other options and modes of recompense are unsteady or have failed, symbols stand for points of intersection with, as Achebe would have it, the very present divine: as introjections of spirit, 'transactions' between the marketplace and goddesses.[44] □

As the critics discussed in this chapter illustrate in different ways, *Anthills of the Savannah* reads as the text of a changed, perhaps more ambivalent Achebe. Without a doubt, the author's fifth novel retains the sense of political responsibility that we see in his earlier work. A quarter of a century after independence, however, it is unsurprising to see that his sense of colonialism's legacy, as well as the nature of his commitment to Nigerian national development, have changed very significantly. In *Anthills of the Savannah*, as we have seen, Achebe invests considerable importance in gender as an axis of positive political change. As with other aspects of his work, the novel's strategy in this regard still excites considerable differences of opinion. What *Anthills of the Savannah* does undeniably communicate, however, is the powerful sense of intellectual engagement and ethical seriousness, fused with stylistic flair and imaginative boldness, which characterizes all of Achebe's writing from the 1950s onwards. It is this unusual combination of qualities, arguably, that has sustained critical interest in his work so strongly for the past half-century. If his fictions still continue to be the subject of painstaking scrutiny and heated debate in the twenty-first century, then this is because they continue to deserve, and reward, such attention.

CONCLUSION

During the twentieth century, the novel was taken in radical new directions, partly under the influence of African authors working through the turbulent circumstances of colonialism and independence. In the early years of the century, writers like Thomas Mofolo (1876–1948) were experimenting with prose fiction in vernacular languages: a translated and expurgated edition of his novel *Chaka* (about 1909) was published in English in 1925.[1] Slightly later, Nigerian writers such as Abubakar Tafawa Balewa were producing novellas in Hausa.[2] Encouraged by British Council sponsorship, short fiction by Nigerians working in English started to be published from the late 1940s.[3] By midcentury, a market for locally published, pamphlet novels had begun to thrive in centres like Onitsha. Growing up only a few miles away in Ogidi, Chinua Achebe would have been well aware of Onitsha's developing literary culture. Ten years before his own emergence, authors like Cyprian Ekwensi already enjoyed a significant following in South-Eastern Nigeria. As the literary historian Emmanuel Obiechina says in his study *An African Popular Literature: A Study of Onitsha Market Pamphlets* (1973):

■ These pamphlets were instantly popular. They were widely read and discussed, especially among young grammar school boys and girls. Other pamphlets soon joined them, and other pamphlet authors quickly appeared. The production of pamphlet literature soon involved a swarm of people in the different functions of publications: authors, promoters, publishers, printers, distributors. Pamphlet publishing became a booming industry, so that, by the early 1960s, any active collector swooping down on Onitsha Market might be rewarded with as many as two hundred different titles. The printing of the pamphlets was later to spread from Onitsha to Aba, Port Harcourt, Enugu and the other towns of eastern Nigeria, and even beyond.[4] □

The development of pamphlet novels in Nigeria was accompanied by concerted efforts at more self-consciously 'literary' fiction: in 1952, Amos Tutuola's *The Palm-Wine Drinkard* was the first novel to win significant international acclaim.

When Achebe published *Things Fall Apart* in 1958, he was, then, by no means the first African or Nigerian writer to turn his hand to the novel. For at least two decades, home-grown literary talent had been strongly encouraged by authorities ranging from the nationalist leader (later President) Nnamdi Azikiwe to the London based United Society for Christian Literature. At the same time, as independence loomed, international publishers such as Heinemann were keen to defend their African markets by developing lists more appropriate to the changing political and educational circumstances of the continent. In the late 1950s, the time was ripe for a significant literary figure to emerge: *Things Fall Apart* could not have appeared at a better moment.

As the critic Simon Gikandi argues, the force and distinctiveness of Achebe's first novel and his subsequent writing must be ascribed to more than his unusual command of style and form, however. It must also be considered in terms of the way his work seems to capture the mood of change in this crucial turning point in Nigerian history. Using a literary form which, although increasingly popular, could still be seen as problematic for African writers – drenched as it was in the culture and values of imperial Europe – Achebe's fiction encouraged Nigerians to see how many taken-for-granted, negative representations of Africa and Africans might begin to be displaced, and a new spirit of self-scrutiny and self-determination installed in their place. According to Gikandi, Achebe's special importance in the development of African literature is exactly this: his recognition of the political as well as aesthetic potential of the novel, if confidently remoulded by African hands. In an interview with Kalu Ogbaa in 1980,[5] Achebe set out his own conception of fiction's role in comparable terms:

■ I mean, we don't have the social institutions that we had in the past in which the values of the community were transmitted. How do we transmit a national culture to Nigerians if not through works of imagination? This is something that our people have not paid attention to. We are talking about modernization, industrialization, and so on, but we do not realize that we cannot even industrialize unless we have tackled the mind, the imagination, and thus the attitude of people to themselves, to their society, to work, and so on. How do you do these things if you cannot get to their minds, to their imagination? So literature is not a luxury for us. It is a life and death affair because we are fashioning a new man.[6] □

As we have seen in this book, many of the early critical responses to Achebe's fiction, especially in Britain, tended to focus on its formal literary qualities, especially in relation to recognized Western influences such as W. B. Yeats and T. S. Eliot. Amongst Achebe's compatriots, meanwhile, critics initially tended to stress his achievements as a cultural archaeologist. In later years, as Achebe's global reputation became consolidated, a much wider range of responses began to appear. Feminist critics such as Ifi Amadiume, Linda Petersen and Florence Stratton challenged the author in interesting ways, questioning the authenticity of his portrayals of Ibo women and uncovering some of the masculinist assumptions that seemed to underlie his writing. Commentators like Herbert Ekwe-Ekwe, Neil Ten Kortenaar and Umelo Ojinmah helped to reveal, in different ways, the political complexity of Achebe's texts, and the sense of ambivalence that often seems to haunt them. Re-examining his historiographic methods, Richard Begam, Michael Valdez Moses and others illuminated the representational strategies of the novels in ways that had not previously been considered.

For a considerable period, including most of the 1970s and 1980s, Achebe remained one of a very small group of Nigerian writers to enjoy sustained critical attention. As Femi Osofisan points out in her essay 'Eagles in the Age of Unacknowledged Muse' (2004),[7] other writers in Nigeria faced major struggles in these years to secure any kind of publication:

■ After the corruption, profligacy and gross incompetence of our governments during the oil boom years of the 1970s, and the inevitable collapse of our economy that followed, the publishing industry, like most enterprises, virtually folded up.
The readership market shrank drastically, in the wake of growing poverty and mass unemployment. Books became rare on the bookshelves, and rarer still the bookstores which displayed them. The international publishers – and particularly Heinemann which had

founded the flourishing African Writers imprint and had so laudably promoted our writing – shut down or sold out their stock and fled back to Europe.

   The local publishers, never very adventurous in the first place or much interested in the area of general publishing, kept even more exclusively to the narrow but fairly lucrative market of educational books.[8] □

After their initial burst of enthusiasm for African fiction, as Wole Soyinka[9] confirms, international publishers became 'far more circumspect, more critical, more choosy',[10] with the result that most writers were limited to local, shoestring publication houses, with distribution at their own expense. In the 1980s, official government censorship in Nigeria, targeted at journalists but also sometimes at creative writers, was also a serious threat. As late as 1995, the poet and novelist Ken Saro-Wiwa (1941–95) was imprisoned and hanged by the Nigerian military government, in what the well-known critic Charles R. Larson (b. 1938) described as 'a travesty of justice, a mockery of human rights and a failure of international diplomacy'.[11] In this period, as Larson says in his book *The Ordeal of the African Writer* (2001), attempting to convince non-specialist publishers to embrace and support struggling African writers was also an uphill task.

   More recently, in the context of a comparatively liberalized public sphere in Nigeria and against the backdrop of a resurgent book market, these problems have receded significantly. Achebe's texts can now be studied alongside a wide range of his contemporaries, including 'third generation' writers such as Ben Okri (b. 1959) and Biyi Bandele-Thomas (b. 1967) who have taken up the baton of literary experimentation with vigour, pushing the African novel in directions not considered by their predecessors. According to the critic Stephanie Newell, 'With no formal alliances between them as West Africans and no literary journal or aesthetic "school" in the manner of the *negritude* poets, these authors have formed a surprisingly coherent *avant garde* which has taken many critics by surprise'.[12] For critics of Achebe's work, the emergence of such writers offers the opportunity to view his oeuvre in important new light. If Achebe's texts have, in the past, often been considered in terms of their revisionist, backward gaze, especially as expressions of historical loss, contemporary readers now also have the opportunity to consider them as building blocks in the development of a dynamic, continuing literary–intellectual tradition.

At the same time, as Thomas Hale argues in his essay 'Bursting at the Seams: New Dimensions for African Literature in the 21st Century' (2006),[13] the tendency of many teachers and critics of African literature to focus almost exclusively on the works of the 1960s and after – as if nothing of significance was written on the continent before that date – needs to be readdressed. The challenge for scholars interested in Achebe's writing, in this sense, is to consider his work not only in relation to European forebears like Joyce Cary and Joseph Conrad, but also in relation to earlier West African writings, including the popular fiction of the 1940s and 1950s and the important, older traditions of Hausa and Fulani writings in Arabic. As Hale reminds us, 'Africans have been writing all kinds of texts for 5,000 years'.[14] Our tendency to focus on Achebe as an 'inaugural' figure in West African writing inevitably obscures his complex relationships to the region's pre-existing literatures. Critical work which approaches Achebe's work in the light of a more richly developed understanding of West African literary traditions, both historical and current, can only deepen and extend our understanding of this strange and familiar, engaging and perplexing writer.

Notes

INTRODUCTION

1 Ezenwa-Ohaeto, *Chinua Achebe: A Biography* (Oxford: James Currey, 1997).
2 Ibid., p. 13.
3 Ibid., p. 56.
4 Idowu Omoyele, 'The Legacy of Chinua Achebe', *West Africa*, 16–29 March, 1998, pp. 346–8.
5 Ibid., p. 346.
6 Ibid.
7 Stephanie Newell, *West African Literatures* (Oxford: Oxford University Press, 2006).
8 Ibid., p. 98.
9 Ibid., p. 99.
10 Kirsten Holst Petersen, 'Working with Chinua Achebe: The African Writers Series; James Currey, Alan Hill and Keith Sambrook in conversation with Kirsten Holst Petersen', in *Chinua Achebe: A Celebration*, ed. Kirsten Holst Petersen and Anna Rutherford (Oxford: Heinemann Educational Books, 1991), p. 150, cited by Ezenwa-Ohaeto (1997), pp. 149–59.
11 Ibid., pp. 150–1.
12 Ibid., p. 152.

CHAPTER ONE

1 Ezenwa-Ohaeto, *Chinua Achebe: A Biography* (Oxford: James Currey, 1997).
2 Kirsten Holst Petersen, 'Working with Chinua Achebe: the African Writers Series; James Currey, Alan Hill and Keith Sambrook in conversation with Kirsten Holst Petersen', in *Chinua Achebe: A Celebration*, ed. Kirsten Holst Petersen and Anna Rutherford (Oxford: Heinemann Educational Books, 1991), p. 150, cited by Ezenwa-Ohaeto (1997), p. 65.
3 Ezenwa-Ohaeto (1997), p. 65.
4 *Times Literary Supplement*, 2938 (20 June 1958), p. 341.
5 Honor Tracy, 'New Novels', in *The Listener*, 59:1526 (26 June 1958), p. 1068.
6 Ibid.
7 G. D. Killam, *The Writings of Chinua Achebe* (London: Heinemann, 1977), p. 1. This study was first published in 1969 as *The Novels of Chinua Achebe*. References here are to the revised 1977 edition.
8 Ibid., p. 10.
9 Ibid., p. 11.
10 Ibid., p. 2.
11 Ibid., p. 15.
12 Ibid., pp. 16–17.
13 Ibid., pp. 19–20.
14 Ibid., p. 29.
15 Ibid., p. 32.

16 Eustace Palmer, *An Introduction to the African Novel* (London: Heinemann, 1972).
17 Ibid., pp. 51–2.
18 Ibid., p. 53.
19 Ibid., p. 57.
20 Ibid., p. 60.
21 Ibid., p. 61.
22 A. G. Stock, 'Yeats and Achebe', in *Journal of Commonwealth Literature*, 5 (1968), pp. 105–11.
23 Ibid., pp. 105–6.
24 Ibid., p. 106.
25 Ibid., p. 107.
26 Ibid., p. 110.
27 Oladele Taiwo, *Culture and the Nigerian Novel* (New York: St. Martins Press, 1976).
28 Ibid., xiii.
29 Ibid., iii.
30 Ibid., p. 114.
31 Ibid., p. 124.
32 Nahem Yousaf, *Chinua Achebe* (Tavistock: Northcote House, 2003).
33 Chinua Achebe, 'An Image of Africa: Racism in Conrad's *Heart of Darkness*', *Massachusetts Review*, 18:4 (Winter 1977), reprinted in revised form in *Hopes and Impediments: Selected Essays* (New York: Anchor, 1990), pp. 1–20.
34 Yousaf (2003), pp. 18–19.
35 Ibid., pp. 27–9.
36 C. L. Innes, *Chinua Achebe* (Cambridge: Cambridge University Press, 1990).
37 Ibid., p. 22.
38 Ibid.
39 Ibid., p. 23.
40 Ibid.
41 Ibid., pp. 24–5.
42 Ibid., p. 29.
43 Ibid., p. 41.
44 Chinua Achebe, 'English and the African Writer', *Transition*, 4:18 (1965), pp. 27–30.
45 Ibid., p. 27.
46 Ibid., p. 28.
47 Ibid.
48 Ibid., p. 29.
49 Ibid.
50 Ngũgĩ wa Thiong'o, 'The Language of African Literature', in *Decolonising the Mind: The Politics of Language in African Literature* (London: James Currey, 1986), pp. 4–5.
51 Ibid., pp. 6–7.
52 Ibid., p. 9.
53 Ibid., p. 20.
54 Gareth Griffiths, 'Language and Action in the Novels of Chinua Achebe', in *African Literature Today*, 5 (1971), pp. 88–105.
55 Ibid., pp. 88–9.
56 Ibid., pp. 89–90.
57 Ibid., p. 90.
58 Ibid., pp. 91–2.
59 James Snead, 'European Pedigrees/African Contagions: Nationality, Narrative and Communality in Tutuola, Achebe and Reed', in *Nation and Narration*, ed. Homi Bhabha (London: Routledge, 1990), pp. 231–49.
60 Ibid., pp. 241–2.

61 Ode Ogede, *Achebe and the Politics of Representation* (Trenton, NJ: Africa World Press, 2001).

62 Rhonda Cobham, 'Making Men and History: Achebe and the Politics of Revisionism', in *Approaches to Teaching Achebe's Things Fall Apart*, ed. Bernth Lindfors (New York: MLA, 1991), pp. 91–100.

63 Ibid., p. 93.

64 Ibid., p. 94.

65 Ibid.

66 Ibid., p. 95.

67 Ibid., p. 96.

68 Ibid., p. 97.

69 Kirsten Holst Petersen, 'First Things First: Problems of a Feminist Approach to African Literature', *Kunapipi*, 6:3 (1984), pp. 35–47.

70 Ibid., pp. 37–8.

71 Florence Stratton, *Contemporary African Literature and the Politics of Gender* (London: Routledge, 1994).

72 Ibid., p. 25.

73 Ibid., pp. 27–8.

74 Ibid., pp. 34–5.

75 In the 1990 collection *Hopes and Impediments* (cited above) the phrase 'a bloody racist' in Achebe's original essay is amended to the more ameliatory 'a thoroughgoing racist'.

CHAPTER TWO

1 Robert Wren, *Achebe's World: The Historical and Cultural Context of the Novels* (Washington DC: Three Continents, 1980).

2 Ibid., pp. 26–7.

3 Ibid., p. 27.

4 Ibid., pp. 28–9.

5 Raisa Simola, *World Views in Chinua Achebe's Works* (Frankfurt am Main: Peter Lang, 1995).

6 Ibid., p. 25.

7 Ibid., pp. 25–6.

8 Ibid., p. 28.

9 Ibid., p. 29.

10 Ibid., p. 43.

11 Ibid., p. 47.

12 Ibid., p. 47.

13 Herbert Ekwe-Ekwe, *African Literature in Defence of History: An Essay on Chinua Achebe* (Dakar, Senegal: African Renaissance, 2001).

14 Ibid., p. 76.

15 Ibid., p. 77.

16 Ibid., p. 78.

17 Ibid., p. 79.

18 Ibid., pp. 80–1.

19 Ibid., p. 82.

20 Ibid., p. 91.

21 Ibid., p. 105.

22 Ibid., p. 107.

23 Neil Ten Kortenaar, 'How the Centre is Made to Hold in *Things Fall Apart*,' in *Postcolonial Literatures: Achebe, Ngũgĩ, Desai, Walcott*, ed. Michael Parker and Roger Starkey (Basingstoke: Macmillan, 1995), pp. 319–36.

24 Ibid., pp. 31–2.

25 Ibid., pp. 33–4.
26 Ibid., p. 35.
27 Ibid., p. 37.
28 Ibid., pp. 43–4.
29 Richard Begam, 'Achebe's Sense of an Ending: History and Tragedy in *Things Fall Apart*', *Studies in the Novel*, 29:3 (Fall 1997), pp. 396–411.
30 Ibid., pp. 396–7.
31 Ibid., p. 398.
32 Ibid., p. 398.
33 Ibid., p. 401.
34 Chinua Achebe, *No Longer at Ease* (London: Heinemann, 1962), p. 39.
35 Begam (1997), pp. 405.
36 Ezenwa-Ohaeto (1997), p. 68, quoting Alan Hill, *In Pursuit of Publishing* (London: John Murray, 1988), p. 121.
37 Ibid., p. 84.
38 Ibid., p. 148.
39 Chinua Achebe, 'The Novelist as Teacher', in *Hopes and Impediments: Selected Essays* (New York: Anchor, 1990), pp. 40–6.
40 Ibid., pp. 40–1.
41 Ibid., p. 44.
42 Chinua Achebe, 'The Writer and His Community', in *Hopes and Impediments: Selected Essays* (New York: Anchor, 1990), pp. 47–61.
43 Ode Ogede, *Achebe and the Politics of Representation* (Trenton, NJ: Africa World Press, 2001).
44 Ibid., p. 1.
45 Ibid., ix.
46 Ibid., p. 3.
47 Ibid., pp. 3–4.
48 Ibid., p. 7.
49 Ibid., pp. 4–6.
50 Romanus Okey Muoneke, *Art, Rebellion and Redemption: A Reading of the Novels of Chinua Achebe* (New York: Peter Lang, 1994).
51 Ibid., pp. 60–1.
52 Ibid., pp. 63–4.
53 Ibid., p. 68.
54 Ibid., p. 69.

CHAPTER THREE

1 Ezenwa-Ohaeto, *Chinua Achebe: A Biography* (Oxford: James Currey, 1997), p. 86.
2 Arthur Ravenscroft, *Chinua Achebe* (Harlow: Longman, 1977).
3 Ibid., p. 17.
4 Ibid., p. 18.
5 Ibid.
6 Ibid., pp. 18–19.
7 Ibid., p. 18.
8 Ibid., pp. 19–20.
9 Ibid., p. 23.
10 Carroll's study *Chinua Achebe* was first published in 1970. References made in this chapter will be to the revised and expanded edition, David Carroll, *Chinua Achebe: Novelist, Poet, Critic* (Basingstoke: Macmillan, 1990).

11 Ibid., p. 65.
12 Ibid., p. 68.
13 Ibid.
14 Ibid., pp. 80–1.
15 Ibid., pp. 83–4.
16 Ibid., p. 85.
17 Philip Rogers, 'No Longer at Ease: Chinua Achebe's 'Heart of Whiteness'', Research in African Literatures, 14:2 (1983), pp. 165–83.
18 Ibid., pp. 165–6.
19 Ibid., p. 166.
20 Ibid.
21 Ibid., pp. 168–9.
22 Ibid., pp. 169–70.
23 Ibid., p. 171.
24 Ibid., p. 172.
25 Ibid., p. 173.
26 Ibid., p. 177.
27 Ibid.
28 Arnd Witte, 'Things Fall Apart: The Portrayal of African Identity in Joyce Cary's Mister Johnson and Chinua Achebe's No Longer at Ease', in Exiles and Migrants: Crossing Thresholds in European Culture and Society, ed. Anthony Coulson (Brighton: Sussex Academic Press, 1997), pp. 125–35.
29 Ibid., p. 126.
30 Ibid.
31 Ibid., p. 127.
32 Ibid.
33 Ibid., p. 130.
34 Ibid., pp. 131–2.
35 Umelo Ojinmah, Chinua Achebe: New Perspectives (Ibadan: Spectrum, 1991).
36 Ibid., p. 37.
37 Ibid., p. 38.
38 Michael Valdez Moses, The Novel and the Globalization of Culture (New York: Oxford University Press, 1995).
39 Ibid., pp. 134–5.
40 Ibid., p. 135.
41 Ibid., p. 136.
42 Ibid., pp. 136–7.
43 Ibid., p. 138.
44 Ibid., p. 141.
45 Ibid., p. 142.
46 Simon Gikandi, Reading Chinua Achebe: Language & Ideology in Fiction (Oxford: James Currey, 1991).
47 Ibid., p. 79.
48 Ibid., p. 80.
49 Ibid.
50 Ibid., p. 89.
51 Ibid., p. 91.
52 Ibid., p. 92.
53 Ibid.
54 Ibid., p. 100.

CHAPTER FOUR

1 Chinua Achebe, 'Chinua Achebe on *Arrow of God*: Conversation with Michael Fabre', in *Conversations with Chinua Achebe*, ed. Bernth Lindfors (Jackson: University of Mississippi Press, 1997), pp. 45–51.
2 Ibid., p. 45.
3 Ibid., p. 46.
4 Ibid., pp. 50–1.
5 Robert Wren, *Achebe's World: The Historical and Cultural Context of the Novels* (Washington DC: Three Continents, 1980).
6 Ibid., p. 105.
7 A. E. Afigbo, *The Warrant Chiefs: Indirect Rule in Southeastern Nigeria 1891–1929* (London: Longman, 1972).
8 Wren (1980), pp. 116–17.
9 Ibid., pp. 117–18.
10 Ibid., p. 117.
11 Charles Nnolim, 'A Source for *Arrow of God*', *Research in African Literatures*, 8 (1977), pp. 1–26.
12 Simon Alagbogu Nnolim, *The History of Umuchu* (Enugu: Eastern Press, 1953).
13 Nnolim (1977), p. 1.
14 Ibid., pp. 2–3.
15 Ibid., p. 3.
16 Ibid., p. 4.
17 Ibid., pp. 5–6.
18 Ibid., p. 6.
19 Ibid., p. 1.
20 C. L. Innes, 'A Source for *Arrow of God*: A Response', *Research in African Literatures*, 9 (1978), pp. 16–18.
21 Ibid., p. 16.
22 Ibid.
23 Ibid., pp. 16–17.
24 Ibid., p. 17.
25 Ibid., p. 18.
26 K. Indrasena Reddy, *The Novels of Achebe and Ngũgĩ: A Study in the Dialectics of Commitment* (New Delhi: Prestige, 1994).
27 Ibid., p. 49.
28 Ibid., pp. 50–1.
29 Ibid., p. 53.
30 Ibid.
31 Ibid., pp. 57–8.
32 Ibid., p. 62.
33 David Carroll, *Chinua Achebe: Novelist, Poet, Critic* (Basingstoke: Macmillan, 1990).
34 Ibid., p. 87.
35 Ibid., pp. 88–9.
36 Ibid., pp. 93–4.
37 Ibid., p. 100.
38 Tejumola Olaniyan, 'Chinua Achebe and an Archaeology of the Postcolonial African State', *Research in African Literatures*, 2:3 (2001), pp. 22–8.
39 Ibid., p. 22.
40 Ibid.
41 Ibid.
42 Ibid., p. 23.

43 Ibid., pp. 26–7.
44 Ibid., pp. 27–8.

CHAPTER FIVE

 1 Ezenwa-Ohaeto, *Chinua Achebe: A Biography* (Oxford: James Currey, 1997).
 2 Chinua Achebe 'The Novelist as Teacher', reprinted in *Hopes and Impediments: Selected Essays* (New York: Anchor, 1990), pp. 40–6.
 3 Ezenwa-Ohaeto (1997), p. 108.
 4 Major Chukwama Kaduna Nzeogwu, speech broadcast by Radio Kaduna (January 15, 1966), reprinted in Ezenwa-Ohaeto (1997), p. 109.
 5 Ezenwa-Ohaeto (1997), p. 115.
 6 Bernth Lindfors, 'Achebe's African Parable', *Présence Africaine*, 66 (1968), pp. 130–6.
 7 Ibid., p. 131.
 8 Ibid., p. 132.
 9 Ibid., pp. 132–3.
10 Ibid., p. 134.
11 Ibid., p. 136.
12 Ngũgĩ wa Thiong'o, 'Chinua Achebe's *A Man of the People*', reproduced in *Homecoming: Essays on African and Caribbean Literature, Culture and Politics* (London: Heinemann, 1972), pp. 51–4.
13 Ibid., p. 52.
14 Ibid.
15 Ibid., p. 53.
16 Ibid., p. 54.
17 Joe E. Obi, Jr., 'A Critical Reading of the Disillusionment Novel', *Journal of Black Studies*, 20:4 (1990), pp. 399–413.
18 O. Chinweize and I. Madubuike, 'Towards the decolonization of African Literature', *Okike*, 7 (1975), pp. 78–9, quoted by Obi (1990), p. 399.
19 Obi (1990), p. 401.
20 Ibid., p. 402.
21 Ibid., p. 404.
22 Ibid.
23 Ibid., pp. 404–5.
24 Ibid., p. 407.
25 Ibid., p. 408.
26 Ibid.
27 Ibid.
28 Onyemaechi Udumukwu, 'Achebe and the Negation of Independence', *Modern Fiction Studies*, 37:3 (1991), pp. 471–91.
29 Ibid., p. 473.
30 Ibid.
31 Ibid., p. 483.
32 Ibid., pp. 485–6.
33 Chinua Achebe, 'I Had to Write on the Chaos I Foresaw: Interview with Tony Hall', *Conversations with Chinua Achebe*, ed. Berth Lindfors (Jackson: University of Mississippi Press, 1997), pp. 18–26.
34 Ibid. (1997), p. 21.
35 Ibid., p. 22.
36 Jago Morrison 'Chinua Achebe *A Man of the People*: The Novel and the Public Sphere', in *Scandalous Fictions: The Twentieth Century Novel in the Public Sphere*, ed. Jago Morrison and Susan Watkins (Basingstoke: Palgrave, 2006), pp. 117–35.

37 Achebe/Hall (1997), p. 23.
38 Morrison (2006), pp. 119–20.
39 Ibid., pp. 128–9.
40 Obi (1990), p. 408.
41 Morrison (2006), p. 130.
42 Ibid., p. 133.
43 Chinua Achebe, 'Chinua Achebe on Biafra', *Transition*, 36 (1968), p. 31.
44 C. L. Innes, *Chinua Achebe* (Cambridge: Cambridge University Press, 1990).
45 Innes (1990), p. 133.
46 Achebe (1977), pp. 118–19.
47 Innes (1990), p. 133.
48 Umelo Ojinmah, *Chinua Achebe: New Perspectives* (Ibadan: Spectrum, 1991).
49 Ibid., pp. 76–7.
50 Ibid., p. 79.
51 Ode Ogede, 'Oral tradition and Modern Storytelling: Revisiting Chinua Achebe's Short Stories', *International Fiction Review*, 28:1–2 (2001), pp. 67–77.
52 Ibid., pp. 67–8.
53 Ibid., p. 69.
54 Ibid., p. 74.

CHAPTER SIX

1 Chinua Achebe, 'Interview with Jane Wilkinson, 1987', in *Conversations with Chinua Achebe*, ed. Bernth Lindfors (Jackson: University Press of Mississippi, 1997), pp. 141–54.
2 Ibid., p. 141.
3 Ibid., p. 143.
4 Ibid.
5 Ibid., p. 145.
6 Simon Gikandi, *Reading Chinua Achebe: Language & Ideology in Fiction* (Oxford: James Currey, 1991).
7 Ibid., p. 126.
8 Ibid., p. 127.
9 Ibid., pp. 129–30.
10 Ibid., p. 140.
11 Ibid., p. 145.
12 Ibid., p. 148.
13 Supriya Nair, 'The Story and the Struggle in *Anthills of the Savannah*', in *South Asian Responses to Chinua Achebe*, ed. Bernth Lindfors and Bala Kothandaraman (New Delhi: Prestige, 1993), pp. 104–21.
14 Ibid., p. 105.
15 Ibid., pp. 106–7.
16 Ibid., p. 107.
17 Ibid., p. 110.
18 Ibid., p. 112.
19 Ibid., pp. 119–20.
20 Ibid., p. 120.
21 Neil ten Kortenaar, ''Only Connect': *Anthills of the Savannah* and Achebe's Trouble with Nigeria', *Research in African Literatures*, 24:3 (1993), pp. 59–72.
22 Ibid., p. 60.
23 Ibid., p. 61.
24 Ibid.

25 Ibid., p. 62.
26 Ibid., p. 66.
27 Ibid., p. 70.
28 Ifi Amadiume, 'Class and Gender in *Anthills of the Savannah*: A Critique', *Okike: An African Journal of New Writing*, 30 (1990), pp. 147–57.
29 Ibid., p. 148.
30 Ibid., p. 149.
31 Ibid., p. 151.
32 Ibid., p. 152.
33 Ibid., p. 155.
34 Rose Acholonu, 'Outsiders or Insiders?: Women in *Anthills of the Savannah*', in *Eagle on Iroko: Selected Papers from the Chinua Achebe International Symposium 1990*, ed. Bernth Lindfors and Bala Kothandaraman (Ibadan: Heinemann, 1996), pp. 311–21.
35 Ibid., p. 314.
36 Ibid., pp. 315–6.
37 Ibid., pp. 317–8.
38 Elleke Boehmer, 'Of Goddeses and Stories: Gender and a New Politics in Achebe's *Anthills of the Savannah*,' *Kunapipi*, 12:2 (1990), pp. 102–12.
39 Ibid., p. 102.
40 Ibid., p. 103.
41 Ibid., p. 104.
42 Ibid., pp. 104–5.
43 Ibid., p. 106.
44 Ibid., p. 110.

CONCLUSION

1 Thomas Mofolo, *Chaka* (Morjia, Basotholand: Paris Evangelical Missionary Society, 1925).
2 Graham Furness, 'Hausa Creative Writing in the 1930s: An Exploration in Postcolonial Theory', in *Readings in African Popular Fiction*, ed. Stephanie Newell (Bloomington: Indiana University Press, 2002), pp. 11–17.
3 T. Cullen Young, ed., *African New Writing* (London: Lutterworth, 1947).
4 Emmanuel Obiechina, *An African Popular Literature: A Study of Onitsha Market Pamphlets* (Cambridge, Cambridge University Press, 1973), p. 4.
5 Chinua Achebe, Interview with Kalu Ogbaa, in *Conversations with Chinua Achebe*, ed. Bernth Lindfors (Jackson: University of Mississippi Press, 1997), pp. 64–75.
6 Ibid., p. 75.
7 Femi Osofisan, 'Eagles in the Age of Unacknowledged Muse: Two Major New Writers in Contemporary Nigerian Literature, Akachi Ezeigbo & Promise Okekwe', *African Literature Today*, 24 (2004), pp. 21–42.
8 Ibid., p. 21.
9 Wole Soyinka, interview in *Talking with African Writers: Interviews by Jane Wilkinson*, ed. Jane Wilkinson (London: James Currey, 1992), pp. 91–108.
10 Ibid., p. 92.
11 Charles R. Larson, *The Ordeal of the African Writer* (London: Zed, 2001), p. 140.
12 Stephanie Newell, *West African Literatures* (Oxford, Oxford University Press, 2006), p. 183.
13 Thomas Hale, 'Bursting at the Seams: New Dimensions for African Literature in the 21st Century', *Research in African Literatures*, 25 (2006), pp. 10–21.
14 Ibid., p. 15.

SELECT BIBLIOGRAPHY

WORKS BY CHINUA ACHEBE

FICTION

NOVELS

Things Fall Apart (London: Heinemann, 1958).
No Longer at Ease (London: Heinemann, 1960).
Arrow of God (London: Heinemann, 1964).
A Man of the People (London: Heinemann, 1966).
Anthills of the Savannah (London: Heinemann, 1987).

SHORT STORIES

The Sacrificial Egg and Other Short Stories (Onitsha: Etudo, 1962).
Girls at War and Other Stories (London: Heinemann, 1972).

CHILDREN'S FICTION

Chike and the River (Cambridge: Cambridge University Press, 1966).
How the Leopard Got His Claws (New York: Third Press, 1973).
The Flute: A Children's Story (Enugu: Fourth Dimension, 1977).
The Drum: A Children's Story (Enugu: Fourth Dimension, 1977) (with John Roper).

POETRY

Beware Soul-Brother, and Other Poems (Enugu: Nwankwo-Ifejika, 1971).
Christmas in Biafra, and Other Poems (Garden City, N.Y: Anchor, 1973).
Collected Poems (New York: Anchor, 2004).

EDITED COLLECTIONS

Achebe, Chinua, Nwankwo, Arthur, Ifejika, Samuel and Nwapa, Flora, eds., *The Insider: Stories of War and Peace from Nigeria* (Enugu: Nwankwo-Ifejika, 1971).
Achebe, Chinua, and Okafor, Dubem, eds., *Don't Let Him Die: An Anthology of Memorial Poems for Christopher Okigbo (1932–1967)* (Enugu: Fourth Dimension, 1978).
Achebe, Chinua and Innes, C. L., eds., *African Short Stories* (London: Heinemann, 1984).
Achebe, Chinua and Innes, C. L., eds., *The Heinemann Book of Contemporary African Short Stories* (London: Heinemann, 1992).

ESSAYS

COLLECTED

Morning Yet on Creation Day: Essays (London: Heinemann, 1975).
Hopes and Impediments: Selected Essays, 1965–1987 (London: Heinemann, 1988).
Home and Exile (Oxford: Oxford University Press, 2000).

OTHER ESSAYS

'English and the African Writer', *Transition*, 4:18 (1965), pp. 27–30.
'The Black Writer's Burden', *Présence Africaine*, 59 (1966), pp. 135–40.
'Culture and International Understanding', *Daily Times* (Lagos), (22 May 1971), p. 7.
'This Earth, My Brother', *Transition*, 41 (1972), pp. 69–70.
'The Bane of Union: An Appraisal of the Consequences of Union Igbo for Igbo Language and Literature', *Anu Magazine*, 1 (1979), pp. 33–41.
'Metaphor of the Rain and the Clock', *Daily Times* (Lagos), (10 Nov 1979), p. 7.
'The Uses of African Literature', *Okike*, 15 (1979), pp. 8–17.
'Why Writers Need an Association', *West Africa*, 3339 (27 July 1981), pp. 1692–4.
'The Okike Story', *Okike*, 21 (July 1982), pp. 1–5.
'Africa Is People', *Massachusetts Review,* 40:3 (1999), pp. 313–21.
'The Day I Finally Met Baldwin', *Callaloo*, 25:2 (Spring 2002), pp. 502–4.

OTHER BOOKS

The Trouble with Nigeria (Enugu: Fourth Dimension, 1983).
The World of the Ogbanje (Enugu: Fourth Dimension, 1986).
The University and the Leadership Factor in Nigerian Politics: Strategies for Nigerian Development (Enugu: Abic, 1988).
Achebe, Chinua, in association with the Beyond Hunger Project, *Beyond Hunger in Africa: Conventional Wisdom and an African Vision* (London: Heinemann, 1990).
Achebe, Chinua and Lyons, Robert, *Another Africa* (New York: Anchor, 1998).

INTERVIEWS

COLLECTED

Lindfors, Bernth, ed., *Conversations with Chinua Achebe* (Jackson: University Press of Mississippi, 1997).

OTHER INTERVIEWS

Achebe, Chinua and Farah, Nuruddin, 'Chinua Achebe with Nuruddin Farah: Writers in Conversation', Guardian Conversations (London: ICA, 1986).
Baker, Rob, and Draper, Ellen, ' "If One Thing Stands, Another Will Stand Beside It": An Interview with Chinua Achebe', *Parabola* 17.3 (Fall 1992), pp. 19–28.
Brooks, Jerome, 'The Art of Fiction', *The Paris Review*, 133 (Winter 1994), pp. 142–67.
Samway, Patrick H., 'An Interview with Chinua Achebe', *America* (22 June 1991), pp. 684–7.
Serumaga, Robert, 'Interview [with Chinua Achebe]', in Duerden, Dennis and Pieterse, Cosmo, eds., *African Writers Talking: A Collection of Interviews* (London: Heinemann, 1972).

CRITICISM

TWO OR MORE NOVELS

Agetua, John, *Critics on Chinua Achebe 1970–76* (Benin: Agetua, 1977).

Booker, M. Keith, *The Chinua Achebe Encyclopedia* (Westport, CT: Greenwood, 2003).

Carroll, David, *Chinua Achebe: Novelist, Poet, Critic* (Basingstoke: Macmillan, 1990).

Egejuru, Phanuel Akubueze, *Chinua Achebe, Pure and Simple: An Oral Biography* (Ikeja: Malthouse, 2001).

Ekwe-Ekwe, Herbert, *African Literature in Defence of History: An Essay on Chinua Achebe* (Dakar: African Renaissance, 2001).

Ezenwa-Ohaeto, *Chinua Achebe: A Biography* (Oxford: James Currey, 1997).

Gates, Henry L. and Appiah, K. A., eds., *Chinua Achebe: Critical Perspectives Past and Present* (New York: Amistad, 1997).

Gikandi, Simon, *Reading Chinua Achebe: Language & Ideology in Fiction* (Oxford: James Currey, 1991).

Griffiths, Gareth, 'Language and Action in the Novels of Chinua Achebe', *African Literature Today*, 5 (1971), pp. 88–105.

Ihekweazu, Edith, ed., *Eagle on Iroko: Selected Papers from the Chinua Achebe International Symposium 1990* (Ibadan: Heinemann Educational, 1996).

Innes, C. L., *Chinua Achebe* (Cambridge: Cambridge University Press, 1990).

Innes, C. L. and Lindfors, Bernth, eds., *Critical Perspectives on Chinua Achebe* (Washington, DC: Three Continents, 1978).

Khayyoom, S. A., *Chinua Achebe: A Study of His Novels* (London: Sangam, 1999).

Killam, G. D., *The Writings of Chinua Achebe* (London: Heinemann, 1977).

Lindfors, Bernth and Kothandaraman, Bala, eds., *South Asian Responses to Chinua Achebe* (New Delhi: Prestige; 1993).

Moses, Michael Valdez, *The Novel and the Globalization of Culture* (New York: Oxford University Press, 1995).

Muoneke, Romanus Okey, *Art, Rebellion and Redemption: A Reading of the Novels of Chinua Achebe* (New York: Peter Lang, 1994).

Newell, Stephanie, *West African Literatures* (Oxford: Oxford University Press, 2006).

Njoku, Benedict Chiaka, *The Four Novels of Chinua Achebe: A Critical Study* (New York: Peter Lang, 1984).

Ogbaa, Kalu, *Gods, Oracles and Divination: Folkways in Chinua Achebe's Novels* (Trenton, N.J: Africa World Press, 1992).

Ogede, Ode, *Achebe and the Politics of Representation* (Trenton, N.J.: Africa World Press, 2001).

Ogu, Julius N., 'The Concept of Madness in Chinua Achebe's Writings', *Journal of Commonwealth Literature*, 18 (1983), pp. 48–54.

Ojinmah, Umelo, *Chinua Achebe: New Perspectives* (Ibadan: Spectrum, 1991).

Okechukwu, Chinwe, *Achebe the Orator: The Art of Persuasion in Chinua Achebe's Novels* (Westport, Conn: Greenwood, 2001).

Omotoso, Kole, *Achebe or Soyinka? A Study in Contrasts* (London: Hans Zell, 1996).

Owusu, Kofi, 'The Politics of Interpretation: The Novels of Chinua Achebe', *Modern Fiction Studies*, 37:3 (1991), pp. 459–71.

Palmer, Eustace, *An Introduction to the African Novel* (London: Heinemann, 1972).

Parker, Michael and Starkey, Roger, eds., *Post-Colonial Literatures: Achebe, Ngũgĩ, Desai, Walcott* (Basingstoke: Macmillan, 1995).

Ravenscroft, Arthur, *Chinua Achebe* (Harlow: Longman, 1977).

Reddy, K. Indrasena, *The Novels of Achebe and Ngũgĩ: A Study in the Dialectics of Commitment* (New Delhi: Prestige, 1994).

Scafe, Suzanne, '"Wherever Something Stands, Something Else Will Stand Beside It": Ambivalence in Achebe's *Things Fall Apart* and *Arrow of God*', *Changing English: Studies in Reading & Culture*, 9:2 (2002), pp. 119–32.

Simola, Raisa, *World Views in Chinua Achebe's Works* (Frankfurt am Main: Peter Lang, 1995).

Stratton, Florence, *Contemporary African Literature and the Politics of Gender* (London: Routledge, 1994).

Taiwo, Oladele, *Culture and the Nigerian Novel* (New York: St. Martins Press, 1976).

Ugah, Ada, *In the Beginning: Chinua Achebe at Work* (Ibadan: Heinemann, 1990).

Wren, Robert, *Achebe's World: The Historical and Cultural Context of the Novels* (Washington DC: Three Continents, 1980).

Yousaf, Nahem, *Chinua Achebe* (Tavistock: Northcote House, 2003).

THINGS FALL APART

Aji, Aron, 'Ezinma: The Ogbanje Child in Achebe's *Things Fall Apart*', *College Literature*, 19:3–20:1 (1992), pp. 170–5.

Begam, Richard, 'Achebe's Sense of an Ending: History and Tragedy in *Things Fall Apart*', *Studies in the Novel*, 29:3 (Fall 1997), pp. 396–411.

Bloom, Harold, *Chinua Achebe's* Things Fall Apart*: Modern Critical Interpretations* (Philadelphia: Chelsea House, 2001).

Cobham, Rhonda, 'Making Men and History: Achebe and the Politics of Revisionism', in Lindfors, Bernth, ed., *Approaches to Teaching Achebe's Things Fall Apart* (New York: MLA, 1991), pp. 91–100.

Criswell, Stephen, 'Okonkwo as Yeatsian Hero: The Influence of W. B. Yeats on Chinua Achebe's *Things Fall Apart*', *Literary Criterion*, 30:4 (1995), pp. 1–14.

Gikandi, Simon, 'Chinua Achebe and the Invention of African Culture', *Research in African Literatures*, 32:3 (2001), pp. 3–9.

Hoegberg, David, 'Principle and Practice: The Logic of Cultural Violence in Achebe's *Things Fall Apart*', *College Literature*, 26:1 (1999), pp. 69–80.

Iyasere, Solomon O., *Understanding Things Fall Apart: Selected Essays and Criticism* (New York: Whitston, 1998).

JanMohamed, Abdul, 'Sophisticated Primitivism: The Syncretism of Oral and Literate Modes in Achebe's *Things Fall Apart*', *ARIEL*, 15:4 (1984), pp. 19–39.

Jeyifo, Biodun, 'Okonkwo and His Mother: *Things Fall Apart* and Issues of Gender in the Constitution of African Postcolonial Discourse', *Callaloo*, 16:4 (1993), pp. 847–58.

Kortenaar, Neil ten, 'Becoming African and the Death of Ikemefuna', *University of Toronto Quarterly*, 73:2 (2004), pp. 773–94.

Kortenaar, Neil ten, 'How the Centre is Made to Hold in *Things Fall Apart*', in Parker, Michael & Starkey, Roger, eds., *Postcolonial Literatures: Achebe, Ngũgĩ, Desai, Walcott* (Basingstoke: Macmillan, 1995), pp. 319–36.

Lindfors, Bernth, ed., *Approaches to Teaching Achebe's Things Fall Apart* (New York: MLA, 1991).

Lindfors, Bernth, 'Achebe at Home and Abroad: Situating *Things Fall Apart*', *Literary Griot*, 10:2 (1998), pp. 10–16.

MacKenzie, Clayton G., 'The Metamorphosis of Piety in Chinua Achebe's *Things Fall Apart*', *Research in African Literatures*, 27:2 (1996), pp. 128–39.

McLaren, Joseph, 'Missionaries and Converts: Religion and Colonial Intrusion in *Things Fall Apart*', *Literary Griot*, 10:2 (1998), pp. 48–60.

Nnolim, Charles E., 'The Form and Function of the Folk Tradition in Achebe's Novels', *ARIEL*, 14:1 (1983), pp. 35–47.

Ogbaa, Kalu, *Understanding Things Fall Apart: A Student Casebook to Issues, Sources, and Historical Documents* (Westport, CT: Greenwood, 1999).

Okpewho, Isidore. *Chinua Achebe's Things Fall Apart: A Casebook* (Oxford: Oxford University Press, 2003).

Osei-Nyame, Kwadwo, 'Chinua Achebe Writing Culture: Representations of Gender and Tradition in *Things Fall Apart*', *Research in African Literatures*, 30:2 (1999), pp. 148–64.

Petersen, Kirsten Holst, 'First Things First: Problems of a Feminist Approach to African Literature', *Kunapipi*, 6:3 (1984), pp. 35–47.

Robertson, P. J. M., '*Things Fall Apart* and *Heart of Darkness*: A Creative Dialogue', *International Fiction Review*, 7:2 (1980), pp. 106–12.

Snead, James, 'European Pedigrees/African Contagions: Nationality, Narrative and Communality in Tutuola, Achebe and Reed', in Bhabha, Homi, ed., *Nation and Narration* (London: Routledge, 1990), pp. 231–49.

Stock, A. G., 'Yeats and Achebe', *Journal of Commonwealth Literature*, 5 (1968), pp. 105–11.

Traore, Ousseynou B., ed., *Discourse on Iroko: 40th Anniversary Symposium on Things Fall Apart*, *Literary Griot*, 10:2 (1998) (Special Issue).

Turkington, Kate, *Chinua Achebe: Things Fall Apart* (London: Arnold, 1977).

Wise, Christopher, 'Excavating the New Republic', *Callaloo*, 22:4 (1999), pp. 1054–71.

NO LONGER AT EASE

Aizenberg, Edna, 'Cortázar's *Hopscotch* and Achebe's *No Longer at Ease*: Divided Heroes and Deconstructive Discourse in the Latin American and African Novel', *Okike*, 25–6 (1984), pp. 10–26.

Criswell, Stephen, 'Colonialism, Corruption, and Culture: A Fanonian Reading of *Mister Johnson* and *No Longer at Ease*', *Literary Griot*, 10:1 (1998), pp. 43–64.

Davis, Richard, 'In Search of Agency among Colonized Africans: Chinua Achebe's *No Longer at Ease* and Joyce Cary's *Mister Johnson*', *Journal of Commonwealth and Postcolonial Studies*, 2:1 (1994), pp. 12–26.

Inyama, Nnadozie F., 'Genetic Discontinuity in Achebe's *No Longer at Ease*', in Ogbaa, Kalu, ed., *The Gong and the Flute: African Literary Development and Celebration* (Westport, CT: Greenwood, 1994), pp. 119–27.

Munro, Ian H., 'Textual Dynamics in Chinua Achebe's *Home and Exile* and *No Longer at Ease*', *International Fiction Review*, 31:1–2 (2004), pp. 54–64.

Rogers, Philip, '*No Longer at Ease*: Chinua Achebe's "Heart of Whiteness"', *Research in African Literatures*, 14:2 (1983), pp. 165–83.

Wilson, Roderick, 'Eliot and Achebe: An Analysis of Some Formal and Philosophic Qualities of *No Longer at Ease*', *English Studies in Africa,* 14 (1971), pp. 215–23.

Witte, Arnd, '*Things Fall Apart*: The Portrayal of African Identity in Joyce Cary's *Mister Johnson* and Chinua Achebe's *No Longer at Ease*' in Coulson, Anthony, ed., *Exiles and Migrants: Crossing Thresholds in European Culture and Society* (Brighton: Sussex Academic Press, 1997), pp. 125–35.

ARROW OF GOD

Adeeko, Adeleke, 'Contests of Text and Context in Chinua Achebe's *Arrow of God*', *ARIEL*, 23:2 (1992), pp. 7–22.

Awuyah, Chris Kwame, 'Chinua Achebe's *Arrow of God*: Ezeulu's Response to Change', *College Literature*, 19:3–20:1 (1992–3), pp. 214–19.

Brown, Hugh R., 'Igbo Words for the Non-Igbo: Achebe's Artistry in *Arrow of God*', *Research in African Literatures*, 12:1 (1981), pp. 69–85.

Innes, C. L., 'A Source for *Arrow of God*: A Response', *Research In African Literatures*, 9 (1978), pp. 16–18.

Jabbi, Bu-Buakei, 'Myth and Ritual in *Arrow of God*', *African Literature Today*, 11 (1980), pp. 130–48.

Kalu, Anthonia C., 'The Priest/Artist Tradition in Achebe's *Arrow of God*', *Africa Today*, 41:2 (1994), pp. 51–62.

Lindfors, Bernth, 'Ambiguity and Intention in *Arrow of God*', *Ba Shiru: A Journal of African Languages and Literature*, 5:1 (1973), pp. 43–8.

Lindfors, Bernth, 'The Folktale as Paradigm in Chinua Achebe's *Arrow of God*', *Studies in Black Literature*, 1:1 (1970), pp. 1–15.

Machila, Blaise N., 'Ambiguity in Achebe's *Arrow of God*', *Kunapipi*, 3:1 (1981), pp. 119–33.

Mathuray, Mark, 'Realizing the Sacred: Power and Meaning in Chinua Achebe's *Arrow of God*', *Research in African Literatures*, 34:3 (2003), pp. 46–65.

Nnolim, Charles, 'A Source for *Arrow of God*', *Research in African Literatures*, 8 (1977), pp. 1–26.

Okechukwa, Chinwe Christiana, 'Oratory and Social Responsibility: Chinua Achebe's *Arrow of God*,' *Callaloo*, 25:2 (2002), pp. 567–84.

Olaniyan, Tejumola, 'Chinua Achebe and an Archaeology of the Postcolonial African State', *Research in African Literatures*, 2:3 (2001), pp. 22–8.

Osei-Nyame, Kwadwo, Jr., 'Gender and the Narrative of Identity in Chinua Achebe's *Arrow of God*', *Commonwealth Essays and Studies*, 22:2 (2000), pp. 25–34.

Sabor, Peter, 'Structural Weaknesses and Stylistic Revisions in Achebe's *Arrow of God*', *Research in African Literatures*, 10 (1979), pp. 375–9.

Wren, Robert M., 'Achebe's Revisions of *Arrow of God*', *Research in African Literatures*, 7 (1976), pp. 53–8.

Wren, Robert M., 'From Ulu to Christ: The Transfer of Faith in Chinua Achebe's *Arrow of God*', *Christianity and Literature*, 27:2 (1978), pp. 28–40.

Wren, Robert M., 'Mister Johnson and the Complexity of *Arrow of God*' in Narasimhaiah, C. D., ed., *Awakened Conscience: Studies in Commonwealth Literature* (New Delhi: Sterling, 1978), pp. 50–62.

A MAN OF THE PEOPLE

Lindfors, Bernth, 'Achebe's African Parable', *Présence Africaine*, 66 (1968), pp. 130–6.

Morrison, Jago, 'Chinua Achebe *A Man of the People*: The Novel and the Public Sphere', in Morrison, Jago and Watkins, Susan, eds., *Scandalous Fictions: The Twentieth-Century Novel in the Public Sphere* (Basingstoke: Palgrave, 2006), pp. 117–35.

Ngũgĩ wa Thiong'o, 'Chinua Achebe's *A Man of the People*', in *Homecoming: Essays on African and Caribbean Literature, Culture and Politics* (London: Heinemann, 1972), pp. 51–4.

Obi, Joe E., Jr, 'A Critical Reading of the Disillusionment Novel', *Journal of Black Studies*, 20:4 (1990), pp. 399–413.

Osei-Nyame, Kwadwo, Jr, 'Gender, Nationalism and the Fictions of Identity in Chinua Achebe's *A Man of the People*', *Commonwealth Novel in English*, 9–10 (2001), pp. 242–62.

Sample, Maxine. 'In Another Life: The Refugee Phenomenon in Two Novels of the Nigerian Civil War', *Modern Fiction Studies*, 37:3 (1991), pp. 445–55.

Udumukwu, Onyemaechi, 'Achebe and the Negation of Independence', *Modern Fiction Studies*, 37:3 (1991), pp. 471–91.

Udumukwu, Onyemaechi, 'Ideology and the Dialectics of Action: Achebe and Iyayi', *Research in African Literatures*, 27:3 (1996), pp. 34–49.

GIRLS AT WAR AND OTHER STORIES

Balogun, F. Odun, 'Achebe's "The Madman": A Poetic Realisation of Irony', *Okike*, 23 (1983), pp. 72–9.

Burness, Donald B., 'Solipsism and Survival in Achebe's "Civil Peace" and "Girls at War"', *Ba Shiru: A Journal of African Languages and Literature*, 5 (1973), pp. 64–7.

Elias, Mohamed, 'Time in Achebe's *Girls at War*: Presence of the Nigerian Past', *Commonwealth Quarterly*, 2:6 (1978), pp. 17–23.

García Ramírez, Paula, 'Women in Achebe's Short Stories: Akueke, Veronica and Gladys', in Guardia, P. and Stone, J., eds., *Proceedings of the 20th International AEDEAN Conference* (Barcelona: Universitat de Barcelona, 1997), pp. 467–72.

Ogede, Ode, 'Oral Tradition and Modern Storytelling: Revisiting Chinua Achebe's Short Stories', *International Fiction Review*, 28:1–2 (2001), pp. 67–77.

Slaughter, Joseph R., 'One Track Minds: Markets, Madness, Metaphors, and Modernism in Postcolonial Nigerian Fiction', *in* Falola, Toyin et al., eds., *African Writers and Their Readers: Essays in Honor of Bernth Lindfors, II* (Trenton, NJ: Africa World Press, 2002), pp. 55–89.

ANTHILLS OF THE SAVANNAH

Abah, Okwute J., '*Anthills of the Savannah*: A Historical Mythology', *Literary Griot*, 4:1–2 (1992), pp. 126–37.

Acholonu, Rose, 'Outsiders or Insiders?: Women in *Anthills of the Savannah*', in Lindfors, Bernth, and Kothandaraman, Bala, eds., *Eagle on Iroko: Selected Papers from the Chinua Achebe International Symposium 1990* (Ibadan: Heinemann, 1996), pp. 311–21.

Amadiume, Ifi, 'Class and Gender in *Anthills of the Savannah*: A Critique', *Okike*, 30 (1990), pp. 147–57.

Ehling, Holger G., *Critical Approaches to Anthills of the Savannah* (Amsterdam: Rodopi, 1991).

Farah, Nuruddin, 'A Tale of Tyranny', *West Africa*, 3658 (21 Sept 1987), pp. 1828–31.

Ibironke, Olabode, 'Chinua Achebe and the Political Imperative of the African Writer', *Journal of Commonwealth Literature*, 36:1 (2001), pp. 75–90.

Ikegami, Robin, 'Knowledge and Power, the Story and the Storyteller: Achebe's *Anthills of the Savannah*', *Modern Fiction Studies*, 37:3 (1991), pp. 493–507.

Kanaganayakam, Chelva, 'Art and Orthodoxy in Chinua Achebe's *Anthills of the Savannah*', *ARIEL*, 24:4 (1993), pp. 35–51.

Kortenaar, Neil ten, '"Only Connect": *Anthills of the Savannah* and Achebe's *Trouble with Nigeria*', *Research in African Literatures*, 24:3 (1993), pp. 59–72.

Ogwude, Sophia O., 'Achebe on the Woman Question', *Literary Griot*, 13:1–2 (2001), pp. 62–9.

Index